Timely and Timeless

The Wisdom of E. Burdette Backus

Edited by Edd Doerr

HUMANIST PRESS

Amherst, New York

Printed and bound in the United States of America.

Library of Congress Catalog Number: 98-070361

ISBN 0-931779-10-3

E. Burdette Backus
1924

E. Burdette Backus
circa 1950
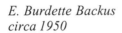

Table of Contents

Foreword

Finding or being found by a worthy mentor is an exhilarating experience. It happened in the early 1950s, when I found myself regularly in the company of Burdette Backus as a fellow member of the Western Unitarian Conference Board. He was the distinguished veteran minister of All Souls Unitarian Church in Indianapolis and I the youngish minister of the Unitarian congregation in Rockford, Illinois. What began as an acquaintanceship deepened in time into a friendship.

Burdette was then a celebrated representative of humanistic liberal religion, widely respected for his popular radio ministry and as spiritual leader of a congregation noted for its activist support of civil rights, First and Fourteenth Amendment civil liberties, world peace, mental health, and religious expressions deeply rooted in principles of freedom, reason, tolerance and social responsibility. He became for me a shining example of a broad-gauged liberal minister, rich in compassion, gentleness, courage, personal dignity, scholarly grounding, equally appreciative of scientific method and democratic values – a good person, a good parson, a good world citizen.

Because of our friendship, Burdette opened to me his searing grief that a small but influential cadre of his parishioners was actively challenging his ministry for its avowed humanism and for its active support of the American Civil Liberties Union, the United Nations, the Mental Health Association, and, wittingly or unwittingly, "a communist conspiracy to overthrow the government of the U.S." Recall this was the era of what we now remember as "McCarthyism," and Indianapolis was the national headquarters of the American Legion. The anti-Backus minority, failing to gain ground among the majority of congregation members, withdrew from All Souls and formed a separate congregation.

The ordeal devastated Burdette emotionally. In one of our private conversations, he asked me if I might consider succeeding him. He felt he probably had to resign and to remove himself in order to recover. My Rockford congregation was flourishing, but I was young and ambitious. In spite of the confidential advice of one of my revered older colleagues that All

Souls was "a contentious congregation," I told Burdette I could be interested.

I've never known, given our vaunted "congregational polity," what Burdette did or didn't do to influence the result, but in due course I was invited to be his successor, and accepted.

Burdette retired to a tragically short period of notable service and personal happiness. The Rockford congregation went on to a prosperous future. All Souls, building on the Backus inheritance, including the radio ministry, became a kind of liberal, humanistic megachurch, necessitating constructing an architectural gem of a new church center. The dissenting congregation disbanded, some of its surviving members returning to the All Souls fold. In time, I moved on to become minister of historic Arlington Street Church in Boston, ever grateful for my Backus inheritance.

Thus it is a delight that many of his choice radio addresses and sermons are once again to be available, and fresh readers inspired by how clear, spare, persuasive and eloquent he was as a preacher. Savor, then, as I do, this recovery of Burdette's radio and pulpit sermons, and be amazed, as I have always been, at how current, gripping and challenging they are.

-- Jack Mendelsohn

The Reverend Dr. Jack Mendelsohn served as minister of Unitarian and Unitarian Universalist congregations in Rockford and Chicago, Illinois; Indianapolis, Indiana; Santa Barbara, California; and Boston, Beverly, and Bedford, Massachusetts. He has taught at Meadville/Lombard Theological School and is the author of many articles and books, including Being Liberal in an Illiberal Age; Channing: The Reluctant Radical; God, Allah, and JuJu; The Forest Calls Back; *and* The Martyrs. *In 1997 he received the Award for Distinguished Service of the Unitarian Universalist Association.*

Preface

As a college student at the beginning of the Korean War, I had already made a rapid and painless transition from a traditional religious orthodoxy to Humanism, which, for the sake of brevity, I would define as a compassionate ethical naturalism. One day, after I had published a few letters to the editor in Indianapolis newspapers, I received a note from the Reverend E. Burdette Backus, minister of All Souls Unitarian Church in that city, expressing interest in what I had written and inviting me to visit his church. Some time not long thereafter I did so, and thus began an association with Unitarian Universalism that has lasted for well over forty years and significantly affected my life.

Burdette Backus, I found, was a forceful but gentle man, brilliant but not arrogant, learned but never pretentious, extraordinarily well read and intellectually gifted but a clear and plain speaker, at once a thinker and an activist. His writing, his work, and his life are to me among the finest expressions of the best in both Humanism and Unitarian Universalism, and illustrate the very considerable overlap between these two traditions.

In those early days at All Souls I could not have dreamed that one day I would speak from Backus's pulpit, succeed him as a president of the American Humanist Association, meet my future wife in his church and be married by his successor (Jack Mendelsohn), devote most of my life to causes he held dear, and eventually edit and publish some of his best writing.

* * *

Edwin Burdette Backus was born in Blanchester, Ohio, on December 27, 1888. His father, Wilson Marvin Backus, was a leading Universalist minister. His mother, Estelle Campbell Backus, also a Universalist minister, died before Burdette was a year old.

Backus received his A.B. degree from the University of Michigan in 1909 and his B.A. from Meadville Theological Seminary in 1912. He pursued postgraduate studies at Oxford, Harvard, the University of California, and universities in Berlin and Jena, Germany, and was awarded a D.D. degree in 1940 by Meadville. After serving as minister of Unitarian congregations in Lawrence, Kansas; Erie, Pennsylvania; and Des Moines, Iowa; as well as the Chicago Humanist Society, he was called to the pulpit of All Souls Unitarian

Church in Indianapolis in 1938. There he served until the end of 1953. He died on July 7, 1955, at the age of 66.

Like Frank C.S. Wicks, his predecessor at All Souls, Backus was one of the 34 signers in 1933 of "A Humanist Manifesto." Along with other Unitarian ministers such as John H. Dietrich, Curtis W. Reese, and Edwin H. Wilson, Backus was one of the eminent popularizers of the Humanist movement. From 1944 to 1946 he served as the second president of the American Humanist Association.

During the mid-1940s Backus's weekly fifteen-minute radio sermons influenced many people and contributed to the formation of Unitarian congregations in several other Indiana cities.

In addition to his thoughtful, stimulating, and remarkably well constructed sermons, Backus's activities included membership on the board of the Indianapolis Children's Bureau and on the Indiana White House Committee on Child Welfare. He was active in the American Civil Liberties Union and played an important part in the formation of the Indiana Society for Mental Hygiene, which he served for many years as its president. And he led opposition to "released time" religious education in public schools, one result of which was the organization of the Citizens Committee for Separation of Church and State.

His radio and pulpit sermons were regrettably not published for a truly large audience. But better late than never. This volume brings together his two small collections of radio sermons, *If Thought Be Free* (1946) and *The Sheep and the Goats* (1948), together with his final twelve pulpit addresses delivered during the fall of 1953. Also included is his September 23, 1945, sermon on the Champaign, Illinois, *McCollum* case challenging "released time" religious instruction in public schools. (The U.S. Supreme Court's 1948 *McCollum* ruling was a landmark in the development of church-state law. Vashti Cromwell McCollum, mother of the plaintiff in the case, later became president of the American Humanist Association. Her son James, the plaintiff, became an attorney, a church-state separation activist, an active Unitarian Universalist and Humanist, performing the first Humanist wedding at West Point Military Academy. In October 1997 I had the pleasure of lunching with Mrs. McCollum and her son Dan, the three-term mayor of Champaign, when I spoke at the University of Illinois.)

More than four decades have passed since Burdette Backus's death, but he remains firmly in the memory of many as a man of great wisdom, sensitivity, dignity, energy, and courage. When he spoke it was impossible not to listen. When one reads his work today, one finds not so much of the flash and fire, the *Sturm und Drang,* of a symphony by Dimitri Shostakovich as the calm steadiness, solidity, warmth, and confidence of a work by Ralph Vaughan Williams.

The reader will note in Backus's writing the sort of grammatical masculinity typical of the period in which it was produced but now happily out of fashion. There is no doubt in my mind, however, that were he alive today Backus would be on the frontlines in the defense of women's rights.

The reader should also be reminded that Backus's radio talks, comprising the first two sections the book, were delivered on a popular Indianapolis radio station to a general public audience, few of whom were likely to have had the slightest acquaintance with either Humanism or Unitarianism, and – remarkably – this in a state which less than two decades earlier had been largely in the grip of the Ku Klux Klan.

* * *

I am happy to play a part in bringing the timely and timeless wisdom of Burdette Backus to a new generation of readers.

Let me acknowledge my gratitude to Virginia Backus Lyon for permission to republish her father's work, Jack Mendelsohn for contributing the foreword and for the influence he has had on my life and thinking, Nick and Nikki Gonis for lending me a battered copy of Backus's radio talks and thus inspiring this book, Teri Grimwood for her skill in preparing this book for publication, and Karen Gajewski for designing the cover.

Edd Doerr
President
American Humanist Association

If Thought
Be Free

The Atomic Bomb and Religion

The Atomic Bomb has been described as perhaps the greatest invention of all time. Involving as it does the first large scale, practical use of atomic energy, the basic stuff of which the universe is made, it inaugurates a new era in the history of mankind. Every new invention, every new source of power which man has tapped, has brought in its wake profound changes affecting not only the gadgets which we use but also our social life and even our individual thoughts and feelings. We must expect that the changes which will come as a consequence of the control of atomic power will be even greater than those which were produced by the introduction of the steam engine which caused what we call the "industrial revolution." Slight wonder that Mr. Raymond Swing has warned us that we have perhaps five years to adjust our mentality to the atomic age or perish. Let us look at some of the probable consequences which justify such a dire prediction.

First, there is what it means for any future war. On that fateful August day when President Truman announced the use of the atomic bomb in the destruction of Hiroshima I was visiting in the home of my daughter whose husband is a physicist in a naval research laboratory. He immediately said that the atomic bomb in combination with the type of robot planes which the Germans were developing at the conclusion of the war in Europe could readily knock out all the major cities of the United States almost over night; this could be accomplished from a distant continent without ever an enemy soldier setting foot on our soil or flying through our air. I have since seen his judgment confirmed by other scientists.

How are we going to meet a menace like that? President Truman has assured us that we, along with the British and the Canadians, will keep the secret of the bomb. There has been talk of putting the control of it in the hands of the Security Council of the United Nations. Representative Louis Ludlow has introduced in Congress a resolution calling for the United Nations to ban the atomic bomb forever as an instrument in war. But at best such measures are only stopgaps; they will not bring us real security. Scientists are well agreed that the secret of atomic power can not be kept for long; the knowledge on which the achievement was based is the common property of the scientific world and what we have been able to do others will succeed in accomplishing, with or without our help. Nor can the proposal to ban the use of the bomb allay our fears; the effort to "civilize" warfare is foredoomed to defeat. If we are to have further wars, sooner or later the contestants will resort to the use of the most destructive weapons available in spite of any such bans. There is merit in the suggestion of using the atomic bomb as an instrument in the hands of the United Nations for the sake of preserving peace, but even this does not go to the root of the matter.

What is needed is that we shall attack the institution of war itself and eliminate it from human life. General MacArthur, in his magnificent address at the surrender of Japan, put the matter in a nutshell. He said: "The utter destructiveness of war now blots out this alternative." We must find some other way or perish. This means that we shall have to take much bolder steps in uniting the peoples of the earth than anything we have been considering to date. The atomic bomb announces that our thinking on this subject is already outmoded, and that we shall have to have "One world or no world." Not only shall we have to go much farther in the matter of achieving world federation than we have been contemplating, but also we shall have to speed up the establishment of those basic conditions of economic and social equality among the peoples of earth which alone provide a secure foundation for enduring peace.

This directs our thoughts to the positive program which we must develop in our use of atomic power; we shall get farther by learning to exploit its possibilities for the benefit of mankind than by seeking to restrict its use. Already a number of scientists have pointed out something of what may be accomplished by this approach. J.D. Bernal, of the University of London, likens this new step which men have taken in the control of nature's own energy, to the discovery of America by Columbus. It opens out a whole new world for development by men. Its possibilities are limited only by our capacities. Here is energy of an order a million times greater than we have ever had at our disposal before. It can be harnessed to the work of the world in a thousand different ways: to provide us transportation, turn the wheels of industry, heat our homes, cultivate our fields, improve our health. Moreover, the manner in which the secret of atomic control was wrested from nature by scientific research on a scale never before attempted, holds in it the promise that other equally important scientific problems will yield to the same kind of methods and that our knowledge and control of our environment can be vastly extended.

The title of the article in which Prof. Bernal sets forth these possibilities is "Everybody's Atom." He is at great pains to point out that the question of how these possibilities are to be exploited is of the utmost importance. If ever any source of wealth ought to be used in the interests of all mankind and not be permitted to gravitate into the hands of a few to use for their own selfish interests it is this atomic energy. It has been made available by the accumulated scientific knowledge of the past half century. Men and women of many nations have contributed; it is particularly noticeable that a number of them were scientists driven out of their homelands by the Nazis. The final achievement was accomplished by a great pooling of scientific intelligence and industrial skill; by the cooperation of some 65,000 persons; by the expenditure of two billion dollars of public monies. There are ugly rumors abroad that certain of the rights to this control of atomic power are to be signed over to private companies. This must not be unless at the same time the rights of humanity in it are adequately safeguarded. As one of our American scientists has said: "Let us not blindly throw the whole business in the street to be scrambled for." We are here confronted in acute form with the great problem of combining individual initiative with social wellbeing.

If atomic power is used for war it will atomize us. If it is used intelligently under social control for the benefit of mankind it can lift the level of life all round the globe and promote prosperity and welfare of every type. The energy of the atom is itself neutral, ready to destroy or serve humanity according to the use to which it is put. We are much more disturbed by what we know about the frailties of human nature than we are by the new knowledge we have acquired of how to control the power locked in the atom. The final answer to the question with which we are confronted lies in the minds and hearts of men. It is here that religion comes in, for it is the business of religion to establish in men the kind of character which can use the power of the world for creative rather than destructive ends; it is the business of religion to build men who are equal to the demands of the atomic age.

We shall have to confess that religion has failed tragically in its task. One of the most potent reasons for the present dilemmas of humanity is that religion has not kept pace with science, it has not enabled man to secure a control over himself equal to his control over the powers of the world around him. The reason for this failure is that men of religion have not seen their task clearly; their attention has been centered on the superficial, the unimportant, to the exclusion of the vital. They have been blinded by inherited creeds and ancient forms to the true work they should be doing. It fairly made me sick to read in a Chicago newspaper that a minister had interpreted the atomic bomb as a sign that the end of the world is at hand, and that the question which it poses to every man is, "Are you prepared to meet your God for eternal Judgment?" The futility of that sort of thing, its unrelatedness to the crying needs of the world today would be comic were it not a tragic reminder of how much human energy is thus misdirected.

We need, oh how desperately we need a religion which is in tune with the mentality of our day; a religion which takes as its central task the creation of the kind of men and women who can build the only sort of society capable of mastering the world in which we live for human ends. It must be a religion which brings the scientist's own temper of mind to bear on its problems and thus learns how to control the energies of human nature as effectively as the scientist controls the energy of uranium. It must be a religion which does not content itself with pious injunctions to love our neighbors as ourselves, to forget ourselves in the service of the common good. These commands are basic, but we shall never be able to get men to heed them unless we press further and discover *why* it is that men destroy where they should create, grasp where they should give, hate where they should love. Religion must learn to establish in men desires in harmony with its ideals, character equal to the requirements of the Great Society of Humanity we dream of building on earth. It is a task of exceeding great difficulty, but it can be done.

A cartoon appeared recently in a magazine: it presents a baby, labeled "Humanity," crawling on all fours over the globe and looking up at a bespectacled scientist who has in his pocket a document bearing the inscription "The Atom." Between his thumb and forefinger he holds out to the baby a pellet under which appears the words "Life or Death." The caption of the cartoon is the query, "Baby play with nice ball?" It is the function of religion to enable that baby to grow in stature so that he can stand erect, mature in intelligence and emotional power, able to make certain that the choice is "Life."

The religion that can do this will not exist in a vacuum; it can succeed only as it is made flesh in the lives of the millions of men and women of earth. It can develop among us only as we recognize that the religion which did for the age of the bow and arrow will not suffice for the age of the atomic bomb; only as we recognize that religion must be progressive, and feed itself on all the knowledge that men acquire, utilize all the intelligence they possess, as well as their idealism and devotion. The responsibility for making sure that such a religion grows from more to more among men rests with each one of us. It is important that a man do his personal work in the world by which he earns his living. But it is equally important that he give of the best of himself to make certain that the character of his world is such that he can be satisfied to live in it himself, and to have his children inherit it after he is gone. This he cannot do if he stands in dread that atomic bombs in the hands of power-mad individuals or nations constantly threaten to destroy all he holds most dear. We must become masters of our own souls to the end that we may master the forces of the external universe and make them obedient servants of the highest human purposes.

Hell is a Myth

There is one fear which I would lift from every heart in the world were I able to do so, for it is so dreadful and so unnecessary: that is the fear of hell. I find it incredible that in this day of the world any one does still believe in a literal hell as a place of torment in which the souls of the damned suffer eternal punishment. It ought to be unnecessary for anyone to announce at this late date that hell is a myth, for that should be taken as obvious by all men. But I am continually having it thrust on my attention that there are multitudes whose minds are still preyed upon by this horrible fiction.

Early in my ministry some people came to me to ask me to conduct a funeral service for a member of the family who had died. They explained that the last death in their immediate circle had been that of a baby, and that the minister who had officiated stood by the tiny casket and announced to those who had assembled that since the infant had not been baptized he was now burning in hell. For any man to make a statement like that to grief stricken parents seems to me utterly inhuman and the reverse of all that I deem to be religious. The father and mother were suffering from the loss of their little one and instead of sympathizing with them, seeking to do what he could to comfort them in their sorrow, this minister added to their burden by invoking the ancient superstition of hell fire and infant damnation; he made the occasion, which is hard enough to bear anyway, well nigh intolerable. I doubt not that the man was sincere and really believed in his infamous doctrine; but he was terribly mistaken and his mistake exacted a heavy price from heavy hearts. The parents explained that they had come to me because they understood that I did not believe in hell and would not use the funeral as an occasion to harrow their feelings. I assured them that such was the case, that I did not believe in hell, and that a funeral was to me a time for such sympathy and help as is possible for us to extend to those in sorrow.

If this were an isolated case we might dismiss it lightly, but alas, over the years I have discovered that it is all too common. Again and again people have come to me for similar reasons; they have told me how the fear of hell has burdened their childhood and continued as a dark shadow over their minds even in maturity; mothers have come to me with deep concern in their hearts for their sons, half believing, half doubting the dreadful doctrine that their beloved boys, because of unbelief or evil deed, are doomed to eternal punishment. Every time I have stood in the presence of such agony I have felt as Lincoln is reported to have felt when he first saw the iniquities of slavery and resolved that he was going to smite it some day.

When we come to examine the history of the belief in hell and see something of its origins as they are disclosed by modern scholarship we can see clearly enough that it is but the mistaken idea of ancient peoples who knew far less about the world than we do today, and their error, becoming part of accepted religious doctrine, has continued long after the best thought of men has outgrown it. In those ancient days men were disturbed, as we are often disturbed, by the fact that the circumstances of life frequently do violence to our sense of justice; the good man does not always receive the rewards of his virtue in the prizes of this world; the evil man does not suffer the punishment that his deeds would seem to require, but lives in prosperity and may even go to his grave honored by his companions. It is this problem which constitutes the theme of the book of Job in the Old Testament. Eventually the thoughts of men hit on the idea that the inequities of this life are redressed in another world; that if the good man does not get his just reward in this life it is reserved for him in the next, and that likewise the evil man will there receive the penalty which he escaped here. We can trace the whole development of the idea of heaven and hell, and see how this early demand for justice was built into the picture of the world which existed in the minds of men in antiquity. We can see, also, how once established, the doctrine of rewards and punishment in the after life became a powerful tool in the hands of men who exploited it in their own interest, making it a source of revenue and power. Having a vested interest in it they did all they could to perpetuate it and fix it in the minds of the people.

But the progress of knowledge has changed our whole picture of the world so that the ancient conceptions of heaven and hell no longer have any place in it. We see that this was a mistaken idea just as the belief that the world was flat, as held in antiquity, was a mistaken idea. And the development of religion itself has led us beyond the crude ideas of reward and punishment with which our ancestors of several thousand years ago sought to solve the riddle of evil. Many of the best minds in the Christian church have long since repudiated the doctrine of eternal punishment. Dean Shaler Matthews of the Divinity School at the University of Chicago was wont to say that we must read the golden rule Godward and demand of God that he shall do nothing to us that He would not have us do to Him. No human father who loved his son would ever doom him to eternal hell fire; why should we believe that God would do such a thing? And one of England's leading churchmen, Dean Inge, has said: "When we remember the character of God the Father was revealed to mankind by and in Christ, the blasphemy of regarding Him as an implacable and ferocious torturer seems almost incredible and must remain a heavy reproach against European Christianity."

My own repudiation of the doctrine of hell does not rest on theological grounds so much as it does on my conviction that the belief is utterly inconsistent with the whole conception of the universe that the modern mind has achieved. The astronomer's telescope has searched the vast reaches of space and not even among the remote galaxies has it found any place where it would be possible to locate the hell of traditional theology. The other sciences have helped us establish a conception of a world of law and order and vastness in which the old idea of a hell to which the souls of erring men are sent for punishment seems childishly fantastic and out of place. I reject the doctrine because I can see that it is a ghastly mistake; because it is untrue. I reject it also because it revolts my moral sensibilities by the wholly unnecessary suffering it has inflicted and continues to inflict on myriads of helpless victims. I would erase it from the mind of the world at once, if I could.

But it would be urged by those who still believe in the doctrine of future punishment that in the absence of that belief, men will no longer restrain their passions and their selfish desires, and that it is necessary to hold the threat of hell over men to secure conformity to the moral law. I am convinced that the efficacy of this threat has been vastly over-estimated; some persons may have been restrained from evil deeds by it. But a morality that is based on fear is on a very low level and is never secure. There is no danger that the world will go to pieces morally when it gets rid of the fear of hell, for fortunately morality has a much firmer foundation in human life than fear. Most of us meet the moral requirements because we are members of a society that expects it of us, because it is only on the basis of good conduct that we can get along well with our neighbors, and live at peace with ourselves. Social habit, conscience, intelligence and love are much stronger safeguards of morality than is fear, and have the added advantage that they lead us toward the heights of the ethical life, where we can never climb in the chains of fear. The majority of the men and women I know do not believe in hell and yet they are very fine people, quite as high in their standards of conduct as any with whom I am acquainted. No, the moral life of the world will not be endangered by the disappearance of the doctrine of hell. On the contrary it will be strengthened, fortified by more positive and creative powers.

During my senior year in theological school I served as minister of a Universalist church in a village in western New York. There was still current in the village the story of a woman whose husband died. She was orthodox and her minister was on vacation; the only other orthodox minister was also away. A member of the Universalist church suggested to the woman that she have the Universalist minister conduct the service, whereupon she threw up her hands in horror, exclaiming: "Oh, I couldn't have a man who doesn't believe in hell bury my husband!" We get a good laugh out of the implications of that exclamation. Would that we could laugh the whole concept of hell out of existence and free the minds of men for more profitable beliefs.

There is, of course, a kind of hell which we cannot laugh out of existence, because it is not simply a theological fiction but a very tough reality of human existence. I mean the hell of war, of poverty, of ignorance, of disease, of crime, of moral degradation. We do not have to invent cruelties and fears: they are all too prevalent in our lives, and a perpetual challenge to us to alter conditions, so to use the forces of our own minds and hearts, that we shall alleviate the sufferings which they cause and rescue men and women from the hells that are of human making.

Warwick Deeping, the novelist, has said: "Hell is to look back at the dim, reproachful faces of those who loved us, those whom we betrayed." Yes, it is hell to know that you have failed those who relied on you and that because of you their lives were filled with frustration and pain; it is hell to know that you are not the man you might have been, that idealism has given away to cynicism, that generosity has been swallowed up in selfishness. But it is the kind of hell that you can do something about, not as much, perhaps, as you wish you could, yet something. A contrite recognition of the way in which you have failed, a genuine resolve to do better, will help you to learn from your mistakes and build your past failures into a better future. It is worth trying; on the slender threat of your own endeavor you can climb out of the pit of your personal hell.

The same is true of the social hells which men have created in their ignorance, selfishness and evil. We need not accept them as inevitable. Men need not go on forever killing each other on the field of battle, exploiting each other in the market place and factory; poverty and insecurity are not fixed in the nature of things;

ignorance and disease are not inexorably fastened upon us. All of these evils which place an intolerable burden on so many hearts are to some extent within our control. If we bring our intelligence, our skill, our determination, our love to bear on these hells we can wipe out some of the worst of them; we may not succeed as rapidly or as completely as we desire, but that we can do much is certain, and in the doing of it we shall find life's highest meaning. It were far more profitable for religion to give over its concern with what happens to a man after death, for that is hidden in the mystery of the inscrutable universe of which we are the children, and concentrate its splendid energies in seeking to redeem the dark places of misery and woe on this earth, taking as its supreme purpose the making of the lives of all the children of men fairer, happier, more deeply satisfying; freeing the minds and hearts from necessary fears; helping men and women to grow into that stature of manhood and womanhood which is heaven.

In Time of Trouble

A letter which I received recently contained this sentence: "Life is tragic for most people." It is indeed; none of us can escape certain tragic experiences. Anyone with imagination reading the casualty lists in our newspapers these days must interpret them in terms of the personal suffering which they bring to the families affected -- parents mourning for sons who have laid down their lives on foreign battlefields; wives knowing that the dreams of their hearts for the normal fulfillment of their marriage have suddenly become impossible; men returning to try to take up life anew under the handicap of severe physical and emotional disability. It is a sorry picture of suffering, frustration, anguish that is conjured to our minds, all of it a part of the inevitable price of war.

But war simply enables us to see as under a magnifying glass the element of tragedy that is always a part of our lives. Indeed in some respects the tragedy of war is less terrible, less sordid than much that afflicts us in the ordinary course of experience. The wounds inflicted on our hearts when our loved ones give the last full measure of devotion in the service of their country are clean wounds, and our sorrow has in it the element of pride that they have met a patriot's death. But there are many of the tragedies of life which are poisonous because they seem so unnecessary and futile. Here is a man whose career has been blasted by the betrayal of a friend, or a woman whose life has been made one long agony by her relation with the one person with whom she expected to find her greatest bliss. Worse still is the lot of him who has betrayed himself, and because of inner weakness has lost sight of the ideal self he might have become and fallen into degradation; there is no worse hell than that of the man who must despise himself. Yes, life always carries its full quota of tragedy.

What are we going to do about it? How shall we fortify ourselves to deal with this element in our existence? Much of the thought and energy of men has been devoted to the attempt to try to find an adequate answer to these questions. Perhaps the most widely accepted and effective answer achieved to date is that of religion which has taught men that everything which happens in this world does so under the will of God and that even our sorrows and sufferings have meaning in his sight and are intended for our good though it is beyond our power to understand. For millions of stricken human souls this has worked; because they have piously resigned themselves to the will of God, the poison has been extracted from their wounds and they have risen superior to their tragedy.

But my concern this morning is not with these people; they have an answer that to them seems satisfactory, one that meets their needs. There are, however, multitudes in our modern world for whom that traditional answer no longer suffices; for one reason or another they cannot accept it as true, and its efficacy depends upon its seeming true to him who holds it. But these moderns have to meet the same portion of tragedy that is the lot of their brothers and many of them are perplexed in mind and disturbed in heart; they have not found a satisfactory alternative to the answer of religion, and are at a loss to know how to deal most effectively with the trouble that comes into their own lives. It is to them in particular that I am addressing my words, and in so doing I shall deal with tragedy not as a mystery to be explained but as a practical situation to be met. I have my explanation but this is not the place to advance it.

The first thing to do is to take stock of the resources which we have for dealing with the trouble that comes to us. These are far greater than we usually realize; when the blow has struck us it leaves us in a daze and the situation is apt to seem far more hopeless than it really is. Our most immediate resources are those within ourselves and it is important that we avail ourselves of them to the full.

We human beings are far tougher than we ordinarily realize; we can take a great deal of punishment and still come up for more. This is because of our heritage; our bodies were fashioned for us by a long line of ancestors who had to battle for their existence in a hard and cruel world, and as a result there is built into the very texture of our blood and bone extraordinary powers of endurance and recuperation. We marvel at some of the tales of heroism that are coming out of the war, men who like those of the PT boat that was cut in two by a Japanese destroyer managed despite severe wounds and incredible exposure to win their way back to safety. They were enabled to do this by virtue of the tremendous vitality that is built into the human body. In the same way we see apparently frail old men and women fool the doctors and return to life and vigor after all hope for them had been abandoned. As long as there is life there is hope.

The counterpart of this amazing physical vitality is our equally marvelous mental or spiritual endowment. Men survive not only because of the toughness of muscle and bone, but also because of the ruggedness of the will to live, because they have refused to give up the struggle, and have availed themselves of every opportunity and created opportunities where none existed. Theoretically we are all aware of this; we know the supreme importance played by the unquenchable human spirit in the battle of life, but it is much easier to recognize and applaud it in the other fellow than it is to recognize it in ourselves and make use of it in our own time of trouble. We are apt to assume that only heroes have this spark; but the truth is that the stuff of which heroes are made is well-nigh universal in its distribution among men; it is in you and in me as an untouched reserve to be called upon in the time of need.

The supreme triumph of this spirit which resides in each of us is when it takes the very tragedy that has threatened to overwhelm us and makes it the means of greater achievement than would otherwise have been possible. Consider the story which A. de Seversky, the great authority on aviation, tells of himself. He was an aviator with the Russian army in the first world war and lost a leg in action. At first he felt completely crushed, sure that his anticipated career was at an end and that there was nothing left for him but to drag out his days as a miserable cripple. But actually he turned the loss of his leg from a liability into an asset. Because of what had happened to him he turned to a study of the theoretical side of aviation, and as he himself has said he has won his place of distinction not *in spite of the handicap* of having only one leg, but *because* of it. This is something that each one of us would do well to remember in his own time of trouble. There are few situations so desperate that ordinary human courage and intelligence will not suffice to wring out of them some otherwise impossible good; we do have the magic power of transmuting the base metal of apparent tragedy into the pure gold of high achievement.

There is something else that we should remember in taking count of our resources, and that is that we are not alone but can count on the help of our comrades. The papers recently told the dramatic story of how a paratrooper was saved from certain death when his parachute collapsed and he was hurtling toward the ground. A buddy who had made the jump at the same time saw what had happened and managed to reach out and grab the parachute and held on until they had both landed in safety. We might take this story as a symbol of the help that man can yield to man. It is not often rendered as dramatically, but none the less effectively. The wounded soldiers at the front are saved in large numbers by the labors of the stretcher bearers, the skill and devotion of the doctors and nurses, the cooperation of a transport system that gets them rapidly to hospitals, the advance in medical science, and perhaps the blood plasma that you have donated. In the same way the life of each one of us is enmeshed in a social structure which is ready to spring into action and help us in our time of trouble; friends and even strangers of whom we have never heard are ready to help us in a thousand different ways. We are strong not with our own strength alone, but with that of all mankind.

Let me remind you of a fact from another realm of human experience which will serve to fortify this sense of a strength derived from our membership within the great community of mankind. One of the great ministers to the human spirit is music; it speaks a language without words that can meet our every mood. And how richly we are endowed with music from out the past and the present to serve us in our needs! Consider the case of Beethoven; it has been said of him that his whole life was like a stormy day, heavy with clouds, the flashing of lightning, the approaching hurricane. He had a difficult life, full of sorrow, tempestuous. Yet he made the motto of his life: "Joy through suffering." He to whom the world refused joy, created joy himself to give to the world; he forged it from his own misery. He has been called the "grandest and best friend of those who struggle and suffer." Sometimes Beethoven would go and play to a mother grieving over the loss of her child and without speaking a word bring her consolation with his music. It retains that power to help us in our sorrow because it speaks out of his own conquest of grief.

Yes, we do have great resources within ourselves and within the human community of which we are members which we can call upon in our time of trouble. They will not always be sufficient to our need, and we will many times wish that they were much more effective than they are. Part of the lesson which we must learn in arriving at a mature attitude toward life is to accept the fact that the world is not arranged to gratify all our desires; that we must do the best that can be done and then resign ourselves to the inevitable. This brings my thoughts around again to the religious method of meeting trouble by accepting "the will of God."

Though the modern mind cannot accept this teaching in its traditional form of belief in a personal deity who guides every step we take in life, it does recognize that there was a truth in this ancient doctrine which we must carry over with us into the thought of today. That truth is that we human beings are dependent on a great universal order of which we are the children, the order that reveals itself in the movement of the stars, that springs up in the beauty of the flowers, and in the wonders of the mind and heart of man. It is futile for us to complain and rebel because this universal order brings us tragedy as well as joy; it sets the conditions of our lives and we have to learn to accept them. But within certain limits our world home is subject to our control and can be made to yield us more of joy and less of suffering.

If we think of God as this stable order of nature, if we think of him as that indwelling spirit of life which manifests itself in the courage of the man who rises to turn disaster into triumph, the sympathy that soothes the suffering and nurses the sick of heart back to life, if we think of him as the will to victory within humanity as it marches down the centuries adding to its stores of wisdom and understanding, then we can still say that God is our refuge in time of trouble. Then we know that Providence works in and through us and our concern is to see that such Providence becomes ever more effective. Shortly after I came to Indianapolis I met a woman who was engaged in seeing to it that no child in our city schools should go hungry. That is the way in which God comes to the help of his children in time of trouble; forever incarnating himself anew in human life, he goes forth to redeem the world from misery and woe.

Unitarians Believe

We begin this morning a series of talks on the general subject, "Unitarians Believe." These Sunday broadcasts which began last April have for the most part dealt with the broadly human aspects of religion and only seldom has doctrine been specifically considered. But I have observed that there have always been more requests for copies of the address when it has taken up some particular belief; this indication of listener interest has led me to undertake the present series in which I shall set forth the Unitarian doctrine on the major articles of religious belief such as God, Man, the Bible, etc.

I wish to preface the series by making as clear as possible our attitude toward those who hold beliefs very different from our own. We do not regard them as heretics or infidels, and we have no desire to compel them to believe as we do. We know that in these great matters of religious belief no one has the absolute and final answers; all our truths are relative, with a large admixture of error. Consequently it behooves us to be tolerant, charitable toward one another when we differ. Unitarians reverence sincere belief wherever it is found, and recognize that to him who holds the doctrine it is precious truth. So if you discover that you disagree with some of the things I say please remember that we respect your right to your own beliefs; indeed what we want above all else is that a man shall be true to his own thinking. The purpose of this series is not controversial; rather it is to express the beliefs at which a great many persons have arrived without knowing that there is a church which embodies those beliefs.

There is an initial difficulty which confronts us when we are asked what Unitarians believe and that is that most persons expect an answer in terms of a creed: "I believe in God, the Father Almighty, etc." But we cannot give that kind of an answer because Unitarians do not have a creed; we are a creedless church. The reason for this is two-fold. In the first place we do not believe it is possible to state the intellectual content of religious belief in a fixed and final form; we are convinced that men grow in their understanding of the truth and that it may be necessary to change the statement which we draw up today because tomorrow may bring new truth that compels revision. So we have decided that a formal creed is a hindrance rather than a help in religion and we have eliminated it from our church. In the second place we are bound together by ties which we find deeper than those of intellectual agreement; we are bound together by our spirit and our purpose is to enrich our individual lives and to improve the social order. Within the unity of this purpose we discover that it is possible for us to hold a wide variety of beliefs; we do not demand uniformity of belief among our members.

Consider, for example, the covenant of the particular Unitarian Church of which I am minister -- All Souls of Indianapolis. It reads as follows: "Love is the spirit of this church and service is its law; to dwell together in peace, to seek the truth in love, and to help one another; this is our covenant." You will note that there are no theological doctrines set forth in this statement; it says nothing about God or Jesus. It simply formulates a human purpose in which we are all united and it allows a wide latitude of belief. A Methodist, or a Baptist, or a Catholic could join our church; of course practically they would not want to because our statement leaves out matters that they would want included, but there are no barriers as far as we are concerned to anyone who wants to join us in furthering the purpose set forth in our covenant. This applies to the Jew, the Buddhist, the atheist as well as it does to the Christian. One of our great leaders of more than a century ago, William Ellery Channing, described this attitude by insisting that he was a member of the Church Universal "from which no man is excluded save by the death of goodness in his own heart."

Another Unitarian leader in the generation following Channing formulated the basic principles of our church in a brief statement which has continued to command our approval and enthusiasm. This was William Channing Gannett. He said: "*Freedom* is our method in religion; *reason* is our guide in religion; *fellowship* is our spirit in religion; *character* is our test in religion; *service* is our aim in religion." Again you will note that there is nothing about theological doctrines here; it concerns itself entirely with a spirit, a method, a purpose. Each one of those phrases which Mr. Gannett used is so important as to deserve a brief elaboration. Let us take them up one at a time.

"Freedom is our method in religion." The Unitarian church in this country was born in that period which followed the revolutionary war when our nation was being established and when the enthusiasm for freedom ran high. That principle of freedom was adopted by the Unitarian church as basic. It is no accident that Thomas Jefferson, the author of the Declaration of Independence, was himself a Unitarian. We have written, and continue to live by, a religious declaration of independence. We are convinced that the spiritual life of men flourishes best under the conditions of freedom, just as does the political life. Therefore we insist that we will not submit ourselves to this external authority of church or creed; we must be free to develop the inner powers of our lives in accordance with their own genius. The final and supreme authority in religion lies in the individual soul. Whatever may be the pronouncement of the rulers within the church, whatever may be the statement of the creeds. I must find it true in me or I must reject it. I must trust my own mind beyond all else, and it can give me its best results only as it operates in freedom. This is democracy in religion and Unitarians accept it wholeheartedly.

We are not, however, without guidance in our freedom; it is not the freedom of license or anarchy as is clearly indicated in the subsequent phrases which Gannett uses. The second one is: "Reason is our guide in religion." Man is endowed by nature with the power of reason, with intelligence, by virtue of which he can seek out and know the truth. To be sure it is not an infallible guide; many a time it leads us astray and we fall into error. But it is the best, indeed the only, guide we have and in the long run it serves us well. It discovers its own mistakes and corrects them. Susan B. Anthony, the famous champion of woman's suffrage in the early days of that movement, herself a Unitarian, expressed our position regarding the use of reason in a telling phrase. She said: "Truth for authority, not authority for truth." That is it! Don't take what someone else tells you no matter with what authority he presumes to speak; discover what commends itself to your reason as the truth and then accept that as your authority. Would you know what the Unitarian doctrine is on any question, then find out what the truth of the matter is, find out what reason working under conditions of freedom, following the evidence available, has to say and that is Unitarian doctrine. And if tomorrow reason shall modify, expand, or even reverse her decision, then this too is Unitarian doctrine. We are not afraid to acknowledge that we were mistaken; we are ready to receive new truth with gladness, proud to grow in knowledge and understanding. I know that my personal creed is very different from what it was when I began my ministry, and I am sure that it is very much richer and more satisfying.

The third in our list of principles is expressed in the phrase: "Fellowship is our spirit in religion." By this we mean that we seek to be broadly inclusive rather than narrow and sectarian. We consider all human beings as our brothers and do not propose to erect artificial barriers between us and them. We will not say to any man, "because you think differently from us you are therefore outside the circle of our good-will, we will not have fellowship with you." On the contrary we regard it as one of the great obligations resting upon us to tear down the barriers which so needlessly separate men, the barriers of class and race and creed, and to do all within our power to promote the unity of mankind. Even when others exclude us from their fellowship on doctrinal grounds we try not to let it disturb us unduly and to rise above the barriers in the spirit of Edwin Markham's lines:

> He drew a circle that shut me out,
> Heretic, rebel, a thing to flout;
> But love and I had the wit to win,
> We drew a circle that took him in.

"Character is our test in religion." The meaning of this phrase is obvious; it does not make any difference that you may profess to be at one with us in your intellectual convictions, your religion is not genuine unless it bears the hall-mark of character, the kind of character that is on the creative, the constructive side of human life. We used to speak of "salvation by character," meaning thereby that a man was saved by the quality of his character rather than by profession of faith or the alleged supernatural power of a church. But recently we have grown away from that language because we have dismissed the whole traditional conception of salvation as being untrue; the later phrase, "Character is our test in religion" represents our present thought more accurately. "By their fruits ye shall know them," said Jesus and we hold that worthy character is the fruit of true religion.

The final principle of the Unitarian church is expressed in the words, "Service is our aim in religion." Man is not merely individual, he is social, and one of the surest marks of fine character is the deep seated acceptance of the fact that we are members one of another. Any religion deserving the name will be a prophetic religion, crying out against the injustices of the world, against man's inhumanity to man, and taking as its supreme task the constant improvement of the social order. Sometimes, as at present, this involves revolutionary changes. But religion is false to its nature if it timidly shrinks away from those things which mean a greater opportunity for the fulfillment of life on the part of the common peoples of earth. It is in just such times as the present that men of religion should be in the thick of the fight leading those causes which hold in them the promise of a better world. Service to the cause of all mankind is the aim of our religion.

Though I have put the emphasis this morning on the basic principles of the Unitarian religion rather than on those doctrines which go to make up the usual church creed, we have, of course, thought a great deal about doctrinal matters. And while we have no authoritative statement about them, and though we do not all think alike, there is yet considerable measure of agreement among us; that degree of agreement which is the natural result of free minds working by similar methods on the same material. What some of these conclusions are I shall tell you in the subsequent talks of this series. But I want you to bear constantly in mind that the important words in the Unitarian vocabulary are Freedom, Reason, Fellowship, Character, Service. That this is so should in itself speak to your minds and hearts of what is most fundamental in Unitarian belief.

I Believe in Man

The most distinctive doctrine of the Unitarian is his belief in man. More than a century ago William Ellery Channing, who was our outstanding leader at that time, said: "I do and I must reverence human nature; nothing will disturb my faith in its godlike powers and tendencies. I bless it for its kind affections, for its strong and tender love. I honour it for its struggles against oppression, its achievements in science and art, its examples of heroic and saintly virtues." We have continued to cherish this confidence in human nature as the living heart of our religion.

It is interesting to recall how Channing arrived at his conviction of the divinity of the human soul. As a boy of seven he went one Sunday with his father to church and listened to a typical sermon of the time. It was all about original sin, the wickedness of man, the wrath of God, and the eternal fires of hell. It had a very depressing effect on his young mind and as he was riding home in the cart with his father he was plunged into deep gloom. Suddenly his father began to whistle and immediately the dark clouds lifted from the boy's mind, for he thought: "If father can whistle, then what the preacher said can't be true; the world isn't such a dreadful place after all." Thus began his escape from the dark doctrines of Calvinistic theology, and he went on to become the chief spokesman for a religion that proclaimed the essential divinity of human nature.

This Unitarian doctrine is not held in ignorance of the evil aspects of man; no one who has had the least experience of human selfishness and cruelty, lust and greed, will for one moment deny the reality of this evil. We are under no illusion that men, even the best of them, are angels; and we have plenty of evidence before our eyes of the depths of depravity to which some of them can sink. But it does not make us hopeless about human nature. We are deeply persuaded that belief in man and confidence in his future is consistent with a realistic appraisal of the facts.

We deny emphatically the dogma of original sin which declares that every child is conceived in sin and comes into the world with an inescapable heritage of evil. It seems to us monstrous to denounce as essentially wicked, the natural process by which little babies come into the world. On the contrary we hold that when a man and woman love each other, establish a home, and participate in the creative process by which the miracle of new life is achieved, they are fulfilling one of the highest functions of human life, and that the whole process should be surrounded with the reverence which inspires a strong sense of the values involved. It is incredible to me that any mother can really believe in her heart of hearts that her darling baby is a creature of total depravity. The little child is the supreme symbol of the divine possibilities of human life. "Of such is the kingdom of heaven."

The tragedy is that we avail ourselves so little of the possibilities that are present in that new life. This is not because we are under a curse of God, foredoomed by the inherent wickedness of human nature to failure, to tyranny, and thievery, to murder and war. No, it is because like an ignorant farmer we do not know how to cultivate our soil properly, do not know the richness of the resources that lie right under our hands. If we were not blinded by mistaken notions, if we would deliberately set ourselves to the task, bending all our resources to it, we could vastly improve the results we achieve in human nature, multiplying the good, diminishing the evil. Indeed, we have already made no little progress in this respect since man became man, but as yet we have only scratched the surface. It is my firm conviction that when we turn our attention to the understanding and mastering of the forces of our own natures we shall win victories comparable to those we have already won in compelling the forces of external nature to do our bidding. This is the next great undertaking of humanity; we are now in the initial stages of it; we have become aware of the nature of our problem; we are beginning to give our best thought to it, and I am confident that the marvels of our age of inventions, with its innumerable mechanical devices, will be surpassed by the achievements in the development of human personality and in our social and economic life.

There is no inherent reason why a large portion of the population should be doomed to lives of unhappiness and frustration because their powers of mind and heart have not developed into that fullness of mature personality which should be achieved by every man and woman among us. There is no inherent reason why so many of earth's children should be doomed to spend their lives in poverty and ignorance. There is no inherent reason why war should continue to take its dreadful toll of human lives. There is no inherent reason why countless millions should continue to live under the menacing clouds of fear and want. It is quite within the realm of possibility for us so to elevate the general level of human life that the majority of men and women shall achieve an existence roughly equal to that enjoyed by the more favored among us today. But to do this we shall have to make it our deliberate purpose and bend our every effort to that end. I cannot conceive of any grander objective than the mastery of human life for the benefit of man.

To be sure it is not going to be easy, but when was anything supremely worth doing easy? There are unruly forces in our natures that require much disciplining before they can be made to serve the good of man instead of inflicting him with evil. But the best thought of our day insists that there are none of the native drives of human nature which cannot be harnessed to constructive purposes and that our central problem is to learn how to do that. Do you say that man is incurably selfish and that his selfishness inevitably dooms to failure his efforts to achieve a nobler way of living? Granted that there is a powerful self-regarding instinct, we observe that in the higher type of men and women the forces of this instinct are directed to constructive social ends because they have learned to extend the boundaries of the self to include their family, their community, and even the world. A primitive drive has been redirected to high human purpose.

The problem is not unlike that of the engineer who must harness a swift mountain torrent and convert its energy, which could so easily spread destruction, into the electrical current which lights the homes of men, turns the wheels of industry, and flashes messages around the earth. It is a matter of spiritual engineering, of learning to harness the dynamic powers of our own souls as they flow down from the mountain heights of our primitive past and put them to work in creating character which more nearly conforms with our ideal of what men and women ought to be, in establishing social conditions that are favorable to the best qualities of human nature. If we understand human nature well enough we can make it work in about any way that we want to.

I am well aware that the sorry state of the world at the present time has brought a wave of pessimism concerning human nature. Men like Reinhold Niebuhr have reverted to the gloomy teachings of the past and are once more proclaiming that man is a creature whose original nature dooms him to sin and suffering. I can well understand the mood which has come over such prophets of despair. But I think that they are wrong, terribly mistaken in their interpretation of the facts. You are whipped before you start if you assume, as Niebuhr does, that even the best in human life is sinful in the eyes of God. Such a conception of human nature should logically paralyze all effort to better conditions; fortunately, because of the inconsistency of the human mind, it doesn't, and Dr. Niebuhr is himself very active in trying to improve the situation. But he would be much more effective if he had a greater faith in man.

Those periods in human history which have been most creative, which have seen the greatest progress toward enlightenment and the improvement of the conditions under which men live, have been characterized by a belief in man. I began this talk by reference to William Ellery Channing, the great Unitarian leader of a century ago. Van Wyck Brooks, in his *Flowering of New England,* says that it was William Ellery Channing with his belief in the divinity of human nature who was chiefly responsible for that remarkable upsurge in New England which produced most of the great men of letters this country has had, resulted in notable social reforms like that of the establishment of the public school, and generally quickened the lives of men. They learned to believe in themselves and their faith showed itself in unprecedented achievement.

The pessimistic view of human nature errs in over-stressing the evil and under-valuing the good in man. It has much to say of the sin of pride, the lust for power, the narrow selfishness, the sensuousness of man; but it does not consider as it should the manly pride which is not inconsistent with genuine humility, the power of love and loyalty and devotion which enables him to achieve social order, the searching intelligence which refuses to be baffled by any problems and persistently seeks a way out of every difficulty, a way forward into new victory, the heroism and self-sacrifice with which he serves the common good. A sober optimism, a restrained yet deep faith in human nature, is consistent with the facts and required for the most effective living.

Belief in man is peculiarly necessary in a democracy. Belief in man, the common man, is the core of the democratic creed. If you do not believe in man you are naturally inclined to some other form of government; you put your trust in the state, or in some divinely appointed leaders and you have the makings of a totalitarian form of government in which the people are considered unequal to ruling themselves and are exploited by those who arrogate to themselves superior powers. But a democracy grows out of a belief that the common people of earth have in themselves the qualities which enable them, in the long run, to do a better job of governing themselves than any self appointed rulers can do. If you are going to believe in democracy you have to believe in man; if you believe in man you inevitably believe in democracy.

One of the supreme prophets and exemplars of democracy was Abraham Lincoln. He was an unusual man, yes; but at the same time he was the common man incarnate. He sprang from the people; he felt that he belonged to them; he believed in them and trusted them; he knew that they were the kind of stuff out of which it is possible to build the kind of a civilization we have dreamed of creating here in America, and in all the world. In the same spirit we of the Unitarian church believe in man. To paraphrase the words of the martyr President, ours is a religion of man, by man, for man. Our abiding purpose is to help man realize ever more fully the divine possibilities which we discover in him.

What and Where is God?

We are to consider this morning a very great and important subject, one that has occupied the mind of man from time immemorial. It behooves us to come to it in a humble spirit deeply aware of the limitations of our best thought on the subject. Beware of the dogmatic mind, of the man who can tell you with certainty all about God, just who he is and how he conducts the affairs of the universe; be equally wary of the man who asserts positively that there is no God and offers some substitute theory as a full and adequate explanation of all things in heaven and on earth. The beginning of wisdom in this great matter is to acknowledge that we do not know, to take as our starting point a reverent agnosticism which will keep us from being too certain about any conclusion at which we may arrive.

The best minds in all ages have wrestled with the great mystery of existence, seeking to give a rational explanation of the world and to interpret human experience in terms that would satisfy the demands of reason and the emotions, but they have not been able to come to agreement. Some men have tried to explain all things in terms of the interplay of physical forces, the ceaseless grinding of omnipotent matter rushing on its relentless way. We call such thinkers "materialists," and despite the fact that their system has never found popular acceptance, it has a long and honorable history and has commanded the assent of able thinkers all the way from Heraclitus who lived five centuries B.C. down to Bertrand Russell in our own day.

Other men have said, no, materialism is not adequate to account for all that we experience of the universe; perhaps it would do as an explanation of the movement of the stars, the rushing of the winds, the ebb and flow of tides, but it cannot explain a blade of grass or the love of a mother for her child or the thought of the philosopher. Such men have gone on to seek the explanation in terms of a spiritual order that lies back of the material universe and produces the results we observe. They have given to this spiritual order the name of God. Simple men have thought of God in childlike terms as being a big man up in the sky, who created the world and runs it, and to whom they can turn in prayer to get things done that are beyond their own power. Philosophers have thought of God as a spiritual being who permeates the whole universe and yet transcends it much as we are present in every part of our bodies and yet feel that we are more than our bodies. We call those who believe in God after this wise "Theists." They have been much more numerous, particularly in our western world, than have the materialists.

Now, materialists and theists have not been the only ones to advance their explanations of the world; there have been numerous other systems of thought which have been developed as men have sought to arrive at an understanding of the universe and the relation of their own lives to it. I shall not stop even to name them. The point is that since these differences of belief exist, since there are so many systems each purporting to have the true explanation, we are forced to the conclusion that no one of them has arrived at a really satisfactory answer or we would all be persuaded of its truth. We don't have to debate whether or not two and two make four, or whether water runs down hill. These are established facts. But the existence of God, and what he is like if he does exist, are still in the realm of speculation; they are unsettled questions and so it is possible for men to have different opinions about them.

This being the case, we should be charitable in our attitude towards those who hold opinions different from our own and not damn a man because of the convictions to which his honest thought has brought him. Unfortunately it has been very hard for men to achieve this charity. The believers in God, being usually in the large majority in our society, have been intolerant of the non-believers, treating them as though they were criminals. In earlier days they were put to death and even now they are looked at askance as dangerous or immoral individuals, and in some instances denied legal rights that others possess, as Rupert Hughes, the novelist, was denied the right a few years ago to adopt a child because he acknowledged that he was an atheist.

This is absurd because there is no necessary connection between the particular views which a man holds on this subject and his worth as a human being. He can be a firm believer in God and still be a scoundrel; or he can be a saint. He can be an atheist and be a very superior person; or he can likewise be a scoundrel. The other day I heard of a young man who was unable to join a fraternal organization which made as a condition of membership an avowal of belief in God. He said he didn't know whether or not he believed in God and his conscience would not permit him to profess a belief which he did not have. Yet this same young man was shocked when he discovered that the soldiers with whom he was associated prayed to God only for their own safety when his concern was not for himself but for the welfare of his loved ones at home. I should say that in any valid sense this young man, agnostic though he was, was more deeply religious than were his believing companions. Too much that passes for religion is simply selfishness; the genuine article has wider concerns than the self of the believer.

All of this has been by way of introduction to the Unitarian attitude toward belief in God. The name "Unitarian" means a believer in one God and was given to us originally in distinction to the "Trinitarians" who believe that God is three persons, Father, Son, and Holy Ghost, and that the three yet make one. Unitarians believed that Jesus was a man, not God, and felt that the Holy Ghost was simply a speculative idea which no one really understood and might as well be eliminated. This left them believing only in God the Father. Most Unitarians have been and are today Theists, believing sincerely in God the creator and ruler of this universe, who is in and through and over all his works.

But because the Unitarian church has no creed, because it is a free fellowship whose members recognize that no one knows enough to be entitled to dogmatize on these great questions of belief, because we think that character is even more fundamental than profession of belief, we have room in our church, and do indeed have, many men and women who are not theists. Some of them prefer to say "Nature" instead of God, because they feel that "Nature" more adequately represents their thought about the character of the world. There are others who are known as "Humanists" because for them the center of religion has shifted from God to man. They say, "we cannot fathom the infinite, it is enough for us to love and serve humanity." All of us, Theists, Naturalists, Humanists and Agnostics, are bound together in the Unitarian church by our common interest in promoting that which is best in human life; this is a foundation that lies deeper than agreement in belief. We cannot all think alike, we can all work together for the enrichment of human life. Life and ever more life is the end of religion.

Let me use the remaining moments to give my own answer to our question, "What and Where is God?" It is not binding on anyone else. First negatively: I do not believe in God as a personal being who hears and answers prayer. It seems to me preposterous that the great traffic of the universe should be side-tracked to let my little train rattle through in response to my petition. I can readily understand why our soldier boys in the thick of battle find themselves praying; it is a spontaneous response born out of their helplessness and tremendous need in the presence of over-whelming danger. But the prayers do not deflect one bullet nor cause a shell to deviate a hair's breadth from its course. What they really do, is to help the boys inwardly by providing a channel through which their natural fear can flow and by fortifying their courage. That is a great deal.

Now positively: God is to me a poetic symbol whereby I seek to express my experience of certain qualities in our universe. Let me indicate briefly what some of these are. First is that magnificent order which the sciences reveal as characteristic of our world home from the movement of the stars through their vast courses to the play of the electrons within the infinitesimal atoms. It is a magnificently dependable world because of the quality which we seek to describe in what we call the laws of nature. Closely related to this is the fact that it is a *universe,* not a chaos. All things within it are bound up together; the very air we breathe is as much a part of ourselves as are our lungs or our thoughts, and that air in turn is bound by innumerable ties to the sun and the stars. A poet has put this scientific truth into lines of beauty:

> All things by immortal power
> Near or far
> Hiddenly
> To each other linked are,
> That thou canst not stir a flower
> Without troubling of a star.

I know no better way to express our dependence on the vast whole of which we are parts than by the familiar word "God."

Luther Burbank, the "plant wizard," was keenly sensitive to beauty and much of the joy which he took in his work came from this source. He said that there is a biological reason for the splendor of the flowers with which the plant announces its presence to the world. The blossoms attract the insects and carry the fertilizing pollen from one plant to another. But Burbank noted that there was a greater achievement of beauty than was necessary for the accomplishment of this purpose. The lavish display of color and form and perfume is not alone for the sake of reproduction but is apparently an end in itself. Burbank concluded that there is a definite urge toward beauty in nature. Again, I know no more adequate symbol by means of which we can signify our recognition of the "beauty that created the world" than the time honored word "God."

A woman of mature years had a cherished friend. They had grown up together and had been inseparable companions. Circumstances carried them apart but they continued their friendship and enjoyed occasional visits. During one of these it developed that they had grown far apart in their thought life. The woman of whom I speak was confronted with the question whether or not this precious friendship could survive an honest discussion of their difference of opinion. Then there came to her the overwhelming realization that she could not suppress what she was convinced was the truth; friendship would have to submit to the test. She felt what Emerson has put into his lines:

> 'Tis man's perdition to be safe
> When for the truth he ought to die.

Once more, this loyalty of a woman's mind to the truth speaks in the depths of me saying, "This *is* God."

God is the quality in the universe giving to it the character which it manifests. He is everywhere present, in the orbit of the sun, in the green of the forest leaves, in the upward urge in the heart of man. God is a poetic symbol by which we seek to express the inexpressible, by which we endeavor to give voice to our faith in this living universe as our home and ourselves as its children. To worship him is to think clear thoughts, to add to the beauty and harmony of our world, to fulfill ourselves in generous living which delights in doing for others, to grow in the stature of our manhood and womanhood, to be co-workers with him in the creative work of the world.

Is It God's Word?

The subject on which I am to speak this morning is one in which the feelings of many persons are very deeply involved. I am aware that the conviction that the Bible is the word of God, a supernatural revelation of truth, infallible in all its parts, is a very precious part of the religious belief of multitudes, and that under the dominance of that belief the scriptures have been very helpful to them, a source of comfort and guidance. I have no desire to do violence to their feelings and therefore suggest that any of my listeners to whom it is offensive to have the traditional view of the Bible called into question shall tune me out at this point. I am speaking what I believe to be the truth under the conviction that in the long run the truth is the best friend that man has. I am speaking for those many earnest persons who no longer believe that the Bible is God's word in any supernatural sense, and who are persuaded that religion gains rather than loses from the acceptance of this fact.

In the address of last Sunday I said that it is a basic Unitarian principle to try to keep abreast of truth; discover what the truth is on any subject and we will accept that as our doctrine. This principle is nowhere better exemplified than in our attitude toward the Bible. In recent generations there has been growing up what is known as the science of Biblical Criticism. Some people shy away from that word "criticism" because it implies to them fault-finding. That is not the sense in which it is used. Biblical criticism is simply the application of scientific methods of study to the writings of the Old and New Testaments in an effort to discover the truth about them, the conditions under which they came into being, their real meaning, their genuine nature.

The development of this science has been the work of many different scholars in various parts of the world. Most of them have been churchmen and they have been representative of a number of different denominations: Lutheran scholars in

Germany; men of the Established Church in England; Methodists, Congregationalists, Presbyterians in this country. I emphasize this fact because the conclusions which I am setting forth this morning are not simply Unitarian heresies but the accepted results of impartial scholarship. They are taught alike in such leading theological schools as the Divinity School of the University of Chicago, Harvard, and Union Theological Seminary of New York City. Unfortunately what the scholars have to say about the true nature of the Bible has not been passed on in any adequate way to the people at large so that a wide gap exists between the understanding of it which the well educated minister has and that of his congregation which has inherited the traditional view.

The major result of the science of Biblical criticism has been to overthrow completely the idea that the scriptures are a unique revelation of supernatural truth bestowed from on high and to substitute in its place the view that the Bible has grown naturally out of the life of man just as has any other body of literature. It is divine only to the extent that human insight, wisdom, genius is divine. Walt Whitman put this essential truth in some memorable lines:

You consider Bibles and religions divine? I do not say they are not divine,
I say they have all grown out of you, and may grow out of you still.
It is not they who give them life, it is you who give them life;
Leaves are not more shed from the trees, or trees from the earth than they are shed out of you.

It is commonly argued that Biblical criticism is destructive, and we shall have to acknowledge that it does destroy the dogma of Biblical infallibility. But progress in every science is made by the destruction of error. The astronomy and chemistry of today have given us a better knowledge of our world only at the expense of discrediting many of the theories of those sciences in the past, but we do not therefore say that they are destructive because our attention is centered on our gains. The same is true of Biblical Criticism; it seems destructive only to those who are thinking of the fact that it has discredited the belief in the supernatural character of the Bible. It seems creative to those who have gone on to avail themselves of the positive values to be found in the new understanding of the Bible. Indeed the conviction is growing that you cannot appreciate the Bible aright, you cannot use it to best advantage save in the light that this new knowledge sheds on it.

Let us have a brief survey of the story as the scholars have reconstructed it. The Bible is a small library selected from the literature produced by the Hebrew people, with some additions by the early Christians, over a period of nearly 15 centuries. The earliest portions are fragments of folk songs, like the Song of Deborah which is to be dated about 1270 B.C. It is found in the book of Judges. The latest is the Second Epistle of Peter in the New Testament which was written about 150 A.D. A great many different writers contributed to this literature: we don't know who most of them were. Much of the material has been edited and re-edited. For example, the first five books of the Old Testament which were formerly called the books of Moses because it was thought Moses wrote them, are known to be the work of numerous authors whose stories have been pieced together. Some of the material belongs to a period 500 years after Moses died. These documents do not appear in the Bible in the order in which they were written and that is confusing to the reader.

Different portions of the Bible are of different value from a historical point of view; some of them, like portions of the Prophets, present a fairly accurate picture of the time to which they belong. Others, like the account of the march from Egypt through the wilderness, are largely legend, the products of later imaginative writers who tried to fill in gaps in the story. The same is true of the New Testament; much of the story of Jesus in the Gospels was not written for upwards of a century after his death. Many of the essential facts were lacking and they were supplied by the imagination of pious Christians. This accounts for the discrepancies of the different Gospels.

By no means all of the literature produced over this long period of time is preserved in the Bible. A process of sifting went on; certain documents were held important and were kept, others were discarded. Even among those retained some were considered much more authoritative than others. It was only gradually that the present list of the Bible books was built up and attained the status of scripture. Indeed as late as Martin Luther lively debate went on as to the right of certain books to a place in the Bible. He thought that the Old Testament book of Esther did not belong in the Bible; he pronounced Revelation to be of little or no worth and called the Epistle of James an "epistle of straw." Some persons seem still unaware that the Roman Catholic Bible contains 14 books not included in the Protestant version. All of this is very human and fatal to the theory that the Bible is the Word of God. Obviously it is the work of men like ourselves.

The discovery of this truth brings certain important advantages. It enables us to get away from the dangerous and mistaken idea that all of the Bible is on the same level. We can bring to bear on it the judgment of our own mind and conscience, making use of that which seems to us good and true, rejecting that which does not meet our standards of truth and right. No longer do we have to try, against all reason, to believe that the sun stood still at Joshua's command. No longer do we have to try to square the terrible spirit of the imprecatory Psalms with our own conscience.

When I was in Boston a few days ago the papers carried a story of a bill introduced into the current Massachusetts Legislature to exonerate the last of the alleged witches who had been put to death and whose names still bore that calumny. This recalls a black chapter in our history which relates how many innocent women suffered cruel persecution and were put to shameful death because in the 22nd Chapter of Exodus, the 18th verse, it says: "Thou shalt not suffer a witch to live." That black chapter is symbolic of the evil which the dogma of an infallible revelation has caused in the world. Fortunately its power is now broken and our minds are free to choose that which is of help to me, free to approach life's problems in the spirit of the question addressed by Jesus to the multitude: "Why even of yourselves judge ye not what is right?"

When we see the Bible in all its humanness it becomes a much more valuable instrument of the religious life; no longer does it seek to impose an external authority but only to appeal to an inner sanction in our own minds and hearts. We cannot understand the Bible aright unless we do see it in the light of its origin and development.

When viewed thus, how rich are the treasures which it offers us! In its pages there is preserved for us one of the most complete records that we have of any ancient civilization. In it we can see how generations long before us sought to interpret and to perfect human life; we can learn alike from their failures and their successes. In it there have been preserved for us some of the finest passages of the world's literature--like the best of the Psalms, and portions of the Book of Job. In it we can trace the evolution of religion from crude and barbaric beginnings in which men worshipped fierce tribal gods up to the conception of a universal monotheism in which all men are seen as children of our Heavenly Father. In it we can observe how men have struggled up the difficult path of ethical achievement, from the barbaric code of "an eye for an eye" to the golden rule of doing unto others as you would have them do to you. In it we can study some of the most heroic figures of the human drama; the great Hebrew Prophets, culminating in Jesus, who dared to apply their religious idealism to the immediate social scene even at the cost of their lives.

There is one further advantage to this modern understanding of the Bible and that is that its claims are no longer exclusive. We now know that the divine in life is not confined to the Christian scriptures but has manifested itself wherever the intelligence and good-will of men has succeeded in pointing the way to better things. Our Bible is greatly expanded; it takes in inspiring words whatever their source. It includes the wisdom of Lao Tsze and Confucius, of Socrates and Buddha; it includes the Declaration of Independence and the Gettysburg Address. We say with Emerson: "God *speaks, not spoke!*" Speaks in every effort of the human spirit to attain a higher level.

All of this which flows from the science of Biblical Criticism the Unitarian accepts as a part of his religion because he is persuaded that it is true. His emphasis is on the positive aspects of the whole story. He is not so much concerned to discredit a theory of the Bible which his neighbor still holds as he is to avail himself of the riches which the modern view offers. All that there is of good in the Bible is still there and it is much more accessible, much more usable than it was before. No longer is it a closed book, but open--open for all that prompts the mind and heart of man to its highest attainment, open for the new and more glorious chapters that are writing or to be written in the saga of man's climb through the ages.

The Human Christ

Unitarians believe that Jesus was a man, not a God.

Our emphasis is not on the denial of the orthodox doctrine that he was God himself come to earth in human form, but on the fact that he was a man in all respects like ourselves. We believe that this represents the historic truth; we believe further that the human Jesus is religiously more valuable than the theological Christ. Let me tell you the story, briefly, as we read it.

About nineteen and a half centuries ago Jesus was born in Palestine. He came into the world through that same natural process as does every child; his father was Joseph, his mother was Mary. He grew to manhood among his people; his ideas and his character were shaped by the influences that were brought to bear on him in his Jewish home and community. When he reached mature years there was awakened in him the conviction that he had a special mission to proclaim the coming of the Kingdom of God, as many a young man before him and since has felt that he had a call to become a preacher of righteousness and love. The form which Jesus' mission too was determined by the culture of which he was a product though of course he gave it the bent of his own genius.

There was an expectation, widely held among the Jews of the time, that God was going to intervene and establish his heavenly kingdom on earth. John the Baptist proclaimed it: "Repent, for the Kingdom of God is at hand." Jesus entered into this expectation and went about the country announcing the good news and explaining to the people what it meant. Perhaps he even came to the conclusion that he was to have a special function in the establishment of this kingdom. On this point the evidence is not clear. But there was among the Jews the belief that God was to select a man, a descendant of King David, to act as his agent in setting up the heavenly kingdom. The title which the Jews gave to this expected king and deliverer was the "Messiah," which means the annointed. The Greek equivalent of this is "Christ." The Jews did not think of the Messiah as God himself but simply as a man chosen by God, and that was the original meaning of Christ. It did not acquire the theological meaning now associated with it until much later. As I have previously said, it is not certain whether or not Jesus regarded himself as the Messiah, but if he did it meant to him that he was a man chosen by God, not that he was himself God.

We do know that he went about announcing the speedy coming of the Kingdom and that in so doing he got himself in trouble with the authorities among his own people. This was because his interpretation of the coming kingdom and of what was required for entrance to it was regarded as heretical and subversive of the public interest. Accordingly after a few months of activity he was arrested, brought to trial and put to death as a criminal. Jesus lived and died a Jew; he had no idea that he was founding a new religion.

He had gathered a little band of disciples about him and when he was put to death they were at first completely dismayed, but soon they rallied and continued his work of preparing men for the coming kingdom. They still thought of themselves as Jews, but they were Jews who believed that Jesus was the Messiah and that he would return to establish God's rule on earth. They did not call themselves Christians, but Nazarenes.

Then there joined the little group a remarkable man by the name of Paul, without whom Christianity never would have become a separate religion. Paul was a Jew of the dispersion; that is, he was not born in Palestine but in the city of Tarsus in Cilicia. Growing up there he had come in contact with the main intellectual currents of the Mediterranean world and in his mind there was a seething conflict between them and his Jewish heritage. When he became a convert to the little band that believed Jesus to be the Messiah he put a different interpretation on the role of Jesus than did those who had been his immediate followers, an interpretation that had in it a large admixture of the mystical ideas he had derived from Greek and Oriental sources. Sharp conflict developed between Paul and the others. Finally Paul went his own way carrying his message to the gentile world. It was his converts who were first called "Christians." Paul rather than Jesus was the real founder of Christianity. It was in Paul's mind that Jesus first ceased to be wholly human and began to take on the attributes of a deity.

This process which was begun by Paul was continued over a long period, produced bitter theological quarrels, and finally resulted in the pronouncement of the Council of Nicea in the year 325 by virtue of which the human Jesus is almost lost to sight in the theological Christ described as "the Son of God, begotten of the Father, Very God of Very God." This has continued to be the official view of orthodox Christianity, but there have been many through the centuries who have protested that it is very far from the thought of Jesus himself and that religion would benefit greatly if we could throw off the accumulations of the creeds and recover the historic personage of the man Jesus.

Unitarians are among those who hold this view. We believe that when Jesus is presented as a god whose mission was to come into the world to save mankind by his sacrificial death on the cross religion is all too likely to become a matter of magic by virtue of which believers expect to escape the torments of a mythical hell and enjoy the bliss of an equally mythical heaven. The emphasis is put on the wrong place. People all too easily profess faith in Christ as their savior and neglect to do the things that he commanded, neglect the effort to attain the quality of character which he exemplified. Of course this is not the necessary consequence, as the splendid lives of many orthodox believers testifies, but it is a constant source of danger.

We believe that it is more profitable to think of Jesus as a human being. If he was a god then it does little good to tell us to emulate him for we cannot expect to do as a god does, for we are but men. But when we recognize the fact that he was a man like ourselves it becomes possible for us to seek to attain in our lives the admirable qualities he exemplified in his. The religious value of Jesus lies in what he was as a human being and the influence which his rare personality has on us when we come in contact with it.

Jesus was a lover of humanity; his great heart yearned over its sorrows and tragedies; he desired in the very depths of his being to help men live at their best, to fulfill the finest possibilities of their souls. He rebelled against the narrow petty rules that stood in the way of this. When his disciples and he were charged with breaking the Sabbath he replied, "The Sabbath was made for man, not man for the Sabbath." He set forth a principle there that was his constant guide; he made man central. Let us find out what is best for man, and then do that. This principle was responsible for his denunciations of hypocrisy and exploitation; it was the basis of his moral commandments. In your relations with others seek to call forth the best that is in them and it will call forth the best in you. This means that good-will and love will be your guiding motives, for it is these generous feelings that lead you to identify yourself with others that produce the finest fruits in the relations of men. The Kingdom of God is like the home at its best where all the members are mutually devoted to the best interests of one another.

Jesus exemplified in high degree this simple, homely philosophy in his own character. He loved little children; "Suffer them to come unto me." He loved men and women with spontaneous affection and they responded with like feelings toward him. The things that roused his anger were those which did violence to this friendliness and good-will among men, the things that would shut men out from the enjoyments of the Kingdom of God. And, crowning glory of all, he was so completely loyal to his vision of where the good of man lies that he was ready to lay down his life to promote his cause in the world. We cherish his memory as one of the supreme heroes, one of the greatest servants of mankind and we would make his spirit our own. He is to us not a god to be worshipped, but a companion to counsel with as we seek to walk the difficult way of life; an inspiring example of the greatness of which the human soul is capable.

The true doctrine of the incarnation is not that the great God of all the universe at one point in human history miraculously took form in a single being who was at once God and man. The true doctrine of the incarnation is that the divine in the universe is perpetually incarnating itself anew in men and going forth to redeem the world from want and woe. The same divine nature which expressed itself in the man of Nazareth is latent in you and in me. To the degree in which we triumph over our own selfishness and rise into the realm of goodwill and love; to the degree that we master our appetites and make them serve the higher purposes of our lives; to the degree that we achieve an understanding of truth, an appreciation of beauty; to the degree in which we foster and increase those values which give human life its true significance, in that degree God is incarnate in us. To live in this spirit is to be a disciple of Jesus.

Though Jesus was preeminent among those in whom the divine possibilities of human life were made manifest he by no means exhausts those possibilities; no single individual can do so because those possibilities are so rich and varied. Every personality has its limitations if for no other reason than that there are virtues which are to some extent mutually exclusive; one person, for example, cannot unite in himself both the manly and the womanly virtues in equal degree; if one predominates the other must be subordinate. Every human being, also, has his frailties and weaknesses which betray him at times into doing things which his best self repudiates. Jesus, fine as he was, shared these limitations and weaknesses with the rest of us; this is but to say that he was human.

Such being the case it is well for us to supplement his example with that of other heroic figures in the history of mankind who can help us to round out our understanding of what men are and what they may become. What a goodly company are the leaders of the race as they march across the pages of history; men whose genius was chiefly of the intellect like the Greek philosophers. Plato and Aristotle; men who were great artists, like Shakespeare and Michelangelo and Beethoven; men who were great scientists like Copernicus and Newton and Darwin; men strong in handling practical affairs like our own George Washington; women like Florence Nightingale and Jane Addams; all of these and thousands besides, join with Jesus to reveal the greatness of which our common humanity is capable. In them that creative power which dwells at the heart of our universe is at work seeking to achieve beauty, dignity, worth; in no one of them does it fully succeed; all of them together do not exhaust its resources. Perpetually the unseen artist is at work to put the mark of his divinity on human life, on yours and mine even as on those in whom it has shone unmistakably. In this sense Jesus was divine. In this spirit the Unitarian says with Matthew Arnold:

Was Christ a man like us? Ah! let us try
If we then, too, can be such men as he!

The Ten Commandments

How long has it been since you have read the Ten Commandments? Permit me to refresh your memory by giving them in simplified form:

1. Thou shalt have no other gods before me.

2. Thou shalt not make unto thee any graven image.
3. Thou shalt not take the name of the Lord thy God in vain.
4. Remember the Sabbath to keep it holy.
5. Honor thy father and thy mother.
6. Thou shalt not kill.
7. Thou shalt not commit adultery.
8. Thou shalt not steal.
9. Thou shalt not bear false witness against thy neighbor.
10. Thou shalt not covet anything that is thy neighbor's.

The dramatic story of how Moses received these commandments at the hand of God himself on Mt. Sinai is familiar to all of us. The divine authority attributed to them has given them a place of tremendous importance in the western world. In some respects this has been a distinct advantage, because the Ten Commandments do incorporate certain minimum moral requirements without which any organized society is impossible, and it has doubtless served to make them more effective that they have had the force of religious sanction. But there have been some accompanying disadvantages. The Ten Commandments have become a sort of fetish; men's attitude toward them has been unthinking. They have assumed that this code was adequate to all the requirements of the moral life without stopping to inquire whether or not this is really the case. I propose that we examine it with fresh minds to see just what its value is.

Biblical scholars who approach the subject from a historical point of view tell us that interesting as is the story of Moses receiving the commandments at the hand of God we cannot accept it as a factual account of the origin of this set of rules. As they reconstruct the account it is something like this. The Hebrews, like all early peoples, had to work out some regulations of conduct which would enable them to get along with one another and establish a stable social life. These rules were wrought out in the hard school of experience. Men discovered that if there were not respect for the life and property of other members of the group they would be constantly quarreling among themselves and at a disadvantage with neighboring groups. Gradually they worked the results of their experience into simple codes that were held to be binding on each member of the tribe. The probability is that we have ten commandments because we have ten fingers--an easy device to help people who did not read and write to remember the rules. Then later, when the human origin of the code had been forgotten, the legend grew up that it had been received directly from God. It may have been that Moses had a hand in shaping the code but he certainly did not give it in its present form for some of the requirements belong to a period later than when he is supposed to have lived.

Turning to the contents of the code we find that the first four commandments are theological or ritualistic rather than moral. Some of them, as in the case of the prohibition of making a graven image, are of little significance to us today. The remaining six do deal with ethical requirements. But they cannot be said to represent a high moral level. For the most part they are couched in terms of negations--"thou shalt not." Only one of them, "Honor thy father and thy mother," is positive. Now, while prohibitions are a necessary part of a moral code, because of the unruly forces in human nature that need to be restrained, it is commonly recognized that it is only when we move over into positive injunctions, only when we come to the "thou shalts" that we have begun to climb toward the moral heights.

The Hebrews did reach these greater heights in the Old Testament; they learned to say "thou shalt love thy neighbor as thyself." But that represents a later stage than the Ten Commandments. Commenting on them Powis Smith in his book *The Moral Life of the Hebrews* says that they "do not present anything that would warrant us in bestowing any prize for moral excellence upon the Hebrew people of that age as compared with any other people in a similar stage of progress in the upward course toward full civilization." He goes on to point out that the Ten Commandments were in effect at a time when polygamy was prevalent, when women were regarded as property, when slavery was an accepted institution, when men held that they were not bound by the same rules in dealing with foreigners as they were among their own people. There is nothing in the Ten Commandments to forbid these practices. Obviously they are not nearly as adequate to the requirements of civilized life as they have been assumed to be.

We need to do some careful thinking about the nature of morality and about what is required of men in our own day. It has become clear, as a result of study by many men, that all moral codes grow out of social experience. They embody the rules of the game which men discover they must obey if they are to cooperate with their neighbors for their mutual benefit. As insight deepens, as we become wiser in our understanding of our selves and our relations with others, the moral laws are refined. Jesus, with his quick sympathy and his law of love, stands on a much higher ethical level than do the Ten Commandments.

The conditions of life change and that which was good under certain circumstances becomes evil under different conditions. "New occasions teach new duties." We have a striking example of this in our national history. In the early days of this country the injunction against "entangling alliances" was valid; we then lived in a world in which it was possible for us to be very largely self-contained. But this has all changed and in the close knit world of today no nation can live to itself alone; morality requires that we shall cooperate with other nations. In every situation the moral quality of an act or an attitude is to be judged by the consequences it has in the lives of those whom it influences. If it promotes their well-being, if it adds to the strength and stability of society, then it is good. If it is destructive of personality, if it makes him who does it less a man, if it is contrary to the best interests of society, then it is evil.

Because our lives are very complicated, because our deeds have consequences that we little suspect, it is very hard for us to gauge the moral quality of some of the things that we do. Oh, certain distinctions are obvious enough--kind words are better than nagging criticism, an honest day's work is more moral than soldiering on the job. But there are many instances in which the distinction is not so clear and we need the guidance of a code corresponding to the Ten Commandments but on the higher ethical level of our own day. In response to this need there have been a number of attempts to formulate a modern version of the Decalogue. It is not an easy thing to do as you will quickly discover if you sit down and try to draw up your own Ten Commandments. You probably won't be very well satisfied with the results; none of those that I have seen are sufficiently well done to attain any wide acceptance. But the effort to write such a code has its value, and I should like to share with you one which has come to my attention. You will note that it is couched entirely in positive terms and that it seeks to include both the individual and the social aspects of morality--if we can make a distinction between the two. Here it is:

1. Thou shalt be healthy.
2. Thou shalt be creative.
3. Thou shalt laugh and play.
4. Thou shalt be intelligent.
5. Thou shalt seek beauty.
6. Thou shalt make a happy home.
7. Thou shalt be a good citizen.
8. Thou shalt cultivate the international mind.
9. Thou shalt "accept the Universe."
10. Thou shalt be a rebel.

Obviously it would require a long time to develop the implications of any one of these commandments. I was particularly interested in the explanation which the author of this code gave for his inclusion of the final requirement--Thou shalt be a rebel. He said that he was seeking to express the truth contained in the lines by Don Marquis:

But for the rebel in his breast,
Had man remained a brute.

There is a constant danger, particularly in drawing up a moral code, that too much emphasis shall be placed on conformity to the neglect of the truth that moral progress has come largely through the agency of the rebel who has seen beyond the present good a better to be achieved. "It was said unto you of old time--but I say unto you." We owe a tremendous debt to the men who have dared speak to us in this wise.

There is another matter that we should consider in connection with any conceivable moral code that we might draw up, and that is the matter of motivation. It is not enough to tell men where the good lies; we must somehow touch springs in their lives which shall impel them to seek the good with their whole hearts. It does no good to enjoin a man to love his neighbor as himself if he finds in his heart an antagonism, a hatred toward his neighbor which he cannot surmount. Where shall men find the power to do the thing which they know is good?

There is no one answer to that question. Religion has been the most universal method employed for releasing in men the powers which enable them to achieve the moral life; but other agencies have also succeeded in doing it; a man may be lifted to a high level by a great human love, by having an absorbing work to do, by patriotism, by devotion to a noble secular ideal. We are rich in the variety of ways in which we may be stimulated to high endeavor, and we should not fall into the error of stressing any one of them to the exclusion of the others; we need them all.

When I had reached this point in the preparation of this talk there came to my desk a copy of a letter written by a young man in the United States Navy to his parents on the occasion of his twenty-first birthday. Permit me to quote a few sentences from it. "Through all these years you have guided me in such a way as to give me not only a high sense of morality but also an avid desire not to disappoint or embarrass you by any act of mine . . . But don't get the idea that I have been upstanding and good only to gratify my parents . . . What will do me harm I stay away from because I believe so much in the deliciousness of living, of vigorous living on this earth . . . Just as I have tried to stay away from physical harms, so it must be done with the mind for a more fruitful, radiant, happy and joyous life . . . Have no fear of what I may do on my own from here on out, for the gyroscope has been stabilized and set to run smoothly for the rest of the course."

It is a letter of which any parents could be proud. And it is a fine expression of the Unitarian understanding of morality in which the young man was reared. To us the quality of life which one achieves is the most important concern of religion. We know that continually we must be climbing the mount of vision that we may bring back with us the knowledge of human life as it ought to be, the principles of conduct that will best serve the welfare of men. We know that we must write what the vision has disclosed to us, not on tables of stone, but in the hearts of men, using all our skill and devotion to translate the vision into the texture of our daily living, in our homes, our industry, our public life. Morality is the art of bringing life more abundant to men.

One World at a Time

We are to deal this morning with another of those subjects on which the feelings of men run high because their hopes and their fears are so deeply involved--the subject of immortality. It is particularly important at the present time when so many lives are being lost on the field of battle, most of them snuffed out long before they have had their opportunity to run their full course, or to develop their powers to maturity. My heart-felt sympathy goes out to the thousands and millions round the earth who have had to endure the sorrow of losing their loved ones in war. And it is wholly understandable to me that the majority of these stricken hearts should seek balm for their hurt in the traditional belief in a life after death in which they are to be reunited with those whom they have "loved and lost awhile."

I would not needlessly add to their suffering by calling into question their precious faith, but there is another group of persons who are not satisfied with the conventional answer to the question with which death confronts us and I should like to constitute myself their spokesman this morning. Let us try to consider the matter as dispassionately as possible. After all there is no real reason for getting unduly perturbed or excited about it for nothing we can say will alter the facts. Either we are immortal or we are not. If we are in truth destined to a life beyond the grave then no amount of denial can rob us of that immortality any more than denial of spring can prevent the buds from opening in the spring. On the other hand, if death be indeed the end no amount of passionate protest to the contrary will avail to secure for us the gift of further life.

I would have us emulate that lofty spirit which Socrates exhibited when confronted with his own death. You will remember that this man who was reputed to be the wisest among the ancients was condemned by his fellow Athenians to drink the fatal cup of hemlock because he asked too many questions they could not answer. when he had received the death sentence he delivered a speech which is one of the most remarkable in all history. In the course of it he said: "Either death is a state of nothingness and utter unconsciousness, or as men say, there is a change and migration of the soul from this world to another. Now if you suppose that there is no consciousness, but sleep like the sleep of him who is undisturbed even by dreams, death will be an unspeakable gain, for eternity then is only a single night. But if death is a journey to another place, and there all the dead are, what good can be greater than this? . . . Wherefore, oh my friends and judges, be of good cheer about death, and know this of a truth, that no evil can befall a good man either in life or after death. The hour of departure has arrived and we go our ways--I to die and you to live. Which is better God only knows."

The Unitarian church does not have an authoritative answer to this question; it leaves its individual members free to decide the matter for themselves in accordance with what they deem to be the evidence. Many Unitarians believe implicitly in immortality. I am thinking of one who is a biologist. He tells me that he has started biological experiments which cannot possibly be completed in the course of one lifetime, they need a thousand years or more to run their course. He is firmly convinced that he is going to be able to know how they come out. Other Unitarians believe just as positively that death is the end. I am thinking of some of our younger ministers who say that modern science has made it clear beyond a shadow of doubt that the old dualism which maintained that man is a spiritual soul inhabiting a physical body is no longer tenable, and that we are now aware that man is a mind-body unity; the two are just different aspects of the same thing and when death comes there is no soul to survive. Yet other Unitarians take an agnostic position, saying with Socrates that we do not know. This is my own position; I am an agnostic who inclines to the side of doubt. It does not seem probable to me that we as individuals survive death, but I will not dogmatize about it, chiefly because I have a profound respect for the limitations of my own knowledge and recognize that it is quite within the bounds of possibility that our mysterious universe may have a surprise in store for me.

Let us now examine some of the consequences of each of these alternatives which Socrates presents. First, that death "is a migration of the soul from this world to another." If this be the case what is the best preparation which men can make for that after-life? In the past men have said that the condition under which we are to live beyond death is determined by things that we do in this present life, that it is necessary for us to "be saved" by believing certain theological doctrines, by having a particular emotional experience, by the performance of special rites and ceremonies, by belonging to a particular church. If we did not conform to these requirements we were told that the delights of heaven were closed to us and we should have to spend our future life in hell.

All of this we now recognize to be a tragic mistake that has caused a vast amount of needless suffering. The Unitarian repudiates the whole theological conception of what is necessary as a preparation for the afterlife and says frankly that if there be a life beyond the present one the only possible preparation for it is to be found in the *quality of character* that you achieve here and now. The only thing you could conceivably take with you in your migration to that other world is what you are, the true inwardness of your own being. And if what you are is essentially evil and corrupt heaven could not be heaven to you, whereas if what you are is fine and strong it will make its own heaven in the midst of hell. It is related of Ralph Waldo Emerson that when some of his critics said he would go to hell because he was a Unitarian, a friend of his, a Methodist minister by the name of Taylor, came to his defense and said that if Emerson went to hell he would change the climate there and start the tide of migration in that direction. There is more truth in a quatrain from the Rubaiyat of Omar Khayyam than in all the tomes of theological speculation on heaven and hell.

I sent my soul through the invisible,
    Some letter of that after life to spell,
And by and by my soul returned to me
    And answered; I myself am heaven and hell.

We turn now to the other of Socrates' alternatives in which death is described as a sleep undisturbed even by dreams, a sleep in which all eternity is but a single night. There are certain mistaken notions about this which we need to dispel. The first is that if men believe that death is the end then they have no reason for leading a moral life and will plunge into sensuousness and all manner of evil. A good deal of the responsibility for this mistaken attitude resets on St. Paul because of his statement: "If the dead are not raised, let us eat and drink for tomorrow we die." What? shall I demean my manhood, shall I make a pig of myself, because I am not immortal? By no means. A decent life, a life of discipline and self-control, of intelligence and good will is worth while in itself; it is what I owe to myself as a man regardless of the meaning of death.

It is fortunate for the world that morality is not dependent on a belief in immortality because ever larger numbers of men are abandoning the belief. But does it disrupt their characters, plunge them into wickedness, cause them to violate the standards of decency and high-minded conduct? The answer is an emphatic "No!" They are on the whole quite as moral as their neighbors who do believe that the dead are raised. Some of the finest men and women I have known in every city in which I have lived have been honestly convinced that death is the end. Morality is something that goes much deeper than belief or lack of belief in a future life.

The second error which I should like to dispose of in this connection is that life loses all its worth and that indeed the whole universe is without rhyme or reason unless men are immortal. This strikes me as being about as absurd as to say that it is not worth while for me to be alive on this earth today unless I can be sure that I shall be living here five years from now. The value of life lies not alone in its length, but in its quality; its worth is to be judged by what it is and not by how long it is going to last. One of America's greatest men answered this error. Oliver Wendell Holmes, late justice of the Supreme Court, said that it would be preposterous for him to fling out his arms in defiance of the great universe, saying to it, "Unless you bestow immortality on me, unless you perpetuate forever my little, individual personality, then nothing is worthwhile, the whole thing is a madhouse." This would be the height of egotism. The universe is what it is, and its significance is unimpaired regardless of the fate of man. Let us find the worth of life in the years of our span on earth for of these we are sure.

It is in this spirit that the Unitarian adopts as his slogan, "One world at a time." We are convinced that religion in the past has been too largely other-worldly, too much concerned with preparing men for a life to come, and only incidentally with the life that now is. We would reverse this procedure, making ours a religion of this world, concentrating our attention on seeing how well we can live, how much of an improvement we can effect in the conditions of human life on earth. We are well assured that this is the part of wisdom, for if it be that our earthly span is all there is we shall have made the most of it, and if there is a "beyond" we shall have been preparing ourselves for it in the best possible manner.

Of one kind of immortality we are sure and that is the immortality of influence. We do not know whether or not personality survives the event of death. We do know that personality leaves its mark behind to influence for good or for ill the lives of other men. After a person is dead it remains true that he was one kind of a man rather than another, and that the quality of his character has become a permanent part of the mosaic of human life. This is conspicuously true of great men. The world is a much better place today because of the influence which Jesus has exerted over men through the centuries. It will be worse for a long time to come because of Adolph Hitler. The same is true in lesser degree of all of us; because of what we are, of what we make of ourselves, children to be born a hundred, yes a thousand, years hence will come into a world that is better or worse.

It is supremely important that we should live in the light of this truth. This is the immortality we cannot escape. Let us make sure that it is the kind of which we can be proud. Millions of young men are dying over the earth during these fateful years in the hope that their supreme sacrifice may contribute to the establishment of a world of peace and order, of justice and good-will among men. That is their immortality--that generations yet unborn may spend their years in creative work and die in peace. It can be assured only as we too make it our purpose and so live that these honored dead shall not have died in vain. The contribution of our lives to a fairer world is our assured immortality.

Beyond Christianity

Sir Arthur Keith, formerly President of the British Association for the Advancement of Science, tells us that when he had graduated in medicine he went to Ceylon to begin his practice. There he found himself living in the midst of a Buddhist population. He had grown up in Scotland and had naturally assumed that the church to which his parents belonged represented the one and only true religion. When he got to know the people of Ceylon with the intimacy which the relation of doctor and patient develops it came to him with surprise that these men and women were just as kindly, just as honorable, just as fine characters as any he had known back home, yet they were not even Christians, let alone Scottish

Presbyterians. They were Buddhists, and he had to acknowledge to himself that many of them were more successful in living up to the ideals of their religion than were most of the Christians he knew.

As a result of this experience Sir Arthur Keith came to the realization that the reason why Christianity had seemed to him the one and only true religion was that he had been reared in that idea and had never questioned it, had never made any attempt to compare it with other religions. Now he suddenly understood that Christianity is just one of the sects among the religions of the world even as the Presbyterian church is just one of the sects within Christianity, and that all the religions seem true to the people who have grown up in them, better than any other faith for the simple reason that their experiences are so limited that they know only their own and do not have adequate material on which to judge the others. It brought him to the conclusion, confirmed by the researches of comparative religion, that all religions have grown naturally out of the lives of the people professing them, and that the claim of any of them to an exclusive, supernatural revelation of the truth has no foundation in fact.

The experience which Sir Arthur Keith had is now being shared in large measure by thousands upon thousands of young men who have been reared in a Christian environment and then because of the exigencies of the war find themselves living in the midst of a non-Christian population. Most of them will probably not alter their views to any extent because people get out of their experience largely what they take to it. But those with discriminating insight will come to the same conclusion that was forced on Sir Arthur Keith. As our world is drawn closer and closer together, as its peoples come to know one another better, we are bound to discover that humanity is very much the same around the planet, that the degrees of difference between us are only relative, and that no one people has that absolute superiority which each likes to claim for itself.

What are the consequences of this destined to be for religion? It is natural for Christians, convinced of the superiority of their faith, to say that as the world becomes knit into a single community. Christianity will demonstrate its superiority in contrast with the other religions, and become the universal faith of mankind. That is indeed the slogan of many earnest Christian leaders today -- to unite all the world in Christ. But it is a hope that is not destined to fulfillment, however fine the idealism that inspires it. The march of history is not in this direction. If ever the world is to be united by a single religious faith, and it is highly desirable that it should be thus united, it will have to be a religion which transcends all of the historic faiths, Christianity included. There are a number of factors which make this clear.

In the global war now raging some of our spokesmen have said that the United Nations are fighting for the maintenance of Christian principles, but certain of our allies have protested against this way of putting it. Men in China who are the inheritors of the great ethical teachings of Confucius, men in India who have built into their lives the fine moral precepts, the deep religious insights of Hinduism, Jews who carry on the tradition of their great Prophets, have all protested that the principles for which we are fighting are just as clearly enunciated in their religions as they are in Christianity, and that it is unfair to seek to label them exclusively Christian. These critics are right; the values for which we are fighting belong not to any one segment of mankind but are the common property of all mankind -- even of many within the enemy countries with which we are now at war. If we could but see the matter clearly we would recognize that it is preposterous for us to ask that a man like Gandhi in India, or his close associate, Nehru, should become Christians. The same is true of a leader like Hu Shi, China's former ambassador in this country and the great progressive interpreter of China's cultural tradition. It would be just as absurd as for them to ask that Mr. Hull and Mr. Eden become Hindus or Confucians. By the same token we cannot expect that any of the historic faiths of mankind can become the universal religion.

There is another set of facts that has an equally important bearing on this question. All of the traditional religions were the products of human experience prior to the arrival of the age of science. The consequence is that all of them contain ideas and attitudes which will not bear the scrutiny of science and they must be revised in the light of our more recently acquired knowledge. This is as true of Christianity as of any other religion; much of the framework within which its teachings are set simply does not seem true to the mind that is trained in the scientific teachings of our day. All round the globe a new intellectual atmosphere is developing as a result of the progress of science; the old supernaturalism in which the religions of the past were born is giving way to a new naturalism which is setting the climate to which any religion of the future must accommodate itself.

About once in a thousand years a new religion is born, and there is a growing feeling among men today that out of the travail of the present time it is highly probable that a new faith, truer, more universal will develop to provide spiritual incentive and guidance for mankind in the next stage of its evolving life on the good planet earth. It will be a religion which takes up into itself the tried and tested ethical insights which have been achieved in all the religious traditions of the past, the dreams and visions of poets and seers which still have validity as goals for which we must strive, and will work them into the living structure of the world's growing thought as we move on into the future. A historical analogy will help us to understand what is taking place.

At the beginning of our era Jesus lived and taught and died, leaving behind him a little band of followers who had been devoted to him personally and who now felt that it was their task to carry on his teaching. But this did not mean to them that they should cease to be Jews and found a new religion. They still thought of themselves as good Jews and simply tried to convince their fellow Jews that Jesus was the expected Messiah. Then a man joined them who had a broader conception: he belonged to a larger world that was almost unknown to Jesus and his followers. This man was the apostle Paul who was the real founder of Christianity.

He was a Jew who had grown up in the city of Tarsus where he had come under the influence of all the forces that were seething in the Mediterranean world of that day. It was a period of great social unrest and upheaval; there were great movements of people from one place to another; there was a feeling of insecurity; belief in the old gods had faded and men were groping for some faith that would satisfy their needs; many weird cults flourished; many philosophies contended for the mastery of men's minds. Paul experienced all of this in his own intense, passionate soul. Then he came under the influence of the followers of Jesus and in their teachings he found the answer to the struggle of his own inner life. He became the great missionary of the movement, carrying it outside of Palestine to the whole Mediterranean world. In so doing he transformed it into a new religion, adding elements of Greek philosophy and Oriental mysticism, and sacramentalism, that were not in the original teaching as Jesus proclaimed it. Paul's version succeeded because it met the needs of the men of his world, because it was a synthesis of the mind of the Mediterranean world in the first century; thus Christianity was launched on its triumphant career.

There exists a striking parallel between the condition of our world today and the Mediterranean world of Paul's day -- this time on a global scale. Again there is the same social unrest manifesting itself in revolution; again there is the wide intermingling of peoples and cultures; again there is the feeling of insecurity, the loss of faith in the inherited religions and a groping for something that will satisfy the needs of the soul of man. In the midst of this confusion there are elements of strength -- the valid idealism and ethical insights of all the religions, the democratic faith of men in justice, freedom, equality; the new knowledge and power that science has put into our hands. What is needed is that some modern Paul shall arise among us to synthesize in his own soul the tensions, the needs, the values of our world, and present them to men in a form which shall answer the cry of our souls for a faith to guide us and feed our deepest hungers.

It cannot be done within the confines of any of the religions of the past, not even Christianity. It must be something bigger, grander, truer, than Christianity, at the same time it conserves all the value of Christianity that has meaning for our day. The time is ripe for the birth of a new religion which continues the old dream of the good life which has always lain at the heart of man's faith, but which implements that dream and makes it effective by harnessing to it all the resources of our modern science, our increasing knowledge and skills, our present commitment to the cause of a better world for men.

Such a religion is actually in the process of development. It cannot be the work of one man; it is too big. It must be the creation of many men all over the world. Its progress will doubtless be slow because men are loathe to shift their loyalties from the old to the new. But it will win its way because it alone is

Timely and Timeless

adequate to meet the needs of men in the age upon which we are entering. Just as politically we are slowly moving toward the United States of the world, so religiously we are moving toward a common faith for all mankind. This is the religion beyond Christianity, beyond all our inherited faiths. To recognize clearly the need for its development, to pioneer in its establishment, is to serve humanity at the point of its greatest need. Today we see but dimly what that future faith may be, but that it will flower into glory beyond anything the past has known we may be well assured, for it is heir to all the achievement of the past and has within it the dynamics of a humanity that is about to march into an epoch greater than any yet known. It will be the soul of that greater world; the universal faith of all mankind.

Thomas Paine

The newspapers have recently announced that Thomas Paine has been elected to the Hall of Fame, and his name is thus added to that distinguished list of those great Americans who have contributed most to the life of their country. Seventy-seven persons from out our history have now been elected. In Paine's case it is a much belated recognition. His contribution to America is far greater than that of others who have long since been enshrined in our national Hall of Fame, and it is clear that he has been denied his due because of religious prejudice. We may well rejoice that this has now been corrected.

The first thing which any admirer of Paine wants to do in speaking of him is to clear his name of the unfounded charges which have been made against him. Theodore Roosevelt called him "A dirty little atheist." The trouble that that description, as someone has properly said, is that there isn't a word of truth in it. Paine was not dirty, he was not little, and he was not an atheist. The whole charge is but the perpetuation of the early effort to discredit Paine because his religious views gave offense in certain quarters during his lifetime. But the authoritative biographies, those of Conway and the most recent one by Woodward, dispose of all these accusations most effectively. Paine was human and had his limitations like the rest of us, but he was not a drunken sot, he was not immoral in his personal life, he was not an atheist.

Paine's early life was one of poverty and obscurity. It was not until he left his native England at the age of 37 and came to American that he began to show the quality that was in him. His arrival here coincided with the period when the colonies were in a ferment of discontent in their relations with the mother country. It was Paine more than any other man who crystalized that feeling into the demand for independence. He wrote a pamphlet entitled "Common Sense" in which he set forth his convictions. The result was electric. Paine had the gift of words; Franklin said of him that he was the first master of the English language to appear in the colonies. "Common Sense" immediately attained an immense popularity; it sold half a million copies, which meant one for nearly every literate person in America. It made men's convictions clear to them. With Paine's eyes they saw that the only solution for their problem was independence from England. There is no question that "Common Sense" was one of the most potent factors in producing the American Revolution and in setting its aims. It was Paine who coined the phrase The United States of America. He was the co-author with Jefferson of the Declaration of Independence.

During the war itself Paine, Quaker though he was, enlisted in the army and by the camp fire at night wrote his series of pamphlets on "The American Crisis," which were of incalculable value in sustaining the morale of the revolutionary forces. Indeed Washington himself said that without Paine's assistance he could not have succeeded. The most famous of these pamphlets is the one which contains the immortal phrase: "These are the times that try men's souls." It was written just before the battle of Trenton when Washington had resolved on his desperate Christmas night attack on the Hessians. Before the battle the disheartened soldiers were called together and in little groups listened to the reading of Paine's words. They adopted that phrase, "these are the times that try men's souls" as their pass-word. The men responded to the challenge -- the daring of Washington, the spirit of Paine. The battle was won and the victory renewed the will to carry on the struggle. A historian has said that "The cannon of Washington was not more potent in the American Revolution than the pen of Paine."

After the war was over Paine made a trip back to England and while there wrote a book entitled "The Rights of Man." It has been called the first textbook in republicanism. In it Paine set forth his political and social theories and did it in such plain, forthright language that no one could fail to understand. The book immediately became a center of controversy. Over a million copies were sold. The British authorities decided Paine's democratic ideas were much too dangerous for their safety, so they banned the book, prosecuted the publishers, and ordered Paine tried for treason.

But Paine slipped over the France which was then in the midst of its own revolution. For a time he enjoyed acclaim as the first revolutionary of the world. But as the French Revolution moved into its extreme stages Paine felt obliged to protest, with the result that he fell under the displeasure of the leaders and was thrown into prison. It was while he was in prison that he wrote *The Age of Reason,* the book that has brought him at once the greatest fame and the greatest condemnation, the book that has denied him his legitimate place in the conventional histories of the country he helped to found.

The curious fact is that while *The Age of Reason* has been bitterly denounced as an attack on religion Paine wrote it as a defense of religion. He says specifically at the outset that this kind of a book is exceedingly necessary "lest in the general wreck of superstition and false theology we lose sight of morality and the theology that is true." He was alarmed by the excesses which he saw in France and wanted to stem the rising tide of atheism by a defense of what he believed to be the true religion. As his biographer, Conway, says, "It is the immemorial fate of great believers to be persecuted for unbelief -- by unbelievers." Paine believed in God. On that point he is explicit. Permit me to quote his own words from *The Age of Reason:* "I believe in one God and no more; and I hope for happiness beyond this life. I believe in the equality of man, and I believe that religious duties consist in doing justice, loving mercy, and endeavoring to make our fellow-creatures happy."

Yes, Paine believed in God, but it was not the orthodox God of the Christian churches. When he was a child of eight an aunt had read him a sermon on the vicarious atonement; his mind revolted at the immorality of the kind of a God it presented. From that experience was born his famous saying, "Beware of any system of theology which offends the mind of a child." He burned to clear the name of deity from what he considered the blasphemies of orthodox theology, he was eager to free men from the tyranny of a church which he saw worked hand in glove with the political masters to keep the people in slavery. So he went through the Bible, the Old and the New Testaments, to show that the claim of the church to have in the scriptures the foundation of a supernaturally revealed religion was wholly and entirely false. He was attacking revealed religion at its foundations.

That work has since been done with much more thoroughness and historical accuracy by the Higher Critics. But Thomas Paine, with only his keen intelligence to guide him, anticipated many of the results of later scholarship in his disclosure of the very human character of the Bible. More important still was the effectiveness of his writing. Here is no cloistered scholar, but a crusader battling against the lies that have been made the basis of the exploitation of the common man by the priesthood. It is crude, rough, telling, written so that no one can fail to understand. The result is that *The Age of Reason* has continued down to our own day to be one of the most effective weapons in the hands of those who feel impelled to do battle with orthodox theology. It has probably converted more persons to liberal views of religion than any other book ever written.

That Paine's interest was not purely destructive is made clear by the fact that he and some of his friends founded a church in Paris known as Theophilanthropy -- that is, the church of the love of God and man. The walls were decorated with famous sayings of a moral or humanitarian nature. Readings were introduced from non-Christian as well as Biblical sources, the standard of judgment being the truth and humanity of what the author had to offer. Paine also introduced the custom of having the church decorated with flowers as a symbol of the beauty and joy of his religion. It was he who coined the phrase "the religion of humanity." In his church they had lectures on science because he believed that the chief hope of man lay in applying the method of science to social and moral problems.

Elbert Hubbard in his "Little Journey" to the home of Thomas Paine says that this church of Theophilanthropy was the forerunner of the Universalist and Unitarian churches of today. We are glad to recognize our indebtedness to Paine. He did indeed anticipate many of the ideas, principles, practices which we use today. In All Souls Unitarian Church of Indianapolis a bust of Thomas Paine stands at the right of the pulpit in token of our indebtedness to this great champion of freedom, truth, and humanity.

When Paine was eventually released from prison in France through the intervention of the American government he returned to the United States to spend his remaining years. A very unhappy period it proved to be. His writings had earned a great deal of money but he had never taken it for himself, always giving it to the causes in which he was fighting. The result was that he now had to live in poverty. But this was the least of his ills. The great services which he had rendered America in the revolution were forgotten; all that was remembered was that Paine had written *The Age of Reason*. It had provoked a terrific storm of hostility in this country because of its attack on orthodox religion. Paine was subjected to constant persecution; he was reviled on the street, refused a seat on the stagecoach, and, unkindest cut of all, he was denied the right to vote in the land he had helped to establish.

Even when he was sick unto death he was not free from indignity. Fanatical persons forced themselves upon him for the purpose of getting him to recant his religious views. Failing this they invented stories that he recanted and even bribed individuals to tell false tales of hearing him abjure his *Age of Reason* and call on Jesus to have mercy on his soul. All of these stories are, of course, utterly untrue. A final indignity was reserved for him. He had expressed a desire to be buried in the Quaker cemetery, but because of his heresies even the Quakers rejected his dead body. At his funeral there was only a French woman he had befriended, her two sons, a liberal Quaker by the name of Willet Hicks, and two Negroes won to him because he had championed freeing the slaves.

Now a measure of restitution has been made and he has been enrolled among our immortal great. All hail to Thomas Paine, who had the courage and daring to fling himself into the fight wherever man's need was greatest, who made the cause of the suffering and downtrodden his own, who cried, "Where liberty is not there is my country," and challenged tyranny wherever it raised its ugly head. All hail to him who was the apostle of the religion of reason, the prophet of the republic of the world. All hail to him who said, "The world is my country, to do good is my religion." It is fitting that he has been elected to the national Hall of Fame; even more fitting that we should seek to build his spirit increasingly into the nation of which he was one of the founders.

What is Humanism?

Dean Willard Sperry of the Harvard University Divinity School is the editor of a recently published book on *Religion in the Post-War World.* There is a paragraph in the preface to it which I should like to quote. After stating that the earlier chapters of the book deal with Roman Catholicism, Protestantism, and Judaism, Dean Sperry says: "Then follows a chapter on Humanism which is a recognition of the fact that outside formal organized churches there is a great body of persons, mainly, perhaps, in our educational institutions and in the professions or in the arts, who are idealists and loyal servants of their fellow men, but who find themsleves intellectually unable to profess the traditional faiths in God. An English bishop has said that fifty per cent of the intelligent people of the modern world are humanists." It is my purpose this morning to set forth the beliefs of these humanists who are said to include half of the intelligent people of the modern world in their number.

It is after all, a very simple belief, easy to understand. You do not have to be a college professor, a philosopher, or a scientist to know what it is all about. Anyone with good native intelligence who is able to consider the subject with an open mind has no difficulty in understanding it. In fact there are a great many persons in every walk of life, aside from those listed by Dean Sperry, who are humanists. They may not call themselves such, may not be able to tell you what humanism is; none the less, they are thinking and feeling and acting in terms of this modern belief which has been labeled humanism by those who are conscious of it as a distinct movement in the world's life.

Humanism has in it three elements. First, a philosophy, a world-view; second, a purpose which it desires to achieve; and finally a plan of action by which it proposes to carry out its purposes. Let us have a brief look at each of these in turn.

The world-view or philosophy of humanism we call "naturalism." You will at once recognize that this is derived from the word nature. Modern men are increasingly influenced in their thinking by science. It is the most powerful intellectual influence of our time. Science is a way of studying nature; it begins by studying the outer physical world -- stars, atoms, the earth; it continues by studying living things, the plants and animals and other creatures with which we share this planet; it completes its structure by studying man himself -- not only his body, but his mind, his emotions, his thoughts, his dreams, his actions, his institutions, his economy, his religion -- all that he is.

Now, these various sciences by which we learn about the different aspects of our universe and ourselves, all fit together; they dovetail to make a single, unified structure. They combine to give us an intelligible and consistent picture of our world, and that is what any philosophy is. Again let me insist that you don't have to be a scientist or a profound thinker to understand it. Most of us take it in all unconsciously because it is part of the very air we breathe, part of the intellectual atmosphere of our time. Science has molded our thinking far more than most of us are aware.

The chief characteristic of the picture of the world drawn for us by the sciences is expressed in the phrase "cause and effect." We see that the things which happen do so because they are parts of a great chain of events, because of the relation in which they stand to the rest of the natural order to which they belong. Night gives way to day because the earth rotates on its axis and again brings our section under the sun's rays. Water turns into ice when the temperature falls to the freezing point. Even the inner life of men is subject to the working of cause and effect; we think the kind of thoughts we do, we develop the personalities we have because of our original heritage and the conditions under which we have matured. We might say that the account which the sciences give of our universe is that it is a democratic order ruled by the interplay of the forces within it, the present growing, evolving out of the past; instead of being made, created, like a watch; our world grows like a tree.

Within the naturalistic world-view the emphasis of humanism is on man himself; that is why we call it "humanism." Man is a true child of nature, just as much a part of the natural order as are stars and atoms. This is true of all that he is, including his ideals and aspirations, his loves and devotions, as well as his physical organism and his animal appetites. Archibald MacLeish has defined humanism as "the belief of man in his own dignity, in his essential worth as a man." It is "natural" man of which these words are spoken. Man, the product of the long evolutionary process of life on this planet, is worthy of reverence because of the qualities and capacities which have been established in him. This belief in the dignity and worth of man is not at all inconsistent with a recognition of his defects and limitations. The humanist belief in man is no superficial optimism, but is maintained in the full light of those facts which in some have inspired a contempt for man. Belief in man is the very core of the humanist's philosophy.

But humanism is more than a philosophy. It is a vital human purpose which must be defined in terms of naturalism. That purpose is to make human life on our earth-home as rich and satisfying as possible. We believe that we have, in the natural resources of our world, including human life, all the material necessary to establish an order of existence much more satisfactory than anything which men have attained to date, and that it is the chief business of man to set his own goals and control the course of events for the purpose of bringing himself along the way toward the richer life of which he has had a vision. The fulfillment of life here and now is the purpose of humanism. The evolutionary process which has brought man here has been largely blind and unconscious, but in man it has arrived at intelligence and self consciousness. It has acquired what Julian Huxley calls a "cutting edge." It has now become possible for human beings to give a direction of their own choosing to the process of evolution in this little sector of the universe over which we have won a measure of control.

We know from experience that man's life can be very rich, both in its material and in its spiritual values, but the tragedy of our lot is that we avail ourselves so little of these values. We get in each other's way; "man's inhumanity to man makes countless thousands mourn"; we defeat ourselves, making our values insecure, preventing us from multiplying them, developing them as we should. The humanist recognizes all this, sees that man's greatest obstacles to the good life he has envisioned lie in himself. The humanist therefore sets himself to the major task of human life, namely that of so ordering the affairs of earth, so directing the energies of men, that the good things we covet shall be made more accessible, more secure, more widely shared by all men. We know full well we shall not attain the goal at a single bound; it is the part of wisdom to take the next step, trying to make sure that it is in the direction we want to go. The difficulties and obstacles in the way are mountainous, but the humanist refuses to be daunted; he maintains his faith in man and sees no sufficient reason for setting a limit to the progress we can make in reshaping the world nearer the heart's desire. It is this purpose to build a world worthy of the best in human life which provides the central drive of humanism.

It is in finding a way to accomplish this purpose that humanism develops its program of action. You may have read in the current *Reader's Digest* the account of a church school in the east which is availing itself of the services of psychologists in setting up its program, and in cooperation with the homes and the schools is having remarkable success in taking unhappy, maladjusted children and turning them into happy, successfully adjusted personalities which give promise of growing into mature, normal men and women whose lives will be much richer because of the help which they have had in these early crucial years. Even when you make allowance for the natural enthusiasm of the writer of the article it is clear that the project is achieving very important results. The work of this church school is typical of the program of action set up by the humanist. He says we will take all the skills and insights which our various sciences have brought us and we will harness them to the task of serving the needs of man; we will bring them to bear on the most pressing problems that are crying for solution; we will use them not only to master the forces of the external world, but also to control and direct the drives of our natures, and see what a fine thing we can make out of life on earth.

If we would understand the humanist program of action, all that is necessary is that we examine the actual practice of men in any of the fields where they are pushing forward the quest for the values of life. Humanist practice has far out-run humanist theory, and while the minds of men linger professedly in the realm of the supernatural, their deeds are actually based on the assumption that only the natural has any reality. Whether they want to increase the world's food supply, safeguard an urban population from disease, bring healing to a neurotic personality, or establish a world order for the preservation of peace, the methods men use are those indicated by a naturalistic understanding of our world. The humanist is convinced that the sooner we recognize this to be the case and accept it consciously, the better it will be for the accomplishment of our purpose. Man must do for himself the things that in the past he has asked the gods to do for him.

Such, then, is humanism which the English bishop declares to be the religion of half the intelligent people of the modern world. It sees this universe as a natural order governed by laws which are the results of the interaction between the many forces which are at work within it, a universe always in the process of development, change, growth, because of its very nature. It sees man himself as a child of this process, man with his thoughts that pierce beyond the stars, man with his dreams of life made perfect. And it says: this be our purpose; we human beings will deliberately set ourselves to make of our lives, as best we are able, a thing of beauty and a joy forever. The method we will use for the accomplishment of our purpose shall be that of bending all our resources, our creative power, our skill, our intelligence, our very heart's blood, in cooperation with the forces of nature about us, to the advancement of the cause of human life. It is a religion of man, by man, for man.

In conclusion, just a word about the relation of humanism to the Unitarian church. Many humanists have found their home in the Unitarian church, both as laymen and as ministers. This is possible because the Unitarian church is founded on the principle of the free mind, and discipleship to growing truth. We welcome humanists to our membership as we do all those who believe in man and are eager to join with their brothers in the perpetual quest to make life fairer, stronger, nobler for all the sons and daughters of earth.

Religious Instruction for Children

During the past half century great changes have taken place in the views of thoughtful men and women on the subject of religion. Science has vastly enlarged our conceptions of the universe and has given us a new understanding of its process. This has inevitably altered our thought of God; it has also given us a different view of man in his relation to the vast whole of which he is such a tiny part. During the same period the historical study of the Bible has made us realize that instead of being the supernatural revelation of truth our fathers held it to be, it is the natural work of men, many of them gifted, but none the less human and fallible like ourselves. Indeed our whole conception of religion has undergone a transformation. We no longer think of it as something apart from the rest of our lives, an intrusion from some other realm; rather we think of it as a way of life, as a quality which we try to infuse into all that we do.

The old distinction between the sacred and the secular is no longer valid for us. To quote a recent writer, "Life becomes religious and ethical whenever we make it so; when some new light is seen, when some deeper appreciation is felt, when some larger outlook is gained, when some other nobler purpose is formed, when some task is well done."

Yes, our conception of religion has been transformed, but we have been very tardy in carrying over the consequences of this change into the religious instruction of children. For the most part the churches go on in the old way, identifying religious education with the teaching of the Bible just as though we still believed it to be an infallible revelation from on high; for the most part they continue to indoctrinate young minds with certain beliefs regarded as necessary to salvation, and to surround those beliefs with an emotional pattern of fear and hope the purpose of which is to keep the child bound to those dogmas when he has grown to maturity.

However well intentioned all this may be it is, in my opinion, a tragic mistake. It does not serve the best interests of the children who are subjected to such teaching. It does not serve the best interests of the adult community of which these children are destined to become members. There is a mistaken idea abroad that simply to instruct children in the Bible is to make them better boys and girls, better men and women. The facts do not bear this out. A study was made a few years ago under the auspices of the University of Iowa on the results of the instruction in the Sunday Schools of the state on the moral perceptions of the children. The result was a complete disappointment to those who had hoped that moral superiority was definitely associated with attendance at Sunday School. The investigators discovered again and again that though the boys and girls and the young people had learned many Bible texts by heart and were familiar with the story of Jesus, the meaning of what they had learned, the moral significance of the passages and stories had escaped them entirely. Their perceptions of what is right and what is wrong were not made any clearer by what they had learned; they were not any better because of their Sunday School instruction for the simple reason that such moral content as there was in the instruction had not become part of their lives; they had learned by rote but had not assimilated.

It is very naive, very superficial, to assume that we make better boys and girls simply by teaching them the Ten Commandments; it is no cure for juvenile delinquency to send the young offenders to Sunday School. That may or may not help them, depending on a lot of factors. We have been learning a great deal in recent years about the way in which children develop and why they do the things they do. One of our surest findings is that while verbal instruction in right and wrong, the learning of ethical precepts, has its place, that place is a relatively minor one. Whether or not a boy or girl grows up to be high minded, conforming his life to the best standards, depends far more on the atmosphere of the home in which he is reared, the spirit which pervades the school he attends, the actual practices of the adults in the community of which he is a member, than it does on his learning certain specific rules of conduct in Sunday School or day school. If the ethical practices of the people with whom he associates at home, in the school, on the playground, in the community, are high the chances are great that he will accept those standards as his own. If those practices are not high no amount of preaching at home will offset that influence and enable him to grow into the kind of a man we would like to have him be.

We need a new kind of religious instruction for children, a new kind of a church school; one which is child centered, one which avails itself of the new insights into the way in which children develop; we need to bring into our church schools the knowledge and skills which are now being used in our best public and private schools. A child is not just a small sized man or woman, and it won't do simply to cut down to his size the religion of grown-ups. That is precisely what we have been doing; we have assumed that there were certain great religious truths which we must cram into the minds of children regardless of whether or not they were prepared to understand them. We have said that the understanding would come later; this has proved to be a mistake.

What we should do is to take the children where they are, begin with their own experiences of the world about them and their own feelings for that world; help them to understand; help them to grow, to use their developing intelligence. A mature idea of deity is beyond the grasp of a little child's mind and for an adult to try to force it upon him regardless of his readiness to receive it may do him irreparable damage. The same is true of high moral requirements; it is only slowly that the child acquires the necessary experience to enable him to understand the reason for such requirements, and if we give them to him as so many arbitrary rules we are doing violence to his spirit. Let us respect the integrity of the child's mind; let us content ourselves with allowing him to grow at his own pace, giving him such assistance as we can, and in the end he will go farther, much farther, than if we try to force our own ideas on him before he is ready for them.

In some respects this method is more difficult than the older one of requiring him to learn certain things which we have decided he ought to know. It requires more of us, more patience, more insight, more ingenuity; but in the long run it will reward us by the richer results it produces in the child's life. It is some times easier for a mother to button her child's clothes than it is to wait while the little one fumbles with uncertain fingers at the buttons. But if the mother always renders this service, the child is greatly retarded in learning to do it himself. Even so in religious education, if we are always buttoning our children's minds with our adult ideas we put serious obstacles in the way of their growing to spiritual maturity.

What place would the Bible have in a child centered church school? Definitely a subordinate one. We would have to remember that the child is more important than the Bible. To be sure, one ought to acquire in the course of his education a knowledge of the Bible, both for the sake of the richness of its content and because of the extraordinary influence which it has exerted in our western civilization. But most of this knowledge should be acquired at a mature age, certainly not in early childhood. The Bible has in it some great literature, but it is not a great child's book. On the contrary, it is a very difficult book even for adults to understand. It requires much maturity of mind and background of knowledge before it can be rightly approached. Otherwise the result is very confusing, and can do the children more harm than good. There is some biblical material which lends itself to the teaching of young children; more as they grow older. But the question which we must always ask ourselves about any of the Bible stories or teachings we propose to use is this: Does it meet the needs of the child at this stage of his development; is it something he can understand and assimilate, something that will help him in his growth? If so, well and good, we will use it; if not, then we will withhold it until he is ready for it. The child and his need come first.

More than a century ago a great man wrote as follows: "The great end of religious instruction is not to stamp our minds irresistibly on the young, but to stir up their own; not to make them see with our eyes, but to look inquiringly and steadily with their own; not to give them a definite amount of knowledge, but to inspire a fervent love of the truth; not to burden the memory, but to quicken and strengthen the power of thought; not to bind them by ineradicable prejudices to our particular sect or our peculiar notions, but to prepare them for impartial, conscientious judging of whatever subjects are offered to their decision; not to impose religion upon them in the form of arbitrary rules, which rest on no foundation but our own word and will, but to awaken the conscience, the moral discernment, so that they may discern for themselves what is right and good."

The man who wrote those words was William Ellery Channing, who more than any other one man established the Unitarian Church in America. In them there is an anticipation of the best modern educational theories and practice of our own day. It is not strange that Channing inspired Horace Mann, who was the founder of the American public school system, and Elizabeth Peabody, who developed the kindergarten in this country. These pioneers in education have left us in the Unitarian Church an inspiring heritage which we have sought to use for the benefit of our children and young people.

In recent years our Unitarian national organization has employed the service of men and women who are experts in child psychology, acquainted with the best that is being done in the field of education. They have been producing textbooks and setting up a course in religious education designed to do the very thing we have here been describing -- take the child where he is and on the basis of his own experience help him to expand his vision, to grow in his knowledge of that which is good and true, to increase in wisdom and stature of character. We have adopted this curriculum and this method in our local school at All Souls Unitarian Church, Indianapolis. We expect of our teachers that they shall keep the child and his needs in the center of their attention. That their concern shall not be to pass on to the children certain adult ideas and conclusions, but to stimulate them to think for themselves, to learn to decide for themselves what is good and desirable. We expect of our teachers that they shall be friends and companions of the children as they progress in the difficult art of using well the materials with which life confronts us all.

We human beings have been moving steadily into a larger world which makes greater demands on us. It is vastly broader in its intellectual sweep, far more complex in its social relations, much more complicated to live in than the world of the past. There is only one thing that can make of that new world a satisfactory place in which to live, and that is an improvement in the quality of the men and women who are its citizens. Let us have a religious education which will help enable our children to measure up to the requirements of the world they are entering, help them to achieve the daring of mind, the breadth and depth of sympathy, the freedom and the self discipline needed to make of it a place where they can dwell with confidence and joy.

The Poetry of Christmas

In the first church which I served as minister there was an exceptionally fine family consisting of the father and mother and a six-year-old son. The parents were of high intelligence and strong, wholesome character; the boy was the kind of a lad you would expect in such a home, sturdy, alert and a joy to behold. The first Christmas season after he had begun to attend school he came home with questions about Santa Claus; was there really such a being as his schoolmates were telling him about who came down the chimney the night before Christmas and left presents for boys and girls who were as good as they could be?

Confronted with these questions the parents took what has continued through the years to seem to me as a very wise procedure. They had a scrupulous sense of honor and did not want to tell their boy a set of fictions in the name of truth, for they knew that when he learned the truth he might well feel that they had betrayed his confidence. At the same time they did not want to deprive him of the delight which the childish heart takes in these myths which have become part and parcel of the Christmas festival. So they told him the various stories, including the one about Santa Claus, making it clear that these were like fairy tales with which he was familiar, pretend stories. Then they said wouldn't it be great fun to pretend that the Santa Claus story was true and that he was going to visit their house this Christmas.

Naturally the idea appealed to the boy and, with zest no whit less than that of his companions who believed implicitly in the reality of Santa, he made his preparations, hanging his stocking by the fireplace, and even, on his own initiative, placing a basin of water, soap and towel handy for Santa to wash himself after his descent of the chimney. In the morning he found that not only was his stocking bulging with the coveted toys, but also that the water in the basin was soapy and dirty, and that there was some soot on the towel as though Santa in his hurry had not done a very good job of washing. In relating these events to me he said, "Daddy did it!" but his eyes sparkled with the joy of the game.

The wisdom in the procedure on the part of these parents lay in the fact that they were taking into consideration the whole situation and trying to conserve all the values. They had to safeguard the integrity of the child's mind and his trust in them, and at the same time give him the delights which are childhood's rights. They succeeded remarkably well.

There is a pattern here that we would do well to apply to the whole of the Christmas festival. It is the richest of all our celebrations, having gathered to itself a great storehouse of treasures in its journey down the centuries and through many lands. Much of its stuff is woven of myth and fancy; it belongs to the realm of poetry and imagination. Many of the greatest values of human life *do* belong in this realm, and we are best able to avail ourselves of their full worth when we take them for what they are without confusing them with sober fact. In this spirit let us look at some of the treasures that the Christmas festival brings us.

First there are the decorations with which we make gay our homes, our churches, and public places -- holly wreath and mistle-toe, the evergreen Christmas tree with its tinsel and lights, the yule-log burning in the fireplace, the lighted candles. All these are lovely in themselves and they combine to produce the deep satisfaction that beauty always brings. But beyond that they minister to us in a way of which we are scarcely conscious but which is none the less vital. They whisper to us of a time, long, long ago when men cherished those few plants which retained their green despite winter's storms, as a sign and seal of life's persistence and its coming victory. They whisper to us of a time long before the birth of Jesus when men were poignantly aware of their dependence on the sun, when they looked with dread on his waning strength and feared that he might die; when they heralded with relief and gladness, at this season of the year, the signs that the danger was over and that he was returning to splendor and power, and they signalized their joy by lighting candles as symbols of renewed light, by kindling fires which perchance might exert a sympathetic magic and help the sun regain his strength. In all this we have fellowship with the unending generations of men who have lived in vivid awareness of their dependence upon the great order of nature of which we are the children.

It is equally true that the center and core of the Christmas festival, the Holy Family, long antedates the Christmas era. Men have worshipped before the shrine of the Madonna and Child from time immemorial for the simple reason that it symbolizes one of the most sacred realities, one of the supreme mysteries of life -- the miracle of birth and motherhood. The wise men do well to bow before the cradle; it is inconceivable that an event so fraught with significance should not be clothed in the garments of sacredness, the robes of religion. The value of the Christmas story lies not in its recital of the birth of one marvel child, but in that it takes up the common experience of parents, their joy and wonder over the miracle they have wrought, their tender love toward this helpless creature, their fond dreams for his future, and weaves them into a myth that seeks to express their inherent sacredness. All families are potentially Holy Families.

To be sure, part of the richness of the festival is due to the fact that it celebrates the birth of a particular baby who was destined to grow into a wise, a great and good man who made a remarkable contribution to human destiny. The Gospel stories of the birth of Jesus are to be taken as part of the poetry of Christmas; not as history, but as expressions of the piety and reverence which this great leader inspired in his early followers. As such they are of surpassing beauty and worth.

Jesus is more than a historic person in the sense that he has become a symbol. About his person has gathered the Christ Ideal. His life has been an urn into which generations of men have poured their own heroic idealism and then have found it gushing forth again, a stream of living water. Despite all the perversion and superstition that has been part of men's use of it the Christ Ideal has been an immense influence for good. It continues to be the most persuasive symbol man has fashioned to express the deepest loyalty of his own heart, the hunger and thirst for partnership in the unending process of creation by which the world is shaped nearer the heart's desire. All this, too, belongs to the Christmas festival to give it richness and a quality that is deeply satisfying to the hungers of men's hearts.

Christmas is the time when the idealism of the human heart comes to the fore. It is the reassuring revelation of those qualities in human nature in which our chief hope lies.There is much, oh so much, that is wrong with the world, that mocks the sound of Christmas bells; but as long as the hearts of men respond to the song of "Peace on earth, good-will to men," as long as they have the grace to act on the injunction that it "is more blessed to give than to receive," as long as they sincerely feel that the great ends of life are served in causes that transcend their petty personal interests, there is hope that we shall yet redeem ourselves from our woe.

Christmas is an invitation to come over on the side of the redeeming forces in human life. The poets have sung the invitation in lines we joy to repeat; the music masters have put it into great melodies that capture our hearts; the artists have presented it in pictures to which we turn again and again to feed on their beauty; men gifted in story have woven it into such tales as that of Tiny Tim which we recite again and again; the heroes and common folk of earth have acted it out a thousand, thousand times in the substance of their daily lives. Our own hearts prompt us to accept with eagerness and live in that which is best for mankind.

Christmas is a fadeless tapestry which our forebearers have been busily weaving for untold generations and have given to us as a heritage to enjoy, and to pass on, enriched at some point perchance, to those who come after us. Christmas is a mighty epic poem chanted from out the depths of human experience, not only by one gifted singer but by the unceasing procession of pilgrims that have marched across the centuries, bearing witness to the divine in man. Christmas is a rich and varied drama to which the poets and dreamers, the men of achievement and action, have lent their talents from time immemorial, and to whose cast we too are summoned to take our minor yet significant roles.

Christmas means the inveterate joy of the human heart when the days begin to grow longer and light triumphs over darkness, bringing the promise that life will renew itself and break forth in the pageantry of spring. Christmas means the ineffable sense of sacredness as the whole world bows before the cradle, symbol of the miracle of human lie, eloquent of the tenderness with which we regard each newcomer into our midst, and of the hope that springs eternal round every babe. Christmas means the sacrament of mother love, the precious influence of exalted womanhood in refining and enriching the ways of men.

Christmas means the story of the birth of one of the noblest sons of men who was true in unusual degree to what is best in you and me and who puts us all in his debt by his unflinching loyalty to his ideals even at the cost of his life. Christmas means the glory of the Christ Ideal that has gathered round the man of Nazareth.

Christmas means the accumulated treasures of the artist in man as he has used the festival through the centuries to pour forth his life in song and picture, poetry and legend. Christmas means the laughter of little children around the lighted Christmas tree and bulging stockings. Christmas means gaiety, color, light. Yes, and Christmas means the tender, sad recollection of the days that are gone, the cherished memory of other scenes and other faces.

Christmas means the yearning in the depths of our own hearts to throw all the power of our lives on the side of those things which bring happiness and peace to loved ones, to friends and neighbors, to all the world. Christmas is the prompting of that spirit which shall some day unite all the children of men in one Holy Family of peace and goodwill.

May your Christmas have its full measure of these universal treasures. A Merry Christmas to you! Yes, a Christmas of satisfactions deeper even than those of the merry heart; a Christmas in which the laughter and the tears of life are commingled in transcendent peace. The blessing of such a Christmas be to you.

The Sheep
and the Goats

The Sheep and the Goats

There is a famous passage in the Gospel of Matthew descriptive of the last judgment. It says that when the Son of Man shall come in his glory he shall have all the nations gathered before him and he shall separate them one from another, as the shepherd separates the sheep from the goats. It then proceeds to identify the sheep with the righteous and the goats with the wicked, and concludes that the latter shall go away into eternal punishment but the former into eternal life.

Whenever I read this passage it is with mingled feelings. I admire it greatly because it identifies righteousness with the ministry to human need: "I was hungry, and ye gave me meat; I was athirst, and ye gave me drink; I was a stranger, and ye took me in; naked, and ye clothed me; I was sick, and ye visited me; I was in prison, and ye came unto me." I admire it because it identifies wickedness with the refusal to minister to such human needs. But at the same time my mind draws back from this sharp differentiation of people into the righteous and the wicked. The human heart is a very complicated affair, and no simple classification of people into good and evil can do justice to the actual situation. As a familiar saying has it: "There is so much good in the worst of us and so much bad in the best of us, that it ill behooves any of us to judge of the rest of us." All our lives are curiously compounded of good and evil. And our modern conscience is revolted by the thought of condemning any person, no matter how wicked he may be, to eternal punishment. We have too deep an awareness of the social as well as the individual roots of evil to sanction any such absolute condemnation. We think in terms of redemption from evil, and the idea of eternal punishment does violence to ours sense of justice and humanity.

That figure of the separation of the sheep from the goats was a very natural one, for the two were herded together, and it was a familiar sight in Palestine to see the shepherd at the close of day when he brought his flock into bed them down, separating them according to their kind. It was natural, also, to identify the sheep with the righteous and the goats with the wicked, for in popular thought the sheep has long been a symbol of innocence and the goat has had an unsavory reputation. We think at once of the "scape-goat" on whom the sins of the community were loaded that he might carry them off into the wilderness when he was driven forth. But I should like to turn Devil's advocate this morning and speak in defense of the goat.

My personal acquaintance with this animal is not very extensive, being confined to some boyhood experiences with a billy-goat kept in a livery-stable. He was at once the delight and the terror of the small boys of the neighborhood, and we had many an adventure in taunting him into pursuit of us. My personal knowledge of sheep is also limited, being acquired chiefly from what I saw of them during childhood vacations on my grandfather's farm. But a lively curiosity about these animals has led me to delve into the literature on the subject and my study has given me a much greater respect for the goat than for the sheep.

One of the books which I read was by a man who had started out in life to be a minister, but by the time he had reached his senior year in the theological seminary had departed so completely from the doctrines of his church that he decided he never could be a minister. So he went out to South Dakota to get a fresh start in life by becoming a sheep-herder. He says that he quickly discovered that one part of his theological education had not been wasted, for the vocabulary of the Pastor and the Shepherd are the same, only with decidedly different emphasis! The first qualification for a successful sheepherder, he learned, was an uninhibited capacity for profanity; if he did not possess this, the rage which the sheep would inspire in him was certain to prove fatal.

The chief characteristic of the sheep is their timidity; their psychology is one of fear. This is due to their defenselessness; they have to depend on mass and flight for protection. They are easily driven into panic; they huddle together and then stampede. They have little power of discrimination between real and imaginary danger; a tumble-weed blowing across the range will set them off just as well as an attack by a wolf. Sheep have a reputation, evidently well earned, for being stupid. They apparently make an impression on their herders similar to that of Mortimer Snerd on Edgar Bergen: "How can you be so stupid!"

The most powerful instinct in the sheep is that of gregariousness, the impulse to herd together. They feed together and though they may spread out somewhat as they graze they always maintain contact with one another, and at the first alarm they immediately bunch up. If a herder comes across a single sheep by itself he knows that something is wrong with it; either it is sick, or has suffered an accident, or is lost. Closely associated with this gregariousness is the propensity of sheep to follow the leader. Where one goes, the others will follow; so much so that in case of panic if one rushes over a cliff or plunges into the water the rest will rush headlong to the same fate. There is real point to the story of the small boy who was asked in the arithmetic class: "If there were five sheep in a field and one of them jumped the fence, how many would be left?" He answered, quite correctly, "None!" "Why, Johnny," remonstrated the teacher, "you know better than that. One from five leaves four." "Well," said Johnny, "You may know arithmetic, but you don't know sheep!" Timid, stupid, mass-minded, easily led -- surely it is not much of a compliment to the righteous to identify them with sheep.

And now for the goat. He is much more hardy than the sheep. He has a far better digestive system; he can thrive on brush and weeds where the sheep would perish. In fact goats are often used to clear rough land in preparation for cultivated crops. He prefers this kind of diet though he can also thrive on grasses. However he does not fatten as easily as sheep do. The goat is lively and daring. He prefers the high places where his agility and sure-footedness stand him in good stead. He is much better able to defend himself than the sheep. Like the latter he moves in herds, but of much smaller size; and always one of the number stands sentinel, on watch for a possible enemy. Most important of all is the goat's independence and his quality of leadership. Goats are frequently used in a flock of sheep to keep the sheep spread out and on the move; their greater intelligence, courage, and liveliness make them admirable leaders of the sheep.

With this contrast between the two animals in mind I should like to offer my own interpretation of the figure of the sheep and the goats. It seems to be that religion has placed too much emphasis on the qualities of the sheep and has given too little attention to the virtues of the goat. I appreciate that there is much beauty in the figure of the shepherd caring for his flock, bearing the lamb in his bosom, seeing that they are safe folded at night. Many are the heroic tales that are told of the shepherds in their care for their charges, particularly in time of crisis, the blizzards of winter, the lambing of spring. All this has been transferred to the realm of religion as in the familiar language of the Psalm, "The Lord is my Shepherd."

Certainly we need some of this element in religion. All of us, even the most self-sufficient, have our times of crisis when we feel a great loneliness and the need of receiving help from outside ourselves. Religion should provide for this need, but not at the expense of confirming us in a sheep-like attitude. Too much the leaders of religion have been "Pastors," which means literally shepherds. They have assumed that they have known best what was for the good of their flock; they have wanted followers, not independent souls who would think for themselves. The appeal of religion has been too much to timidity and fear, too much to the desire for conformity, to run with the herd. It has professed to gather men into the safe-fold of rigid doctrine. It has been too much an appeal to the sheep in man.

What we need is more of the goat in our religion. Let it be a summons to our courage and daring; let it call to us to scale the heights. Let it appeal to our hardihood; challenge us to rugged pioneering; to clear away the brambles and weeds, preparing the wilderness for the less hardy stock that will move in to take possession of the land after it has been tamed. Let us have a religion that appeals to the intelligence of men, that refuses to herd them together, but insists that each one shall develop his own personality. Let us have a religion which appeals to the qualities of leadership in men, a religion which appeals not to our weakness but to our strength.

It is in such a spirit that I conceive my work. I prefer not to be called a "pastor" because I refuse to think of my relation to the people of my church as that of a shepherd to his flock. I don't want to shepherd them, to think for them. It wouldn't do me much good if I did, because they are too independent in mind; they don't shepherd worth a tinker's damn! I conceive that I have a much higher function, namely to be their companion in our mutual quest to attain the best of which we are capable. I offer them the results of my thinking, not that they shall take it as their own, but that they shall find stimulus in it to do their own thinking. I share with them my hopes, aspirations, ideals, again, not in any expectation that they shall appropriate them as their own, but solely that they may find in them some spiritual sustenance with which to nourish their own hopes, ideals and aspirations. I want their religion to be their own, not an echo. "Minister" is the appropriate word to describe this function, for a minister is one who serves.

Surely the world stands in great need of a religion conceived in these terms, a religion that impels men not to seek their own ease and safety but to dare greatly for the sake of creating a better world. We live in a time when the old order is breaking up and all things are being made new; the time when things are being made new is the time to make them better. But it is a difficult undertaking and can never be carried through by the sheep-like mind. It is to the goats among men, the innovators, the heretics that we must turn, for despite their unsavory reputation and the inconvenience to which they ofttimes put us, they are the ones in whom our hopes lie in this time of crisis. We might even venture a paraphrase of the ancient passage and say: "Inasmuch as ye were numbered among the competent, lived in the might of your own spirits, thought your own thoughts, hewed out your own paths, pushed forward to the conquest of the human wilderness, ye were companions of mine, co-workers with me in building the kingdom which hath its foundations in the heart of the world. Enter into the joy of those who have been the servants of man."

The Gospel According to Mark Twain

One of the best loved American authors is Mark Twain. His tales of Tom Sawyer and Huckleberry Finn are among our classics. We commonly regard him as our greatest humorist. Now, it is somewhat dangerous for a man to have a reputation as a humorist because it is difficult for us to take him seriously. This has proved to be the case with Mark Twain; it has tended to obscure the fact that he was a profound thinker. A distinguished English visitor to this country has said that abroad Mark Twain is regarded as one of the ablest thinkers, one of the best philosophers America has produced. It is to this more serious phase of his writings that I would direct your attention this morning in an examination of his religion.

The Atlantic Monthly has recently been publishing *The Love Letters of Mark Twain,* written to Livy who was to become his much beloved wife. In one of these letters there is a passage in which he tells of his valiant effort to become a Christian for her sake. He says that he has made good progress in his moral life, that he performs all his duties as well as he can, but, and I quote: "See what I lack! . . . I lack the chief ingredient of piety -- for I lack (almost always) the 'special moral emotion' -- that inner sense which tells me that what I do I am doing for the love of the Savior. I can be a Christian -- I shall be a Christian -- but when I feel as I feel today, it seems a far journey away." Later in the same letter he tells Livy that his moral growth has been motivated by his love for her. Again I quote: "Please don't let my motive distress you, Livy. You know the child must crawl before it walks, and I must do right for love of you while I am in the infancy of Christianity; and then I can do right for love of the Savior when I shall have gotten my growth."

This is to me a pathetic passage in its revelation of the unnecessary struggle and pain that was going on in Mark Twain's soul to bring himself into accord with the conventional conception of what it is to be a Christian. It has long seemed to me that Jesus himself would be the first to repudiate this notion that it is only as you do right for love of him that you are truly a Christian; the first to insist that sincere goodness, whether motivated by the love of a man for the woman of his choice or his own spontaneous desire to cleave to that which is good, is no less the genuine article, no whit inferior, to that which is motivated by the "love of the Savior." "By their fruits ye shall know them" are his own words.

Mark Twain never made that "far journey" of becoming a Christian in the theological sense of that term. He was too honest to profess to believe things which he could not believe. His intelligence was too keen to accept many of the doctrines which have been insisted on in the name of Christianity. There are different phases of his thought which are represented in his books. There is an iconoclastic phase which reminds us of Robert Ingersoll in his attacks on Christian theology. This comes out clearly in *The Mysterious Stranger.* This has been published as a tale for children, but really it is a terrible satire on orthodox theology. Mark Twain's wife regarded it as "indiscreet" and so it was not published till after his death.

A single passage in which he describes Christian theology as a hysterically insane dream will give you the terrific impact of his thought. "A God who could make good children as easily as bad, and yet preferred to make bad ones; who could have made everyone of them happy, yet never made a single happy one; who made them prize their bitter life, yet stingily cut it short; who mouths justice and invented Hell -- mouths mercy and invented Hell -- mouths Golden Rules, and forgiveness multiplied by seventy times seven, and invented Hell; who mouths morals to other people and has none himself; who created man without invitation and then tries to shuffle the responsibility for man's acts upon man, instead of honorably placing it where it belongs, upon himself; and finally, with altogether divine obtuseness, invites this poor, abused slave to worship him."

But by no means all of Mark Twain's thought was in this iconoclastic vein. He went on to work out positively and constructively his own beliefs. These are well represented in one of his serious books called *What Is Man?* The answer which he gives to this question is that man is a machine, a very marvelous, intricate, and flexible machine, but none the less a machine. The quality of the machine is given once and for all by heredity; what the machine will produce is determined by the discipline it receives and the environment in which it works. Shakespeare was a machine; not an ordinary sewing machine like you and me, but a Goeblin loom which wove out of the materials available to an Englishman of his day tapestries of marvelous design and richness of color, but nonetheless a machine; creating nothing himself, always moved by forces outside himself, able only to reshape the material offered him by his environment. Free will is an illusion.

This is pushing determinism to its logical conclusion, but Mark Twain says it does not mean that we shall supinely accept things as they are. It is part of our inheritance to have an active desire to change them for the better. It does show us that the only way we can succeed in that purpose is by accepting the true state of affairs as a basis from which to start. By continued intelligent discipline we can enable our machines to reach a higher capacity and accomplish many things which would otherwise be impossible to them. By manipulating the materials of our environment intelligently we can add immeasurably to the value of the product. The only kind of freedom we have is that which man has exercised in his conquest of the air. He cannot set aside the law of gravitation, he has to work in a realm in which the laws of cause and effect are inexorable; yet working within those laws, he achieves the marvel of the modern airplane. The triumphant flights of his own life can come in no other way than by heeding the laws of his own being.

One of the inexorable laws of the human machine, says Mark Twain, is that only one impulse ever moves a man to do the things he does, namely the impulse to content his own spirit. The act must do him good first; otherwise he will not do it. No man ever sacrifices himself for others. We do many things daily for others, but it turns out upon careful analysis that the reason we do so is primarily to gratify a deep-lying demand in ourselves; we feel that we fulfill ourselves most by doing for others. Mark Twain sums up his philosophy for the general betterment of the race in the following admonition: "Diligently train your ideals upward and still upward toward a summit where you will find your chiefest pleasure in conduct which, while contenting you, will be sure to confer benefits upon your neighbor and the community." He says that this is the same ethical principle which has been set forth in all high religions; but he argues that it has a distinct advantage over the usual statement of it because it is more realistic in frankly placing the contentment of self first and the conferring of benefits of others second. He has caught the essence of this in his famous saying: "So live that when you die even the undertaker will be sorry."

William Dean Howells wrote Mark Twain, "God didn't forget to put a soul in you. He shuts most literary men off with a brain only." This is true; Mark Twain's heart was as warm as his intelligence was keen. At the conclusion of *Eve's Diary* he represents Adam sorrowing over Eve's death and the words which he puts in Adam's mouth are these: "Where she was, there was Eden." This speaks for Mark Twain's feelings on the death of his own wife. This warm and generous love of his went out not only to his own family but to mankind at large whenever its need was greatest. You feel him brooding over humanity in its sufferings much as Jesus did. Out of this love develops the third phase of his religion.

It expresses itself in *A Connecticut Yankee in King Arthur's Court,* which is usually taken as a hilarious farce but which has a serious purpose underneath its surface comedy. In the preface to this book Mark Twain says: "My object has been to group together some of the most odious laws which have had vogue in the Christian centuries, and illustrate them by incidents of a story." This story of a man of the 19th century who becomes part of the 6th century is a fierce heart-cry against man's inhumanity to man. It is a brief for human rights. It is an expression of Mark Twain's democratic faith, his passionate desire to right wrongs and to labor for the improvement of social conditions. He was not only an iconoclast, throwing down the false idols of the past; not only the rational thinker working out his own philosophy of life, but also the passionate hearted lover of human kind seeking to help men move on toward the ideal of mutuality, the recognition that we are members one of another and must act accordingly. His was a religion of the heart as well as the mind.

We shall not agree entirely with Mark Twain in his philosophy; the thoughts of men have moved on since he lived and wrote. But that in no wise diminishes our appreciation of him. Mark Twain belongs to the glorious fellowship of the heretics, to that company of men and women of independent minds, who down the centuries have refused to be bound by creeds or yield to the constraint of authority imposed on them from without by church or state or mob, but have thought their own thoughts and have spoken them with boldness.

Because of them ancient and established error has slowly crumbled. Because of them new truth has slowly emerged and been established in the minds of men.

Mark Twain belongs to the glorious company of the new orthodoxy which substitutes the eternal quest for truth in the place of dogma; which refuses to erect today's understanding into a barrier against tomorrow's new insight. Because of them, humanity is slowly learning to receive new truth with gladness. Because of them, the mind of man grows broader and his hand becomes surer in directing his destiny.

Mark Twain belongs to the glorious company of the lovers of man. His keen mind detected our foibles, our frailties, our imbecilities. Yet they moved him not to wrath and condemnation, but to understanding and pity. His warm heart was moved to indignation by exploitation, by man's inhumanity to man, and he yearned to succor the victims, to lift the burden of suffering and woe that needlessly weighs them down. He used the power of laughter to blast at ancient error and injustice to the end that men might move on toward greater equality and mutuality which he saw as possible to them. And under his laughter there was the solemn note of sadness because his heart was so close to the common sorrows of our kind. Mark Twain belongs to the noble company of those who have identified themselves with our humanity, sharing at once its joys and its woes, and using their splendid powers to stem its tide of tears and enhance its abiding satisfactions. Let us take courage of their daring, strike our blows at the shackles which still enchain the minds of men; labor for the establishment of new truths; right ancient wrongs; give ourselves more fully to the creation of that finer society for which they have toiled, and which shall progressively be established upon the earth.

Peter Pan Religion

One of the most delightful of modern stories is that of *Peter Pan*, by Sir James Barrie. Countless thousands have enjoyed it in the book, on the stage, and on the screen. Peter is one of the best loved characters of fiction. Yet despite the fact that he is so charming, the story of Peter is a tragedy as is indicated clearly enough in the subtitle which the author has given his play, *Peter Pan, or the Little Boy Who Would Not Grow Up.*

That is the trouble with Peter. According to the story he heard his mother and father talking on the day he was born about what he was going to be when he grew up. He didn't want to grow up; he wanted to stay little and have a good time. So he ran away to "Never Land" and became the leader of a band of lost boys. He does have a good time in Never Land, particularly after he persuades Wendy and her brothers to join him. They have many exciting adventures. But always Peter shies away from anything which looks like accepting real responsibility. When Wendy decides to go home and resume the business of growing up she tries to get Peter to come along with her. Mrs. Darling, her mother, says that she will adopt Peter, but he will have none of it. He says, you don't catch me! I'm going to stay little and have a good time.

This tale of Peter Pan is far more than a fairy story. With deep psychological insight Barrie has made it the means of setting before us one of the deep tragedies of human life, -- namely that there are a great many persons, men and women alike, who never do grow up. They remain childish in their emotional life, though they attain their full growth physically and intellectually. They are unable to accept the responsibilities of adulthood; they take refuge in Never Land, a realm of fantasy and illusion, because they can not cope with reality. They may be charming and have many delightful qualities; nonetheless their lives are tragic and bring much heartache to those who love them because after all the world is real, and a large part of the business of growing up is to adjust ourselves to that fact and accept the responsibilities which it entails. No mother who truly loves her child would want him to remain a Peter Pan.

What I should like to do this morning is to indicate that there is much which passes for religion which is all too like the story of Peter Pan; superficially it is charming and appealing, but beneath this fair cloak there lurks an unsuspected tragedy, for it is a running away from the world of reality into the illusions of Never Land. There is a mistaken notion among many persons that all religion is good. That is not true; the worth of a religion depends upon the consequences which it has in the life of him who cherishes it. If it fortifies him for the business of living, if it enables him to deal more adequately with the real world, if it provides him with the courage and the inspiration to help make that world a better place for himself and his fellows, then it may be said to be a good religion. But if it is a method of running away from the world, if it makes him who espouses is less responsible as a man and a citizen, then it is Peter Pan religion and is evil rather than good.

Let us look a little more closely at the dangers of this Peter Pan religion. Like the hero of Barrie's play it runs away to Never Land, rejecting the obligation of meeting the requirements of the real world for the easy delights of a world where everything is arranged in accordance with the heart's desires. It is an other-worldly religion of compensation. It says in effect, the job of dealing with things as they are is too tough for me, I am going to stay little and have a good time. So in imagination it pictures a world where there is no hardship and suffering, but only joy and gladness; where all good things are to be had for the asking. And it says this is my real home rather than the vale of tears in which I now dwell.

There is, of course, much to be said in defense of this kind of religion. The world *is* a hard place, and many times it becomes too much for us. Then it is a welcome relief to slip away into an ideal world in which the good always triumphs over the evil, in which all things are arranged in accordance with our liking. We escape for a time from the strain of things as they are into the heaven of things as they might be, and come back refreshed to take up anew the struggle with things as they are. This is in part the function of art, to rearrange the elements of existence into a more satisfying pattern; here is the appeal of romance, of the exquisite harmony of music, the beauty of great painting and great architecture. It is true that many persons come back from religious fantasy refreshed for the work of the world.

But there is a danger here that the fantasy shall be mistaken for reality; that it shall become a substitute for actuality, a sedative rather than a restorative. The greatest art, that which alone has substance and depth, is that which reveals the ideal possibilities in the real and provides us with incentives to attain those possibilities; it is not a running away from life but a disclosure of the riches of which life is capable. The same is true of religion; it is at its best when it is inspiring us to make the most out of the possibilities of life, when it shows us heaven not as a place to which we may escape from the trials of the world, but as an ideal, the principles of which we can build into the substance of this life. Religion at its best means the acceptance of the necessity for growing up and dealing with the real world on a mature level.

A second danger in the Peter Pan type of religion is that it is self-centered and egotistical. Peter is always concerned about himself and his own pleasures; the stories he loves best are those in which he is the hero. He has very little feeling for other people, little understanding and sympathy for them. This, alas, has been true of much that has passed for religion; it has concentrated on individual salvation at the expense of broad interests and much feeling for the rest of the world. It has been charged, with what justice I cannot say, that industrialists when threatened with labor trouble used to call in the late Billy Sunday to hold a revival, because it had been discovered that he took the minds of laboring men off their efforts to improve their economic position and concentrate their attention on salvation in the world to come. When religion operates in that way it is essentially immoral. The core of its appeal is to selfishness. To be sure salvation may be interpreted to include certain moral requirements, and I know that many times this religious experience does result in an improvement in the life of the individual who has it. But over against such gain we must set the fact that the emphasis on what is to become of the individual in another world, the preoccupation with personal salvation, is a serious obstacle to the wider social purposes which it is the business of religion to promote.

One of the marks of a mature person is that while he can never outgrow his concern for himself he does greatly enlarge the boundaries of that self so that it includes others for whom he is as deeply concerned as he is for himself. Indeed he will sacrifice his own life if need be in their service. The most deeply religious men are not in the least worried about their personal salvation, about what is going to happen to them in the after world. They are so busily engaged on behalf of others to whom their love has gone forth that they forget their selfish interests, and paradoxically thereby serve themselves best. It is a mark of a mature religion that it asks not "what can I do to be saved?" but "what can I do to save the world?"

We have time to consider but one further danger of the Peter Pan type of religion. The Peter Pans of the world do very well as long as they are dealing with fantasy; they can indulge easily in rosy dreams. But when it comes to dealing with actuality they have to fall back on the assistance of someone else; they retain a childlike dependence, a let-mother-do-it attitude. They are not able to stand on their own feet and accept the responsibility for meeting the requirements of life. The same is true of the infantile type of religion; it is perpetually dreaming fine dreams but shoving the responsibility for making those dreams off onto other shoulders. It asks God to do the things that we should be doing ourselves, with the consequence that they do not get done. This dependence shows itself further in the reliance on authority. Instead of thinking for himself, instead of arriving at his own decisions, the follower of an immature religion is always turning to outside authority to tell him what he must believe, what he must do. He has not reached manhood's estate of self-dependence and self-responsibility and is thereby inevitably denied the opportunity to reach the heights.

There is a passage in George Eliot's poem "Stradivarius" of which I am particularly fond because it presents an attitude the reverse of that which we have just been considering. In it the violin maker tells of the philosophy which has guided him in his art and concludes with these lines:

> If my hand slacked
> I should rob God -- since he is fullest good --
> Leaving a blank instead of violins.
> 'Tis God gives skill,
> But not without men's hands: he could not make
> Antonio Stradivari's violins
> Without Antonio.

This is the mature attitude which should characterize religion -- man grown to his full stature, accepting his responsibility as a partner in the Firm of God and Sons.

At the conclusion of Peter Pan, Barrie throws in an aside that is not spoken in the play. When Mrs. Darling wants to adopt Peter and he says no, he is going to remain a little boy and have fun, the author says, "So he thinks, but it is only his greatest pretend; if only he could catch the hang of things he would learn that growing up is the biggest adventure of all." This is equally true in religion; to grow up religiously means to abandon some childish delights and irresponsibilities. It means that we have to leave Never Land behind us, substituting in its stead the actualities of the work-a-day world. It is by no means easy, but it is richly rewarding for it is only there that the true treasures of life are to be found, and any one of them is worth far more than all the Castles in Spain that vanish into thin air at the touch of reality.

"When I was a child I spake as a child, I felt as a child, I thought as a child, but now that I am become a man I have put away childish things." It is high time for the world to adopt this attitude toward religion, and putting away childish things to move on into maturity. Let us have a religion that expresses itself in seeking to mould the real world nearer the heart's desire, a religion that is ethically responsible and self-reliant; a religion whose adherents find their fulfillment in pouring out their lives in the creative work of the world.

The World's Debt to Its Heretics

Ofttimes the derivation of a word gives us an insight into its meaning which does not occur to us as we ordinarily use it. Such is the case with the word heretic; it comes from the Greek word which means "able to choose." The heretic, therefore, is a person of independent mind who does not simply accept his beliefs because they happen to be dominant in the society in which he moves, because they are taught by his church or his party, but he accepts them on the basis of his own examination, his independent thought. He considers different possibilities and is "able to choose" among them that which to his mind best represents the truth.

Today this ability to think for one's self is among many of us regarded as a desirable quality; indeed it is held to be one of the highest achievements of man. How, then, does it come that the name heretic is regarded as a term of reproach, that there still lingers about it an unsavory taint so that there are few who are willing to be known as heretics? The answer is not far to seek. There is still attached to the term the feelings which were born of the time when conformity was regarded as the highest virtue and the man who dared choose for himself some pattern of thought or action other than that commonly accepted among his fellows was considered a traitor, a dangerous individual who was disrupting the unity of the group. Indeed a great deal of this feeling still lingers among us and the non-conformist is looked at askance; he seems disloyal to us, a troublemaker. The word "heretic" is charged with the emotional quality born of this threat to our security. We are passing judgment on a man, condemning him when we call him a heretic.

Yet it is clear from an impartial study of history that the heretic has an invaluable role to play in human society. He is the agent of change, of progress. There are two tendencies among us: the one, we call conservative. It is the tendency to let well enough alone, to keep things as they are. A very powerful tendency it is, too. It is fortified in part by inertia, by our unwillingness to make the necessary effort to change our ways and our thoughts; it is fortified also by our self-interest which we usually come to identify with things as they are. The other tendency is the progressive. The plain truth of the matter is that we do live in a world of change; things do not stand still, they are on the move. Sometimes the rate of change is very slow; then there may be periods when it comes more rapidly. The heretic, the man who is "able to choose," is often only one who has become aware more quickly than his companions of the need for change to adjust to changing conditions, and as such he renders an important service to the community, though it is a service which is rarely appreciated until long afterward.

Usually the conservative forces in society far outweigh the progressive. It is only in revolutionary periods and then for a short time that the "heretics" possess a preponderance of power. The result is that for the most part the heretics of history have fared badly. They have made their contributions only at tremendous cost to themselves. (As one historian has put it, there has been no period in the human story at which it was not more dangerous to be a heretic than it was to lead an attack on a citadel.) The heretics have been ostracized, excommunicated, outlawed, starved, crucified, burned at the stake. Slight wonder that men have been very loathe to let it be known that they were heretics, and have resorted to all manner of devices to disguise their heresy. Nor does this persecution all belong to the past; the same tendencies are active in men today. The fields in which heresies are important have shifted, but we still impose heavy penalties on those among us who are "able to choose," and exercise that power to choose a way that seems to threaten some deeply established, vital interest.

To be sure the heretic is not always right, the conservative always wrong. There have been many instances in which it has later been proved that the defenders of orthodoxy were nearer the truth than were the heretics. And it needs always to be borne in mind that there are substantial values in the conservative position. Life requires a large degree of security which only a relatively stable order can give it. Too rapid or too frequent change can be fatal. But so, equally, can an adamant resistance to change. The course of evolution, both animal and human, is strewn with the wrecks of forms which were so set in their ways that they could not make the adaptations necessary to survival. And if the heretic can be mistaken, history also demonstrates that in a great many instances he is much more nearly right than those who have opposed him. (Some years ago Ambrose Vernon, then a professor at Dartmouth College, stated that in a study which he had made of sixty men selected as the ones who have made the greatest contributions to the world he discovered that in their own lifetime forty of the sixty had been considered heretics and only twenty had been conservatives.) Two-thirds of the men to whom the world is most deeply indebted in all history have been heretics. Surely here is something to give us pause and make us consider.

The best way in which to appreciate the role which the heretic plays in society is to consider the career of an individual who in exceptional degree has shown that he was "able to choose." For this purpose let us select Socrates, reputed to be one of the wisest and best of men in antiquity. He was born in Athens nearly five hundred years before the time of Jesus at a period when the great Greek city was at the height of her glory. Socrates believed that he was divinely commissioned to help the people of his city move forward in their moral and intellectual life. He called himself the "gadfly" of the state, whose business it was to arouse, persuade, and reproach men. In particular he tried to teach men how to think properly so that they would not be content simply to accept inherited and current ideas but would delve deep in their effort to arrive at the truth. He developed what is still known as the "Socratic" method. It consists of a series of questions by which the teacher seeks to guide the pupils into an ever deeper understanding of the truth they are exploring. The purpose which Socrates had in all this is to be found in his conviction that there is a very close connection between knowing the truth and doing the right; if only we could know the full consequences of an evil deed we could never bring ourselves to do it.

In his personal life Socrates was exemplary. In order that he might be free to carry on his work, he refused to accept any office from the state and contented himself with a most meager livelihood. One of his friends said that if a slave were given such scanty fare as that on which Socrates lived he would run away. Though he lived under the sense of a divine commission there was nothing Pharisaical about him. He recognized his own limitations and was humble. He was wont to say that the only way in which he was wiser than the men with whom he debated was that he knew he was ignorant whereas they thought they already had full possession of the truth. And though he was ruthless in exposing their errors, he loved the men with whom he differed with a love of which only the greatest are capable. Again and again he stood steadfast for what he believed to be justice in public affairs no matter how many were arrayed against him.

Inevitably this searching, probing mind, backed by a will which stood resolute in the face of all opposition, brought him many enemies as well as friends. At length his enemies triumphed. They brought him to trial, charged with denying the gods recognized by the state, with introducing new gods, and corrupting the young. The story of his trial and death, as it is told by his disciple Plato, is one of the most profoundly moving dramas in all human annals; it deserves a place right along with the story of the martyrdom of that other heretic, Jesus of Nazareth. The two were kindred spirits. Socrates was found guilty and condemned to drink the fatal cup of hemlock. Thus the man who of all who had lived up to that time had deserved best at the hands of his fellows was put to death as a criminal. He died a heretic; but he has lived in the minds and hearts of humanity through all these 2,500 years and will continue to live down the centuries because he was an agent of change, of progress; because he was "able to choose."

Alas, how much easier it is to look back and discern that the heretic was right and those who put him to death were wrong, than it is to see with equal clarity the right and wrong in the issues of our own day! There are all too many persons whose religion consists largely of worshiping the dead heretics of the past and persecuting the living heretics of today. We are very slow to learn the lesson which the careers of such men as Socrates should teach us, namely, that we ought not to silence the voice of the man who disagrees with us no matter how sure we are that he is mistaken or how dangerous we consider his ideas. It is possible that we are the ones who are mistaken and the heretic the one who has laid hold of a new and fruitful truth. This has been demonstrated to be the case so many times that we should always consider it as a possibility.

In a laboratory which I once visited a sign hung on the wall bearing this statement: "There must be a better way to do it." That motto was indicative of the spirit in which the scientists at work in the laboratory went about their tasks. They accepted the fact of change; they assumed that progress was possible and desirable; they deliberately cultivated the heretical attitude of mind and were "able to choose." Their method got results; continually they were improving their process and their products, and now and again developing some new and unexpected product. The same motto is applicable to human affairs in general, "there must be a better way of doing it." The conservative tendency is so powerful in human life that we do not need to worry about it, for it will take care of its own interests. But we do need to make deliberate provision for the heretic to contribute his full quota to our common human enterprise and he can do that only on condition that he feels free to give us the results of his best and fullest thought. There is only one real, only one deadly heresy; that is to deny any man the right to make his best contribution to our difficult task of finding the most favorable path for our humanity to tread on its difficult trek through the wilderness as it seeks the promised land.

Joseph Priestley

The man whose career I propose to set before you today is famous as a scientist, the discoverer of oxygen, and one of the great founders of modern chemistry. Everyone who ever enjoys a drink of soda water is indebted to him, for it was his discoveries which made this drink possible. But in his own estimation his work in science was of secondary importance. His first great love was the ministry of religion and it was as a Unitarian minister that he would prefer to be remembered. His name was Joseph Priestley.

He was born in England near the city of Leeds on March 13, 1733. His father was a cloth manufacturer and Joseph was one of a large family of children. His mother died when he was seven years old and he was brought up by an aunt who was a woman of strict religious principles and yet withal of a liberal and tolerant spirit. Joseph owed much to her influence in his life. She naturally hoped that this nephew she was raising would join the church of which she was a member and indeed he desired to do so before he went away to school. But here that independence of mind which was to mark him all through his career interfered. When he sought membership in the local Presbyterian church he was refused it because he was found to be unsound in doctrine. He could not believe that all men share in the guilt of Adam's fall, and because of his sincerity he refused to profess something he did not believe.

His heresy stood in the way of his attending the Academy which he had selected for there the students were required twice a year to subscribe to the ten points of the Calvinistic faith and this he would not do. However he found an Academy where the atmosphere was freer. In a few years he had finished his course and had become the minister of a small Presbyterian church.

He did not last long in this position. His views were unorthodox and furthermore he suffered from a tendency to stutter. The combination was too much and his small congregation faded away; with it went his salary of $150.00 a year! Before long he had secured another and freer Presbyterian church. It is interesting to note, in passing, that Unitarianism in England early developed in the Presbyterian churches and to this day a considerable number of churches bearing that name are Unitarian in theology.

While he was serving in this second church Priestley began to teach in an Academy and to take private pupils. He exhibited great gifts in this respect. What marked him in particular was that he encouraged his pupils to express their own views even when they were contrary to his. He wanted them to think for themselves; he respected the rights of the intelligence of others and carried the spirit of freedom into his teaching. I dwell on this because it reveals a quality of his mind which was of the utmost importance for all his career.

Teaching proved so congenial to him that for a time he gave up the ministry to accept a position in Warrington Academy where he remained for six happy years. Teaching, however, did not occupy all his energies. He was an active and versatile mind always looking for new worlds to conquer. In particular the field of science attracted him. He became acquainted with Benjamin Franklin, who was living in England at the time, and under the stimulus of his friendship with Franklin wrote his first scientific work, *A History of Electricity*.

But he could not escape the lure of the ministry and before long he accepted the position of minister to a large "dissenting" congregation in Leeds. By dint of much effort he had overcome to a considerable extent his speech defect and now proved himself an effective and popular preacher. The church flourished under him. He did not, however, give over his scientific interests. It chanced that his home in Leeds was in the vicinity of a brewery and he became interested in the processes of fermentation. He wanted to know the reason *why* and at the age of thirty-five began those experiments which resulted in the year 1774 in his discovery of oxygen, the most abundant of all the elements on earth's surface.

I have already spoken of the use of his discovery in the manufacture of soda water. That, of course, was only a relatively unimportant consequence. Now for the first time men began to understand what happens when we breathe -- the tremendously important role which oxygen plays in the vital processes. A whole new field was opened up for development by Priestley's discovery.

It is interesting to read some of his accounts of his experiments. Judged by the standards of today his chemistry was very crude and he made numerous mistakes. But in the temper of mind which he brought to the work he was a true scientist. He was aware of his own prejudices, of the way in which an accepted opinion can blind a man to a new truth which is simply crying out for discovery. So he forced himself to study the facts with an open mind and let them speak for themselves, with the result that they led him to conclusions which were often very far from his preconceived notions.

As the years went by Priestley's reputation grew, not only as a scientist but as a philosopher and theologian and champion of human rights. The man's versatility was amazing. No field of human interests was foreign to him. As James Martineau said, "To refer to a catalogue of his works is like consulting the prospectus of an encyclopedia." This man brought the same fearless intelligence which made him preeminent as a scientist to bear on all the subjects which he touched. The result was that he built up for himself a formidable host of enemies. In a day of religious conservatism he boldly championed the cause of the disestablishment of the church, maintaining that church and state ought to be separate. Also he insisted that Jesus was a man and that the religion which he had established had been profoundly corrupted during the centuries; he pleaded for a return to the simplicities of the teachings of Jesus.

In politics as well as in religion he was enlisted on the side of freedom. At the time of the American Revolution he was a mature man in the fullness of his powers. He spoke out boldly on the side of the American colonies and said that they were defending the basic principles of Englishmen, the principles embodied in the Magna Charta and the Bill of Rights. When the French Revolution came along his sympathies were with the people, and while he deplored the excesses into which the revolution fell, he still defended its essential aims. As a result he was bitterly attacked in the British Parliament and accused of plotting to overthrow the government. It all has a very familiar ring; the champions of human rights are always denounced as the enemies of society.

All this leads up to the most dramatic incident in Priestley's life. In 1780 he had settled in Birmingham because a number of other distinguished chemists lived there and he wanted the stimulus of their fellowship in the pursuit of his own work. Before long, however, he was pressed into the service of a church, limiting himself to the preaching and teaching while the pastoral work was carried by a younger man. With the passage of the years Priestley's reputation and influence became very great, but all this did not save him from tragedy. On the 14th of July, 1791, there took place in Birmingham an event which one would have thought impossible in a great city of a civilized nation. It was the second anniversary of the destruction of the Bastille and some of the citizens of Birmingham who sympathized with the French revolution celebrated the occasion by a dinner at a hotel. Priestley had nothing to do with this. He was spending the evening quietly at home. But a campaign against him had been carried on by church leaders who resented his views and they took advantage of the inflamed temper of mind of the populace to direct the feeling against the French Revolution toward Priestley.

A mob gathered round the hotel and after breaking a few windows started for Priestley's church. With the cry "For King and Church" on their tongues they burned the building and then set out for Priestley's home with the intent of killing him. Fortunately he was warned in time and found refuge with a friend. But his home was destroyed, his scientific instruments wrecked, and his priceless manuscripts, representing the labor of years, were cast to the winds.

Through it all Priestley conducted himself with courage and equanimity. It was apparent, however, that he could not continue in Birmingham. So he moved to London where he was again invited to become the minister of a church. He accepted and for two years continued his work, but it became evident that even in London he was not safe. Furthermore the hostility to him had been extended to his family and his three sons had had to sever their business connections and seek refuge in America. Priestley decided to join them, and spent the last years of his life in this country.

He settled in Northumberland, Pennsylvania. Occasionally he went in to Philadelphia to give lectures. One result of these lectures is of particular interest to Unitarians. Priestley urged some young men who shared his views to form a Unitarian church in Philadelphia. This they did, the first meeting being held on June 12, 1796, thus establishing the first Unitarian church to bear the name in this country. They urged Priestley to become their minister; he refused to do so but joined the church as a layman. There is to this day a group of Unitarian churches in the vicinity of Philadelphia which continues to be known as the Joseph Priestley Conference.

The best elements of the Unitarian religion are admirably exemplified in Joseph Priestley. First, there was his championship of freedom in all the realms of human activity. Next, there was his acceptance of the guidance of intelligence. We disagree today with many of the conclusions at which Priestley arrived, but the important thing is that he used his reason to arrive at them. Finally he held that the highest good is character, and in his own life he gave a magnificent demonstration of it.

Thomas Huxley, at the dedication of a monument to Priestley in Birmingham on the 100th anniversary of his discovery of oxygen, said that here was a "heretic who was at the same time a saint"; that in all his controversies he never had any animosity toward those who disagreed with him; that the only people who hated him were those who did not know him; and that he never lost a friend. He was humble, simple, sincere. The whole movement of his mind was forward; the whole desire of his heart, to serve the best interests of men. We who cherish his memory as one of the great names of our heritage would seek to emulate his spirit in laboring to advance a religion conceived in liberty and dedicated to the service of humanity.

Who is Important?

I should like to begin by quoting a stanza from the modern English poet, William Watson:

> Momentous to himself as I to me
> Hath each man been that ever woman bore;
> Once in a lightning flash of sympathy,
> I felt this truth an instant, and no more.

The instinctive, spontaneous answer which each one of us gives to the question, Who is important? is "Why, *I* am important!" The next instant we may want to qualify this by saying, "At least I am important to the people who love me, and I am important to myself." Yes, it is easy for us to recognize our own importance; much harder for us to keep the other aspect of the truth in mind, that every human being seems as important to himself as we do to ourselves. The man you pass on the street, the woman who hands you a cup of coffee in a restaurant, carries around within him or her a whole inner world and if you could but enter that world sympathetically you would discover that it is as important to him or her as your own inner world of feeling and thought and experience is to you.

We are dealing here with one of the fundamental facts of our existence; there is an inescapable egoism in human nature. We have to believe in ourselves; it is necessary to our health as personalities that we shall think highly of ourselves and seem important to ourselves. We know that the man with what we call an "inferiority complex," the man who is forever belittling and humbling himself, is a sick soul. What is essential for the attainment of the finest results in character is the achievement of a nice balance in which a normal, wholesome sense of your own importance is offset by a corresponding feeling for the equal importance of others, so that your egoism has in it the needed seasoning of humility. The opposite of the "inferiority complex" is the "Jehovah complex," under the influence of which a man suffers from illusions of grandeur even to the point of thinking that he is God, and we recognize that he is insane. There is many an individual whose egotism is so intense that while it does not carry him to the extreme of insanity it does shut him off from an adequate insight into the lives of others, from sympathy with their feelings, and makes him a well-nigh intolerable person to live with. Yes, it is highly desirable that we modify our native egoism with the salt of humility.

The traditional Christian theology had a very effective way of enforcing this truth. It told man that he was a worm in the dust, a creature of total depravity, wholly dependent on the mercy of God; and yet at the same time it enabled him to feel tremendously important because it taught him that the struggle for the salvation of his soul was the central meaning of the whole drama of the universe; that God himself came to earth in human form to save man from his sin. The modern mind is compelled to reject this story because it simply does not seem true to us. But we ought not lose sight of the psychological values which it contained; it is still necessary for us to achieve this balance of humility and pride; and, even more important, it is still necessary for us to retain our concern for what happens to every human being. I covet for our modern religion that same fervor for souls which has marked sincere revivalists, only we must express that fervor in concern for what is happening to men here and now rather than in some questionable theological future. The core of our religion both in theory and practice should be the recognition of the importance of every human being and the need for helping him to live at his maximum.

This doctrine of the supreme importance of the individual man has suffered serious impairment in recent years. This is partly due to the rise of a naturalistic philosophy concerning human nature which has replaced the older theological view. According to the theological view each individual is of importance because he is a child of God with an immortal soul; according to the modern view man is a product of biological evolution. In the conflict between the two views, special creation on the one hand and biological evolution on the other, the modern mind has decided that the latter is far superior as a theory which harmonizes the known facts. We believe in evolution.

But it does not follow that we must therefore accept all the conclusions which some evolutionists draw from the theory. A psychologist in California is reported to have advanced the theory that: "Men and women have been trained by the demands of civilization to cover their natural impulses with many layers of disguises till it is very difficult to detect the real individual under the cloak. Monkeys are human beings without their masks on. If we want to now what is good for our instincts, we must study the monkeys." This is an absurd conclusion and involves a serious fallacy. It is, of course, true that we can profit by the study of the forms of life which preceded man, and particularly of those closest to him, but it does not follow that the proper study of mankind is monkeys! Even if the theory of evolution is true, as I believe it to be, man is something very different from the highest forms of life in the line from which he is descended, and must be judged by what he is in himself rather than by his origins. Man is what he *is*, not what he *was*. And this, despite all his frailties, defects, and limitations, is something incredibly wonderful. We can say with Emerson, "An individual man is the fruit which it has cost all the foregoing ages to form and ripen." He is not a "mere animal," but something immensely more complex and marvelous. From the evolutionary point of view, rightly understood, there is the same reason for that commingled feeling of humility and pride which was fostered by the earlier theological view. The individual is no less important than he ever was.

There has been an attack on the importance of the individual from another direction in modern times, and that is seen in the theory that the citizen is of value only as he serves the state. This appears at its worst in the Nazi philosophy where it is held that it is right and proper for the leaders to sacrifice their followers ruthlessly for the benefit of the state. This philosophy of "statism" takes a partial truth and elevates it into a colossal error. It is true that not a little of the significance of the individual derives from his membership in society, but an even more fundamental truth is that the values of the state exist only in the individuals who comprise it, and it is fatal to the state for it to try to make itself great by sucking dry the lives of the individuals of whom it is composed. Someone has aptly said that the end result of the philosophy of statism is simply the creation of a colony of termites. An individual is important not because he is a cell within society but for what he is in himself, and in the long run that state will prosper most which most fully recognizes the importance of the individual men and women who are its citizens.

We are in great need of cultivating a philosophy which emphasizes the importance of the individual, not in the sense of the "rugged" individualist who is prone to disregard his social obligations, but in the sense that the man who most fully identifies himself with his fellows makes his greatest contribution to the common life only on condition that he is free to be an individual, a person in his own right. We need to apply this philosophy of the importance of the individual to every phase of our life, to work it into all the patterns of our actions.

Channing Pollock tells of a farmer's wife who, after years of cooking and housework without a word of commendation, one day served a dinner of cattle fodder. When her menfolk protested she explained: "I never heard anything to make me think you'd know the difference." This was a legitimate protest on her part against the failure of the men to give recognition to her importance in the household. How often we are guilty of the same sort of neglect of those about us. How much happier, how much richer, our relations with others are when we feed this hunger of their hearts to know that they are important to us. A little consideration, a few words of appreciation, pay rich dividends in mutual satisfaction.

A friend told me of listening to a structural steel worker as he talked with the owner of a great office building on which the man had worked and which had just been completed. There was pride in the man's words as he talked of the building; he called it "our building." He had a sense of proprietorship in it because he had helped to create it. My friend said that the tone in which the man spoke made him think of the passage in Genesis in which it is written that God looked upon his creation, "and behold, it was very good." This man felt important, not in any little egotistical sense, but in a big way, because he had fulfilled himself by partnership in a great undertaking. How grand that is, how eagerly we ought to avail ourselves of every opportunity which our business and industrial life presents to give to all who participate in it, no matter how humble their capacity, the feeling that they are important because they are making their contribution in sustaining the life of the world. We have scarcely begun to develop the resources of human life because we have not availed ourselves of that great power in men which impels them to want to show their worth, their importance, in partnership with their fellows in doing the work of the world.

Who is important? Every human being in the world. There are vast differences among us, and some are much more highly gifted than others, capable of rendering more conspicuous service than others. But despite all these differences, everyone, even the most humble, is important in his own eyes, and if we could get the hang of it, important to the rest of us as well.

Two things we have to do: first, see to it that we do not fulfill our own sense of importance at the expense of others; there is ample room for us all. And, second, to make such contribution as we can to the fulfillment of our neighbor's sense of his importance. This we can do by recognizing in all our relations with him that he is a person even as we are, by treating him as such, not ignoring him as though he were a shadow, not using him as a means to our ends, but regarding him always as an end in himself; seeking ever to make the interaction of our lives mutually beneficial, trying to carry into every action, every attitude, the rare insight of the poet with whose words we began:

Momentous to himself as I to me

Hath each man been that ever woman bore.

Is Einstein Right?

It is commonly recognized that Albert Einstein, the world renowned physicist, is the man who more than any other one person is responsible for the atomic bomb. To be sure, he was not engaged in the immediate task of preparing the bomb, but he wrote the basic formula which made it possible. His genius has been the crucial factor in enabling men to release the power locked up in the primal stuff of which the universe is made.

Recently Einstein has issued a statement in which he sets forth his conclusions as to what men are going to have to do if the atomic age upon which we have entered is not to mean the end of civilization but, on the contrary, a further step in the progress of mankind. So important does he consider this matter that he, together with eight other atomic scientists, has formed an emergency committee to carry on an extensive educational campaign to inform the public of the terrible danger and the stupendous possibilities for good which lie in this gift of science to men.

It is a good omen when scientists thus accept a portion of the responsibility for the use which is made of their discoveries. In the past their attitude has been very largely that their job was confined to the scientific field itself; they proclaimed their truths, they gave their inventions to the world and felt that their task was done. It was up to the rest of society to decide whether the powers they unleashed were to be used creatively or destructively. Now they recognize that they can no longer disavow their personal responsibility. They are men as well as scientists; they must live in the same world with the rest of us. They are frightened by what they know may happen if atomic energy is used as the major weapon in another war; they feel the bombs bursting over their own heads, annihilating them and their loved ones along with the rest of mankind, wiping out the civilization they have helped to create. They have suddenly developed a strong social conscience and we should be very foolish not to listen to what they have to tell us; listen and act upon the information they give us.

Let us, therefore, examine Einstein's statement to which I have referred. He begins by saying that "a new type of thinking is essential if mankind is to survive and move to higher levels." Over and over again in the history of evolution of life on this planet species have found themselves living under conditions so radically different from those they have formerly experienced that they have been confronted with the necessity of adapting themselves to the new environment or perishing. Man himself is today confronted with precisely this alternative -- adapt or perish.

The advent of the atomic bomb, plus the other inventions used in modern warfare, created a revolutionary situation. For the first time it is possible for one nation to make war on another without sending armies across the border. No center of population on the earth's surface is secure from surprise destruction in a single attack. "Rifle bullets kill men, but atomic bombs kill cities." Should one rocket with an atomic warhead strike Indianapolis, our city would look almost exactly like Nagasaki. There is no foreseeable defense against atomic bombs. Scientists do not even know of any field which promises us any hope of adequate defense.

This is a hard truth for many persons to accept. I was recently in a gathering where the question of military preparedness was being debated. It was argued by some that the history of warfare shows that where a new weapon of attack has appeared it has always been followed by some method of defense which has neutralized it and that the same course is likely to be followed in regard to the atomic bomb -- we will find a way of defending ourselves against it. The scientists present, however, would not agree to this. They did not rule such a defense out as impossible; they did say that it is highly improbable. They agreed with Einstein's pronouncement: "A tank is a defense against a bullet but there is no defense in science against the weapon which can destroy civilization."

This is the radical change in our environment which necessitates a new type of thinking if we are to survive. It is no longer sufficient for us to think in terms of military preparedness. Surely we cannot content ourselves with going underground like moles, or rebuilding our cities as long ribbons stretched across the country in an effort to reduce destruction when war comes. We must think in entirely different terms. We must think in terms of *preventing* wars. This means, according to Einstein, that "a world authority and an eventual world state are not just *desirable* in the name of brotherhood, they are necessary for survival. Today we must abandon competition and secure cooperation. This must be the central fact in all our consideration of international affairs; otherwise we face certain disaster."

It is hard, very hard, for us to wrench our minds around to this way of thinking. We have been accustomed for generations to think in terms of nationalism, in terms of the sovereignty of individual nations. Patriotism, the love of country, has been one of the most lauded of virtues and continues to exert a powerful influence over us. To vast numbers, love of country and the sovereignty of the nation seem completely incompatible with the establishment of a world authority and an eventual world state. They are therefore unwilling, unable, to do the things which the atomic scientists tell us are indispensable if we are to survive. They are oriented to the past instead of the future. They do not realize that the time has come when love of country dictates that we must be ready to surrender something of national sovereignty for the sake of joining with the other peoples of earth to create the kind of international society which is free from war. That is the only adequate defense against the dangers which menace us today.

Dean Christian Gauss of Princeton University examines the validity of Einstein's argument and comes to the conclusion that he is right. Dean Gauss says that the reason why the great Roman Empire died was that it was oriented to the past instead of to the future. Its people and its rulers were incapable of thinking in terms which were adequate to the changed situation in which they found themselves. Rome "failed to recognize that in expanding the empire she had altered the nature of her problem. She never dreamed of creating the technological instruments which might have assured her dominion over her over-extended and increasingly impoverished domain." So, for all her admirable qualities, the Roman Empire perished miserably.

If a like fate is not to overtake us we must avoid the mistake which Rome made. We must look to the future instead of the past. We must discern what is necessary if we are to meet the requirements of that future and have the courage and skill to meet them however difficult and unprecedented they may be. Dean Gauss agrees with Einstein that, "The nation-state with sovereign powers, including the power to make war . . . is now totally obsolete as an instrument for the protection of the culture and life of its people; and any attempt to maintain pretensions to 'sovereign rights' must spell disaster to its own people as well as to our world." If we are not to go the way of Rome we shall have to extend the sphere of law to global dimensions and establish a new and global enforcement agency. "It is a staggering problem of readjustment, reconstruction, and re-education."

There are many among us today who are talking in terms of an inevitable war between the United States and Russia. It is, of course, unhappily true that there are tremendous conflicts of interest between us. None of us can blink that fact for a moment. But let us beware of assuming that war is inevitable, for that can only help to bring about the very result we deplore. Let us pause to consider the probable results of such a war. Within the past ten days I heard the professor of Russian history in a Eastern university -- a man who is as vigorously opposed to Russian totalitarianism as any of us -- make the emphatic statement that if such a war comes the United States will lose it. But regardless of who were to win or lose it the destruction would be so complete that victor and vanquished alike would lie prostrate in the dust. We know how difficult it is proving for Europe to lift herself out of the chaos created by the last war; what do you think the situation would be following an atomic war? The question answers itself.

No! Instead of assuming that war is inevitable and proceeding to act in accordance with that assumption we should be doing every thing humanly possible to create a peaceful world. At this point I wish to quote Einstein's statement again: "Henceforth, every nation's foreign policy must be judged at every point by one consideration: does it lead us to a world of law and order or does it lead us back toward anarchy and death? I do not believe we can prepare for war and at the same time prepare for a world community. When humanity holds in its hand the weapon with which it can commit suicide, I believe that to put more power into the gun is to increase the probability of disaster."

We have made the beginnings in the United Nations Organization of the kind of machinery which we shall have to make effective if we are to have a peaceful world. To date its achievements have not been very impressive. Human nature being what it is we are inclined to lay the responsibility for its failure at other doors than our own. It is true that others have contributed greatly to the difficulties which the United Nations Organization has experienced, but it is by no means one sided and we share the responsibility with them. Upon us more than upon any other one nation, particularly because we alone still have the secret of the atomic bomb, rests the obligation to make the United Nations Organization function. It is the only instrument we have with which to achieve something better. Let us not be unduly pessimistic; only impatient Americans would expect that the difficulties of so gigantic an undertaking could be ironed out in two short years. Infinite patience, understanding, persistence and skill are required.

We must remember, also, that this problem cannot be solved solely on the governmental level. You and I often have a sense of impotence in these great matters; we feel that what we think and do is of no consequence. That is a grave mistake. The ultimate solution of such vast problems lies in the minds and hearts of individual men and women. The machinery of government, whether it be in a city, a nation, or the world, can only make effective those things which the people who are concerned do sincerely desire and are willing to work for. It is of the utmost importance that you and I and the millions like us around the earth learn to think and feel and act in terms of that future which the best minds among us see so clearly stretching before us. If we feel and think and act in terms of the world that is dying we shall only hasten its death.

If we feel and think and act in terms of the better world struggling to be born we shall help it to come. With us lies the issue for the world is what we, the people, make it.

"Ole Man River"

One of the most memorable events of my life was hearing Paul Robeson sing "Ole Man River." I continue to hear with my mind's ear his magnificent voice as it poured out in the recurrent phrase of the song: "He jes' keeps rollin' along." It is not at all strange that "Ole Man River" should be haunting my thoughts at this season when the old year is running out and a new one is about to begin. It is natural for us to depict the passage of time in terms of the flowing of a river; natural for us to say of human life that it "jes' keeps rollin' along." I suspect the analogy is profounder, truer, than we are usually aware when we use it. Life is a stream, a deep stream which moves into the present out of a remote past and sweeps on into an unknown future which somehow grows out of the past and the present. A large part of the art of living consists in accepting the full significance of this and adjusting ourselves to it.

Too often we have a superficial view of life; we see only the surface of "Ole Man River" and are unaware of the murky depths that lie hidden beneath. I mean by this that we judge our own lives, and the lives of others, only by the *conscious* thought and feeling, only by the obvious, and we fail to recognize in ourselves and others those deep-lying motives and impulses, those hidden desires and strivings, which determine the true character of our lives far more than do those aspects of which we are usually conscious. Or we see only the small segment of the river which lies within our present view and forget the long stretch of territory through which it has passed before it reached this point. We are unmindful of the fact that flood waters may suddenly flow in upon us from upstream completely altering the present character of the river. What I am trying to say is that human life has a history, and that the pressure of its past is a much more powerful influence in the present than we usually take into account. It is this that gives it the character of a river that "jes' keeps rollin' along."

It is here that we have the explanation of the strange mixture of good and evil in our lives which so often perplexes us, the curious commingling of clear and muddied waters in the stream. *War,* for example, from the point of view of our intelligent judgment, is wholly irrational. It ought not be allowed to persist; it is frightfully destructive of the values of life; it never accomplishes the purpose which men think they have in fighting, or if it does it is at a price not worth what is gained; it never settles anything. No less an authority than our

Secretary of State, George Marshall, has said that "The only way to win a war is to prevent it." Yet here it still is, in all its hideousness, a present fact towering up in the midst of life. There is no rational justification for it; we can only account for its persistence in terms of "Ole Man River" who "jes' keeps rollin' along."

The same is true of that other great evil which confronts us -- *race hatred.* From the rational point of view it is no more justifiable than war. All the arguments are against it; science has demonstrated very clearly that there is no valid ground for one race to feel superior to other races; religion, with its doctrine of universal human brotherhood, is opposed to it. No one who seriously tries to apply the golden rule of doing to another what he would have that other to do to him can possibly justify the prejudice and the discrimination which exists between the races. Common decency condemns it. Yet, there it is in all its poisonous quality, producing injustice, exploitation, subservience, hostility, and open strife. Again it is because our conscious thought, our reason, our ideals are but glints of sunshine touching the surface of the stream, while underneath "Ole Man River . . . jes' keeps rollin' along." This is why these ancient evils are so difficult to correct.

But it is equally true that the good things in life are part of this mighty, flowing stream. No less than war and race hatred, love and friendship, the desire to organize society for the mutual benefit of all its members, are gifts that "Ole Man River" bears in his flood. The homes in which we are nurtured and which are the source of some of the deepest joys we know, are not the creation of the moment, not the products of conscious thought. They come to us with the pattern already fashioned out of the experiences of endless generations; they are fed from deep springs of living water that have poured into the river all along its course. In consequence they have a vitality, a capacity for endurance, and for the performance of their function which could not possibly be theirs were they the ephemeral creatures of the moment. The might, the surge of "Ole Man River" is in them. The same is true of our religious ideals, our insights into the requirement of the moral law. The same is true of the creative impulses of human nature which express themselves in the building of a bridge, the writing of a poem, the establishment of a business. In all of them there is the surging might of the stream of human life which "jes' keeps rollin' along."

I have been speaking in terms of all mankind, but of course the same thing applies to us as individuals. We are drops in the stream, and take our character from it. We, too, are flowing; we have our individual past, and the past of the race is in us. Far more than we realize, our course in all its success and failure, its joy and sorrow, is determined by its relation to this whole process. Here is a young man who, with high hope in his heart, marries the girl of his choice; they have every expectation of happiness together. Then, alas, an influence from out of the past lays hold of them and wrecks that promise. It may be a constitutional defect that cuts his life short; it may be a perverted conception, born of childhood experience, of what the relation between husband and wife should be. "Ole Man River . . . he jes' keeps rollin' along!" Or, more happily, another young man, a Louis Pasteur, seems to his instructors so far from brilliant that they mark him "mediocre" in chemistry, the very branch he is afterwards to shine in so brilliantly. What they are not able to observe in him is that deep-lying drive which gives him a stupendous capacity for hard work, and a burning will to achieve which more than compensates for the lack of inherited talent. "Ole Man River . . . jes' keeps rollin' along."

Are we impotent in the toils of the great stream; is there nothing that we can do about it, no contribution that we can make toward determining the course it shall take? The answer to these questions is, "Yes, there is something we can do!" It is not as great, not as dramatic and decisive as we in our egotism would like to think it; none the less it is important, vastly so.

Personally I always identify "Ole Man River" with the Mississippi, on whose banks I lived in my boyhood. And it has long struck me that we can take a page out of man's relation to that great stream for our guidance in dealing with that other river in which our lives are immersed. Think of the Mississippi valley before the white man arrived. For many centuries the Indians of the region just accepted the river as one of the great natural features of the territory they inhabited and adjusted themselves to it. They fished in its waters, travelled on it in their canoes and dugouts, found it in a measure a barrier to their movements, fled before its raging floods. When the white settlers came, their relation to the river was for a time essentially the same. Then began the slow process of seeking to master the river. Dykes were built and the lowlands behind them cultivated. At first the efforts were not very successful and the river periodically rose in might and wiped them out. But gradually men's concept of taming the river grew in extent and practice until at length it was seen to be a single project from the head-waters to the delta. It was inclusive of multiple purposes -- soil conservation, the control of the flow of the waters, irrigation, navigation, power plants, etc. It is a tremendous undertaking, and it is at yet by no means complete, its possibilities only partially realized. At times the river still shows its contempt for man's puny efforts to harness it. Nonetheless, human life along its course is much more secure and far richer than it was when men just took the river for granted and accommodated themselves to it, instead of trying to make it their servant.

Something of the same sort must be accomplished with "Ole Man River" of which our lives are a part. We are still largely in the stage of simply accepting the fact that he "jes' keeps rollin' along," and of adjusting our lives to him. It has only begun to occur to us that we can harness his mighty powers, and to some extent at least impose our conscious will, our purposes on his flow. It is a mighty undertaking, infinitely more complex and difficult than the taming of the Mississippi. Our present efforts are very crude and ineffective; the river of human life with its sudden floods of passion and irrationality brushes aside our flimsy devices as easily as the Mississippi in full flood breaks through the mud dikes. Yet it is significant that we have made a start; that we begin to realize that we need not accept war and race hatred, ignorance and poverty, and the selfishness that knows not itself as inevitable. It is significant that we have begun to realize that we can deliberately increase the amount of good will, of constructive effort which the river achieves in its flow.

We are not at all deceived as to the size and difficulty of the undertaking. In one sense the analogy to "Ole Man River" fails; we cannot go back upstream and begin our mastery at the headwaters. That past is closed to us and we have to accept the river as it arrives at this point in time. It has been flowing a very long distance; it has within it the power of a torrent driven on by the pressure of the waters piled up behind the crest; its channel is deep cut and long established. No, we do not expect it to yield easily to our control. But it does no good to curse the stream for its ways, for the evils it brings into our lives, no more good than it does to curse the flood waters that inundate our farms and homes. What we need in dealing with "Ole Man River" is patience, and understanding, and diligence in our efforts to harness his vast powers for our own purposes. We know that we are not going to win sudden and dramatic victories; but slowly, little by little we can learn to master "Ole Man River" and make him yield an increase in the power, the beauty, the fruitfulness of human life. The very meaning of our existence is to be found in this process, and each one of us is responsible for that portion of the process which goes on in his own life. We can meet that responsibility only as we understand the nature of the stream as its powers flow in us.

"Ole Man River" pays no attention to our calendar. He doesn't know we are about to enter a new year. That is just our artificial division of his course for our own purposes. But our divisions are important to us, and my wish for you is that in the year ahead "Ole Man River," by virtue of your understanding and skill and courage, may yield a little more fully to intelligent, purposeful direction, may produce in your lives a greater abundance of the prizes which truly satisfy, as he "jes' keeps rollin' along."

The Vast Drama of Creation

There are three major attitudes toward the conflict which has developed between science and religion, the two most potent forces in shaping the life of man. First there is the attitude of those who are champions of religion in its orthodox form. They hold that in religion they have a supernatural revelation of truth and they are convinced that it is superior to science at any point where there is conflict between the two. Hence they reject science in favor of religion, or perhaps it were better to say in favor of revelation, for the two are often confused although they are by no means the same. There is religion aplenty in the world which is not based on revelation.

The second attitude toward the conflict between science and religion is that of an attempted reconciliation. There are those who maintain that rightly understood all of the truths advanced by science will be found to be in harmony with religion. For example, it used to be taught by religion that God created each kind of living thing separately. Then along came Charles Darwin and established the theory of evolution according to which the present forms of life on earth have grown by a series of changes over a long period of time out of the earlier and different forms. Evolution does *not* teach that man evolved from a monkey, but that both man and the monkey had a common ancestor in the distant past. The theory of evolution has now been so thoroughly established that no scientist of standing at the present time doubts its essential truth. At first the religious world bitterly denounced the theory as contrary to the revelation of the Bible. Many religious men still do. But as the theory of evolution gained prestige and became more thoroughly established an increasing number of men of religion undertook to reconcile the theory and religion. They said that evidently evolution is simply the way in which God has worked to create the different forms of life which we know and that rightly understood there is no conflict between the teachings of science and religion.

The third attitude is that of those who are so impressed by the claims and achievements of science that they decide it must be right and religion wrong. Hence they have been inclined to discard religion as being merely a product of the childhood of the race when men were ill-informed and didn't know any better. They would substitute science for religion. A distinguished Frenchman wrote a book called *The Irreligion of the Future*. His argument was that religion belongs to the past, that it is largely a texture of myth and illusion, and that as man progresses in knowledge he will discard religion, leave it behind him much as a child when he grows to manhood leaves behind him the plaything which occupied him when he was little. There are a great many persons in the world today who take this position; they feel that they are through with religion and that they will try to live by man's more recently acquired understanding of himself and his world, though they are often not very sure what that means or what it implies. But they are sure that religion is wrong.

If I had to choose between these three different attitudes I should take the last one, which rejects religion in favor of science. The sharp distinction which says religion is wrong and science is right seems to me much too simple a solution of a complex problem and therefore a mistaken one. I reject the solution which places revelation above science because I am convinced that what is called revelation is nothing more than the thoughts of men who lived a long time ago and which has become hallowed by tradition and given an authority which does not really belong to it, but is read into it. I reject the second solution which tries to reconcile science and religion because it usually turns out to be nothing more or less than an unhappy compromise. Science is somehow twisted around to make it fit into the preconceived pattern of religious thought. The process reminds me very much of the story of Procrustes and his bed. You will recall that when Procrustes entertained an overnight guest he fitted the guest to the bed. If the man was too long the genial host chopped off just enough so that he was the right length; if the guest was too short Procrustes stretched him out until he fitted the bed. In much the same way many modern theologians have, willy-nilly, "reconciled" science and religion; they have constrained science to fit the religious bed.

I am convinced that the much more fruitful method is that of accepting the full implication of established scientific truth and then, where religious thinking is found to be out of harmony with that truth, make the necessary changes in religious thinking to bring it into line with science. I am persuaded that fine as is the work which has been done by the so-called "Modernists," great as is the service which they have rendered to many individuals, a much more thorough going acceptance of scientific results than theirs is demanded if religion is to meet the requirements of the modern world. Science is still on the march; it is the most potent force shaping the intellectual life of man today and any religion which is to command the allegiance of the best minds among us must square itself with science. I would have religion avowedly, unashamedly, courageously take the material which science offers it and then, without distorting it, transfuse that material with the religious spirit, use it for religious purposes.

This does not at all mean that religion has surrendered to science. It does not mean that we have fallen into the mistake of setting up a new infallibility in place of an old one, substituting science for revelation. We know full well that science is entirely a human creation. It is not a god come in from the outside to put man in possession of all truth and "save" him. Science is simply a tool devised by man's busy brain to help him in the business of living. It is very fallible; it is continually leaving the truth of yesterday behind for the sake of the truth of today, and it fully expects to leave that truth behind for the truth of tomorrow. This is one of its great glories. Science has its very definite limitations; of necessity it confines itself to certain aspects of the world and leaves out of consideration all else. But for all the mistakes to which it is liable, for all the limitations to which it is subject, it is a very remarkable instrument which has served man exceedingly well. It has vastly increased our knowledge of our world and our place in that world, and it has multiplied our power of control of our world many times over.

We shall never succeed in making the relation between religion and science as fruitful as it should be until we get clearly in mind the respective functions of the two. Then we shall see that they are not antagonistic, but supplementary; that they can be united in a marriage to which each contributes what the other lacks. It will probably be a marriage which has some tensions in it as most marriages do, but that is a wholesome thing rather than otherwise. The purpose of science is to provide us with certain generalizations about our world which are descriptive of the way in which it acts; it provides us with what we call the laws of nature, and by working within those laws we are able to produce results which we desire. The purpose of religion, however, is to make us aware of certain qualities in our world and in ourselves; it deals with values, with the things which are worthwhile in life, the ends we should seek; it concerns itself with beauty and truth and goodness. The respective functions of the two have been aptly summed up in the statement that science tells us of the law of gravitation and religion tells us of the beauty of holiness. We need to know both.

To make the whole matter as clear as possible let us apply the principle we have been setting forth to a specific case. In the first chapter of Genesis there is a famous account of the creation of the world. "In the beginning God created the heavens and the earth." This statement is followed by a detailed account of the origins of things. What standing has this story of the vast drama of creation in the science of today, and what is the relation to religion of the account of creation which science now gives us?

J. Arthur Thompson, writing in *The Outline of Science* says: "When we speak the language of science we cannot say, 'In the beginning . . ,' for we do not know and cannot think of any condition of things which did not arise from something that went before." In other words science does not think of the world as having been created at a certain historic time as the Bible story indicates, but as having always been in existence. This is but a slight hint of the tremendous differences which exist between the scientific understanding of the process of creation and that contained in the Biblical account. The astronomers who are in charge of the next two-hundred inch telescope on Mount Palomar in California have a vastly different and truer understanding of the nature of our universe than did the man who wrote the first chapter of Genesis. Let us recognize it frankly.

Does that mean that religion is discredited? By no means; it simply means that what we have in the first chapter of Genesis is the science of 2,500 years ago. It was the best man could do then; we can do much better now. We shall cherish that early account because of its poetry and piety, because of the important place it has held in the thought of men. But as for ourselves we will live in the vast new universe which has been disclosed by science. We cannot return to the tidy little universe of Genesis. But religion is not adversely affected by this at all; religion does not stand or fall with the truth or falsity of that early chapter. All that has happened is that we have moved out of the little cottage into a mansion. The essential thing is that we shall take the spirit of religion, with its deep concern for the values of life, into the new house and expand it in the more spacious rooms of our new dwelling.

The essential thing is that we shall continue to cultivate the reverence for life which resides at the core of religion; the essential thing is that we shall grow in the stature of our manhood and womanhood; the essential thing is that we shall succeed in making the expanded horizons, the deepened insights, the increased power which science has placed at our disposal more fruitful of abundant human living. The respective tasks of science and religion are spectacularly illustrated by the recent discovery of a way to unleash atomic energy. It was the task of science to make this possible; it is the task of religion to see that this magnificent achievement is used not for the purpose of manufacturing bombs to destroy all human life but to create a richer and more harmonious human world. We need them both; science with its knowledge and skills to furnish us the power; religion with its insight and poetry, its feeling for value, its sense of sacredness to set our goal. The best interests of man can be served only as he unites in holy wedlock his science and his religion.

The Emergence of Man

The conflict which has developed in recent years between science and religion can be resolved only when we recognize the distinctive function of each of them. The purpose of science is to discover the facts about our world and to interpret them in terms of certain great generalizations to which we have given the name of the laws of nature. By using the understanding thus acquired we have been able to win a remarkable degree of control over the forces of nature; we have been able to improve the quality and the quantity of our corn crop; we have been able to add years to the length of human life; we have developed radio and all the other wonders of our technological civilization.

The purpose of religion, on the other hand, is to determine the use to which we put the powers science has placed at our disposal. Religion is concerned with using knowledge and power and all the other resources of life for the benefit of mankind. Religion is concerned with the ideal possibilities of human life; with the values which are represented by such words as truth, goodness, beauty, love. Religion seeks to inspire men to live on the highest level of which they are capable. Religion sets the ends; science provides the means. To use a crude analogy, science provides the family income; religion determines that the income shall not be spent in riotous living but expended creatively on behalf of the best interests of the members of the family, supplying them not only with daily bread but also bread of the spirit. United in this manner science and religion turn out not to be hostile but mutually beneficial, and both of them serve human life with a greater effectiveness than before.

Now, it is my purpose this morning to apply the principle here set forth to the doctrine of man. We can best get at this question by briefly reviewing the traditional doctrine and contrasting it with the one given by science. The thought concerning the origin and nature of man which has dominated Christian theology has been derived from the Bible. In the book of Genesis there are two accounts of the creation of man. The first is by a priestly writer who lived about 500 B.C. His words are dignified and have the element of loftiness in them. He contents himself with saying "God created man in his own image." The second account is of a different order; it is much more dramatic and picturesque. It tells how God formed man out of the dust of the ground and breathed the breath of life into him. Then, at a later time, God decided that this man needed a mate so he caused a sleep to fall upon him; took out a rib and from it fashioned woman. This second story is told in a very naive fashion much as though it were intended for children. Biblical scholars, who approach their study from a historical point of view, think that this second account was written at a much earlier date than the first one and represents a more primitive state of mind. The date when this alleged creation of man took place used to be figured as about 6000 years ago.

The doctrine of man was further developed in Christian thought by saying that man had originally been created perfect but that by his own sin he fell from this perfection and became a creature of depravity. God tried to redeem him from his fallen state by setting up certain rules of behavior for him, but man proved unequal to obeying these moral commandments and fell deeper and deeper into sin so that a great debt accumulated against him. Then God, in his mercy, sent his son into the world in the person of Jesus who, by his sacrificial death on the cross, made atonement for man's sins and opened the way to salvation for those who believe in him. This, in a very simplified form, presents the doctrine of man which has dominated the Christian centuries and which continues for millions to represent the truth on this important subject.

Science has a very different story to tell. Instead of saying that man was created by an act of God some 6000 years ago, it says that man emerged, as a result of a process which had been going on for a very long time, from the lower forms of life which were his ancestors. He was not created; he evolved. He had become man perhaps a million years ago, and the process which preceded his attainment of manhood can be estimated only in terms of hundreds of millions of years. Furthermore, when man did at length appear on the scene he was not perfect, but carried in his body and mind the qualities which had been built there by his long animal ancestry. There is in him a curious mixture, from the moral point of view, of good and evil. On the one hand there is the fierceness which was born of the ruthless struggle to keep himself alive in a none too friendly world; on the other hand there is the gentleness and tenderness born of his relations with his immediate family and friends, their need of cooperating for their mutual benefit. Man has not fallen; he is not a creature of depravity. On the contrary, he is slowly rising; learning to master the wild animal impulses within him and to develop more fully his distinctively human qualities of reason and self-direction and of good will extended to all his kind.

This scientific account of the origin and nature of man has become established with increasing firmness by the researches of scientists in many fields since Charles Darwin first set forth his theory nearly a hundred years ago. Confronted with the choice between the story of special creation as told in Genesis and the account given by science, there is no question in my own mind that we have to choose that of science. We have to recognize that the earlier story of man being created perfect and falling from that perfection is a myth, the effort of men before they had adequate knowledge to account for the mystery of their own being. The myth has been hallowed by long acceptance and precious associations but it will have to yield place to fuller truth. The myth contained certain important insights but they are presented in a manner which is no longer a help but a hindrance. The time has come when religion must frankly abandon the doctrine of man as it was developed in the pre-scientific age and base its teaching squarely on the scientifically established truths concerning the origin and nature of man. To do so is not a loss but a gain for religion.

Accepting the evolutionary point of view religion will then go on to inquire how the values which it exists to serve can be most effectively safeguarded and increased. How can human life best fulfill its potentials, express itself more fully in truth and beauty, in goodness and love? We can best come to grips with this problem by taking up a specific item. All of us recognize that selfishness is the source of a very large share of the trouble we experience. Men are so intent on getting the things which they want for themselves that they are largely callous to the consequences for others. According to the view of science this selfishness was bred in our bones by untold generations of ancestors, human and animal, which had to be selfish in order to survive; if the primitive animal does not get his dinner at no matter what cost to the creature upon which he dines he cannot maintain his own life. A lot of that self-interest remains in us; it forms a large part of our drive; it is what makes us go and we would not get rid of it if we could because it would leave us like a watch with a broken main-spring.

But that does not mean that we have to leave the drive of self in its primitive form; we have to take this natural power and tame it, direct it in such a way that it will promote the highest ends of our lives. The way in which this is to be done is very clear; it is not a mere matter of theory but of historic achievement. It is the way of expanding the circle of your self until it includes not only your narrow personal interest but much more which you identify with yourself. We speak of "my wife," "my children"; and when we share our food and all our good things with them we do not think we are sacrificing ourselves, rather we are fulfilling our larger selves, for they are part of us and their well-being is part of our own well-being. We know how the patriot says, "my country!," and in the service which he renders her, even to the point of death, does not feel that he is denying but living out his self more completely than he otherwise could. We know that the highest type of humanity which this earth has produced is to be found in those rare souls who have identified themselves with all mankind; who have felt it their high destiny to give themselves completely to some cause which meant more of justice, or truth, or humanity for their fellows. It is the function of religion to inspire in men the vision of the higher good they can achieve by thus expanding the circle of self and using the powerful drive of selfishness for the achievement of something far above itself. We have to do with our own inner forces what we do with the external forces of nature. We take the power of the waterfall and transform it into electricity to turn the wheels of industry and light our homes. Even so we must harness the power of selfishness to the broad and noble ends of humanity.

The same thing which is true of our use of selfishness is likewise true of intelligence, which we usually think of as belonging not on the debit but on the credit side of the human ledger. The scientists of today tell us that intelligence is not a power which was planted in us full blown by God at the time of our creation. Rather they say that it too has come by a process of evolution. The faint glimmerings of it are to be seen in the lowly forms of life; there is a gradual increase of it and in the effectiveness of its use among the higher animals until in man it has become, perhaps, his most distinctive characteristic; though even in him it is still a fitful gleam. The scientists tell us that intelligence has developed in us in response to our need; in just the same way that we have eyes to see with, so we have acquired intelligence for the purpose of directing our activities more effectively. Here again the gift with which nature has endowed us can be used for good or evil purpose; an intelligent crook is more dangerous than a stupid one, and an intelligent man of good will is much more effective than a stupid one. It is the function of religion to see that intelligence is used on the side of the angels. Let science tell us how intelligence got here and what its nature is; let religion see to it that intelligence is put to work in the service of all that is best in human life. Science helps religion by enabling it to understand better the nature of the force it is using for its ends.

I am profoundly convinced that there opens before religion a new and more splendid period if it will but enter into partnership with science. The account which science gives of the nature of man is vastly more helpful than that of the traditional theology. It assures us that we are not fallen creatures but rising. To be sure the way ahead is long and difficult; we shall doubtless make many a mistake, suffer many a setback. But we have set our face to the heights; we are moving toward the improvement of our individual lives and the perfecting of the social order. We are on the march; great nature has equipped us with the driving power, science is lighting the way increasingly; religion must sustain our morale and keep us ever aware of the distant goal we are seeking.

Science Searches Scripture

The contribution which science is making to our modern religious thought is nowhere more important than in the way science has compelled us to modify our conception of the nature of the Bible. When modern science began to develop some three centuries ago it was inevitable that a few daring thinkers should apply the method which proved so successful in arriving at truths in physics and chemistry to the study of the Bible. This resulted in the production of what is known as the Higher Criticism of the Bible. Needless to say the word "criticism" here is not used in the sense of finding fault but in the technical sense of the dictionary definition as "the scientific investigation of the origin, text, composition, character, history, etc. of literary documents, especially the Bible."

In other words the Higher Critics were men who said in effect, let us make a fresh start in studying the Bible. We shall not begin with what the church has to say about the nature of the Bible, the way in which it was written, the character of the material in it, the degree of authority which it should possess. Instead we will examine the book itself; see what we can find out about the way it was written, decide for ourselves what authority it claims for itself, test for ourselves the truth of its statements, examine the way in which it came into the position which it has held in Christianity. In brief, they decided to study the Bible as objectively as the geologist studies the rocks of the earth, or the botanist studies the plants of the field. Their sole purpose was to discover the truth.

This science of Biblical Criticism was begun about 300 years ago by the famous Jewish thinker Benedict Spinoza who paid for his daring by being excommunicated by the Jewish community, in language which makes your blood run cold. But the science has developed through all the intervening years, carried on by a succession of brave men who took their reputations and even their lives in their hands in order that they might bear testimony to the truth as they discovered it. The story of the achievements of the Higher Critics forms one of the finest chapters in the history of human thought.

It is my purpose this morning to present some of the major results which have been produced by their studies. In doing so I wish to emphasize the fact that what I am presenting are not simply Unitarian views, but conclusions which have been reached by scholars in a number of the leading churches and which are taught to students preparing for the ministry in many of the leading theological schools of this country and of Europe. I have myself taken courses in the Higher Criticism at the Universities of Chicago and Harvard in this country; in Oxford, England, and in two of the German Universities before the first World War. Unfortunately there is a great gap between the understanding of the rank and file of the members of the Christian church and the conclusions to which the scholars have come. The results of the Higher Criticism have been very slow in permeating the thought of the people at large.

The first, and most important, result of the Higher Criticism is that we have to abandon the entire conception that the Bible is the Word of God in any such literal sense as men have assumed in the past. On the contrary we see very clearly that the Bible is throughout the work of men, a natural human product instead of a supernatural one. The truth is that the Bible as a whole does not make any claim for itself as being the word of God. To be sure there are some passages which begin with the assertion, "The Lord spake," and then his alleged words are given. But for the most part no such claim is made for the material presented and it is set forth just as any writer would put forth his own material. The author of that interesting short story in the Old Testament, the Book of Esther, would be very much surprised if he could come back and discover that his tale of the patriotic devotion of a Hebrew girl had become "Scripture" and was regarded as the word of God.

It was only subsequently and as a result of a long process of development that the documents which now make up our Bible were sifted out of the body of literature produced by the Hebrew people and elevated to a position of sanctity and authority. You can read the story of how this all came about in any good book on the development of the Canon, as it is called; that is, the way in which the particular books we have in the Bible came to be chosen and others rejected. It is interesting to note that the Roman Catholic Bible includes a number of books which are not to be found in the Protestant Bible. This process of selection had been concluded by the Jews for the Old Testament in the year 113 A.D. For the New Testament the debate as to what books were to be included went on down to the Council of Trent in 1545 when the matter was officially settled for the Roman church. It is interesting to note that Martin Luther, the leader of the Protestant Reformation, called the Epistle of James, in the New Testament, as "Epistle of straw" and deemed it unworthy of a place in the Bible.

The discovery that the Bible is the work of men and not a supernaturally given body of truth, and that the idea that it is the authoritative Word of God is only a notion which was gradually imposed on it by other men, inevitably changes our whole attitude toward it. We now recognize that there is no reason why we should believe anything in the Bible simply because it is there. Its only authority is that of the inherent truth and wisdom which it possesses. We judge its contents by the same standards with which we judge any other literature, bringing it to the bar of our own reason and conscience, accepting what seems to us good and true, rejecting what seems to us bad and false.

Some years ago one of the country's leading engineers amused himself by taking the dimensions of Noah's ark as they are given in the Bible and figuring out the amount of space available to house the animals which are supposed to have been saved from the flood in it. He discovered that there would have been something less than two cubic inches per animal, which would have crowded them considerably, to say nothing of leaving no room for the provisions which they needed for their long voyage. This is, of course, a trivial instance, but it does illustrate the principle that there is much in the Bible which we must frankly acknowledge belongs to the realm of fiction and myth and is not to be taken by us as truth.

More important than this, more important than the fact that the Higher Criticism has discovered many historical errors in the Bible, is the disclosure that much of it is on an ethical level that does violence to our conscience today. Consider the incident of the Golden Calf as it is related in the 32nd chapter of Exodus. The people had become tired of waiting for Moses to return from Mt. Sinai where he had gone to talk with God, and they asked Aaron to supply them with a God. This he did by making the Golden Calf. When Moses returned he was exceedingly angry on discovering what had happened, and to those who were loyal to him he spoke these words: "Thus saith Jehovah, the God of Israel, Put ye every man his sword upon his thigh, and go to and fro from gate to gate throughout the camp, and slay every man his brother, and every man his companion, and every man his neighbor." They did according to his command and killed about 3000 men, a ghastly slaughter of heretics, allegedly at the direct command of God.

This sort of thing in the Bible does not disturb us if we can see it in its natural setting, a part of the crude, barbaric times which produced it. But if we have to take it as the literal command of God, a revelation of what he is like, then it is inexpressibly horrible. Science has rendered religion a great service in freeing it from the dogma of the verbal inspiration and inerrancy of the Bible, and enabling us to use our own judgment as to what is true and good within this ancient collection of literature. I quite concur in the judgment passed by John Bury in his invaluable little book, *The History of Freedom of Thought,* when he says: "The truth is that Sacred Books are an obstacle to moral and intellectual progress because they consecrate ideas of a given epoch, and its customs, as divinely appointed. Christianity, by adopting the books of a long past age, placed in the path of human development a particularly nasty stumbling block."

When we are able to look at the Bible in the light of the Higher Criticism it becomes a much more understandable book to us. More important still we are able to bring our own ethical discernment to bear upon it and to select those elements from it which can help us in our own lives. We are able to see that it is not all on one level, but that in its pages there has been recorded the story of the way in which man has climbed from crude and barbaric notions of deity to high and noble ones; in its pages we can see how men have had to struggle to learn from their experience those principles of conduct which are most favorable to harmonious human relations and the highest spiritual development of the individual. We see that the great Hebrew Prophets who announced that to do justly and to love mercy was the will of God stood immeasurably above the man who wrote the story of God commanding the people who bowed before the Golden Calf to be put to the sword. We are able to see that the teachings of Jesus with his emphasis on good will and love are immeasurably above the ethical level of the people who wrote the commandment, "Thou shalt not suffer a witch to live," a commandment which cost an untold number of innocent women their lives.

The Higher Criticism tells us in the words of Jesus, "Why of yourselves judge ye not that which is good?" We dare not bind our intelligence and our conscience by what the past has taught. We can learn of the past but we must go on to improve on its lessons. Beyond this, the Higher Criticism opens the way to a much nobler conception of Scripture. It makes us aware that wherever truth and goodness and nobility have found expression in human life, there the divine is speaking to us. It speaks in Lincoln's Gettysburg Address just as it does in the exalted passages of Isaiah; in the Bill of Rights as in the Ten Commandments. The Higher Criticism enables us to know we have a larger, grander Bible than we had hitherto appreciated. Again science contributes to the enrichment of religion.

Science and Salvation

The most recent of the sciences to develop is psychology, which deals with the mind. Indeed this science is yet in its infancy and is still in such a state of confusion that many men deny that it is a science at all. The reason it has developed so late is because it is much easier to be objective and impartial about the stars than it is about ourselves. It has taken us a long time to get around to the point where we are willing to try to study our own feelings, our desires, our thoughts, our hopes and fears, with the same resolution to get at the facts and understand them that we have brought to the study of sticks and stones. Indeed it is probable that one of the reasons men have not been willing to acknowledge that psychology is a science has been that they do not like what it tells us about ourselves. But despite the hostility it has aroused, and the tardiness of its development, this new science has today reached a point where it must be reckoned with; already it has made most valuable contributions to our understanding of human nature and it is not too much to predict that it will prove one of the most important means of promoting the further progress of mankind.

For example, the parents of today who have the advantage of the insights which psychology can give them into what is taking place in the emotional lives of their children are in a much better position to help their children achieve a normal, wholesome, happy development than were the parents of past generations. We can be blind to very important things that are going on in the lives of our children, and because of our blindness permit irreparable damage to be done to their sensitive feelings; or fail of helping them to achieve the good things of which they are capable. Such apparently simple matters as helping an older child adjust himself to the arrival of a new baby in the family turns out to be vitally important to the whole further development of the child's character. There are innumerable ways in which psychology points the path of wisdom, not only in our dealings with our children but also with adults, and with ourselves.

Because this science concerns itself with the inner life of man it inevitably has an important bearing on religion. Indeed it has devoted no little attention to the study of religious experiences, ideas, and practices. The result is that at the present time there is being written another chapter in the history of the unhappy warfare between science and religion, which has persisted through the centuries. It took a long time for religion to adjust itself to Galileo's proof that our earth is not the center about which the whole universe revolves; it proved even more difficult for religion to assimilate Darwin's proof that man belongs in the same class with the other living forms on our earth; it will be many times more difficult for religion to accept and use the truths set forth by Sigmund

Freud, to mention only the foremost name in the science of psychology. The reason is that psychology penetrates to the very citadel of religion, the human soul itself, and dares to offer its interpretation of what goes on there. Yet this new science has come to stay. It will doubtless modify many of its present findings, and become more accurate as it follows the same process of development through which the older sciences have passed. It can be of tremendous assistance to religion if religion will overcome its hostility and avail itself of what psychology has to offer.

To make this statement more specific, let us consider one of the most important experiences of religion and see what psychology has to say about it. For this purpose I have selected the experience of "salvation." This is something which is familiar to all of us, either as a part of our own religious life or because we know one or perhaps many persons who have experienced it. "Salvation" appears in different forms in most of the great religions of the world. In the traditional Christian form it is that experience by which the individual believer feels that he has been rescued from a state of sin by the grace of God and assured of eternal life. The original pattern of this experience was provided in the life of the Apostle Paul. He was a man of very intense nature. Originally an orthodox Jew of the most rigid type, he had failed to find in his religion the satisfaction which his soul craved. For a time he persecuted the followers of Jesus and then had what was for him a tremendously significant experience and became converted to Christianity, finding in his new faith the joyous release of his energies which he had failed to find in his Phariseeism. It made a new man of him and he devoted his great abilities, his extraordinary powers, to try to carry to all the world the wonderful experience that had come to him, becoming the most successful of all Christian missionaries.

Down the Christian centuries millions of men and women have in varying degrees entered into Paul's experience. They have felt themselves saved. Where before they have been unhappy, torn by an inner conflict, oppressed with a sense of unworthiness and sin, they have gone through a radical transformation which has brought them inner peace and a sense of security; a feeling that now, not by their own efforts, but by the grace of God operating through Christ, their eternal happiness is assured, and like Paul they lived on a higher level of achievement as a result of their experience. This has been to multitudes not simply a set of theological ideas to be believed, but a vital and transforming experience, bringing the conviction of "new birth." What does psychology have to say of all this?

It agrees that the experience is a genuine one; there can be no question of the reality of the feelings through which the believer passes, nor of the transformation which is wrought in his life; the change is genuine, and often drastic and enduring. Nonetheless the psychologist is constrained to point out that the interpretation which the believer puts upon his experience is not necessarily the true one. He describes it in the familiar language of the Christian theology, but that is only because he has been trained in that manner of thought; only because he has lived in a society in which the Christian pattern has been constantly before him. The reality lies in his experience and not in the theological interpretation which he and his fellows place upon it. Had he been living in some other part of the world where he was subject to the influence of a different kind of culture, then he would have had the same kind of an experience but he would have put an entirely different interpretation on it. Buddha, for example, rather than Christ, would have been his savior. The psychologist insists that we must try to go deeper, penetrate behind the language in which the man who feels himself saved describes what has happened to him, to the true inwardness of that experience.

When we do so, what we discover is something like this. Every child as he develops is sure to experience within himself certain powerful tensions. These are the products of his own desires as they come into conflict with the necessary rules and regulations of the group to which he belongs. It is basically the conflict between the individual and society. The little child is self-centered; could he have his way, everything would be made the servant of his desires. But he quickly discovers that this cannot be because he has to live with others who have desires of their own which are contrary to his. He begins in the home to have the discipline of social living and it has tremendously important emotional consequences in the deep places of his being. For a time the conflict is pushed down out of sight in the inner life, but at adolescence when the boy is becoming a man, the girl a woman, it comes to the surface and must be resolved in some satisfactory way if the individual is to mature properly. When the adjustment is happily made the tensions are largely released and their energies are available for the business of adult living. Salvation, from the point of view of psychology, is that process by which the naturally selfish and egotistical and in part destructive impulses native to the human being are disciplined to the requirements of social living, with the result that a mature personality is produced, integrated around a social ideal. This is well suggested in Paul's phrase: "When I became a man I put away childish things."

Psychologists recognize that religion has been in large part an instrument which has grown out of human experience for the accomplishment of this purpose; that is, for the resolution of the conflicts in the inner life of man and the production of secure, wholesome personalities capable of using their powers in the service of the common good. The purpose, however, has been obscured by the theological speculations which have been a part of the method. The truth is that salvation is not a guarantee of eternal bliss beyond this earth, but the achievement of a satisfactory manner of living here and now. It is highly probable that the traditional religious method will long continue to be the one by which large numbers of men and women will be helped to achieve emotional maturity, because this method is deeply rooted in the life of the world and still commands the loyalty of multitudes. For the invaluable service which it performs in the lives of men we may well be grateful.

The advantage which our psychological insight gives us over the traditional religious method is that it enables us to see clearly what the purpose is and to achieve it by direct methods. We are now able to chart with a fair degree of accuracy this process by which the individual human being passes from infancy to maturity; we know the character of the tensions to which he will be subjected at each stage in that difficult journey; we now what unnecessary obstacles those about him are likely to put in his way; we know what he most needs from others in order to enable him to achieve the maximum of success, in order to become a man in the fullest sense of that word. We know, also, that in order to be saved, in the psychological sense of attaining mature and socialized character, it is not necessary that one should go through the gateway of traditional religion. There are many methods by which this purpose can be achieved, many different paths by which men can travel to the same goal. We have every reason to anticipate that as our psychological insight increases and as we develop more effective methods of putting those insights to work in the lives of men, we shall succeed in greater degree in fulfilling the purpose of religion, which is to bring life more abundant to men.

The psychologist who is able to help us understand our own nature and the nature of those about us, who is able to mark out for us the desirable pattern of development which we should achieve in our own lives so that they will yield us enduring satisfaction and make us valuable members of society; the psychologist who restores diseased minds to health, who increases the effectiveness of education by showing how the emotions can be educated, as well as the intelligence, this scientist is doing the work of religion; he is helping to save men, not in a theological but in an intensely human sense. Let us acknowledge our indebtedness to him and avail ourselves of his contribution to religion.

Unitarians have for a century stated that they believe in "Salvation by character." That is, we believe a man is saved not by "the blood of the lamb," to use the theological phrase, but by what he is, by what he becomes in his own inner life. Perhaps it were more accurate to say we believe character *is* salvation, for we do not mean that character saves a man from the fires of an imaginary hell or for the bliss of an equally imaginary heaven. We do not profess to know what, if anything, lies beyond death. But of this we are sure, that an inner life shaped in the light of sane ideals brings to a man the finest, most enduring satisfaction of which we are capable and makes him a source of strength to the community of which he is a member. This is the pearl of great price for which a man should give his all.

Biology and Brotherhood

I am going to depart from my usual custom this morning and take a text for our remarks. It is found in a famous speech attributed to the Apostle Paul in the Book of Acts: "God hath made of one blood all nations of men to dwell on all the face of the earth." It is my thesis that biology confirms this religious pronouncement that all men are blood brothers, that science and religion are at one here.

The doctrine of the brotherhood of man is without doubt one of the greatest in all the range of religious teachings. In its most fully developed form it refuses to recognize any of those distinctions and barriers which commonly set men into antagonistic groups, and proclaims a universal brotherhood which transcends all barriers of race, nationality, sex and creed. It proclaims that all men everywhere belong to one great family and that their true welfare is to be found in the recognition of that fact and the establishment of their relations to one another on the basis of the mutual good-will it enjoins.

This lofty conception was not attained at a single bound, nor is it yet accepted as the truth by any large percentage of the earth's population. It has been very largely the product of a few thinkers, dreamers, idealists. Even when men have given lip service to it they have hedged it around with restrictions which have nullified its full force, and have flouted many of its requirements. This is not to be marveled at when we recall the history of man, and it may help us to understand the present status of human brotherhood if we remind ourselves of the way by which it has been achieved.

It has come to us of the western world by way of the history of the Hebrew people as recorded in the Bible. But most of the Old Testament represents a history which is hostile to any brotherhood which extended beyond the few tribes who regarded themselves as God's chosen people. For the greatest part of their history they held themselves as a people apart from their neighbors, superior to them, more holy. They were narrow and nationalistic, super-patriots with different standards for their own people than for the foreigner. In this they were by no means unique; mankind in general has been narrow and nationalistic, each tribe, each nation sure of its own superiority. It is a long, hard path from the clannishness of primitive people to the universalism of the man who looks with genuine good-will on all peoples.

The Hebrew people reached this higher conception. It finds noble expression in the writings of a poet whose lines are included in the Book of Isaiah. He sang that God is the God of all peoples and has laid on the Hebrew people the task of establishing one universal family of mankind. This same strain is caught up and carried on in the New Testament in the teachings of Jesus. It seems to have been an evolution in his own mind. At first he thought of his teachings as applying exclusively to the Jews, but as his experience broadened so did his sympathies and eventually he included the gentiles in the conception of the Kingdom of God. The hero of the parable of the Good Samaritan, for example, belonged to a people despised and hated by the Jews. The universal strain becomes, if anything, stronger in the teaching of Paul, for he deliberately went to the gentile world with his message. Other religions aside from the Jewish and Christian have arrived at the same conception. Confucius in ancient China said: "The good man loves all men; all within the four seas are his brothers; the love of the perfect man is universal."

The violations of the commandment of brotherhood have been more conspicuous than adherence to it. The slave-ship fitted out for the private profit of Queen Elizabeth of England was named "The Jesus," which certainly is about as sad a contradiction of the spirit of that noble man as is conceivable. Yet, despite the violations, the ideal of brotherhood has been there all the while rebuking us for our narrowness, luring us on toward its height. The man of understanding is not too critical of those who fail to conform to it, for he knows how deeply ingrained are the prejudices, how long are the historical roots of the attitudes which must be overcome to achieve genuine brotherhood. Yet we dare not be content with our failures; we must press on toward the ideal.

We turn, now, to inquire what the various sciences which deal with man have to tell us about him. Do they confirm and enforce this doctrine of brotherhood, are they neutral, or do they require that we reject it as incompatible with the facts? The question is one of increasing importance because science is bringing men closer together all the while, shrinking time and space, binding them together in the ties of a single culture. Consequently the attitude which they take toward one another becomes more and more crucial. May I remind you that there are about 400 million more dark skinned people in the world than there are white.

There is an aspect of science which serves mightily to stress the unity and brotherhood of mankind; that is the fact that science itself knows no boundaries but derives its truths, its theories, its inventions from all peoples. It has been truly said: "There is one World Republic today which offers rights of citizenship to all. It is the domain of science, the world of discovery and invention." How true and how grand that is! A Japanese doctor working away in the jungles of Africa to conquer yellow fever, a French woman toiling to wrest the secret of radium from nature, an American Negro discovering an amazing number of uses to which the lowly peanut can be put, an Italian inventing the radio -- all bear eloquent testimony to the reality of the brotherhood of Man within the World Republic of science.

But how is it with that statement of Paul that all the nations of men are of one blood? The answer of science is an emphatic confirmation; those in charge of the blood banks tell us that it is only in response to prejudice that the blood of different races is kept separate; there are different blood types within the same race, but the same types appear in all races. In strict scientific literalness we are all of one blood. The biologist says that existing man constitutes a single species.

Science also has some important things to say about the alleged superiority of some races, the inferiority of others; and what it has to say makes us feel humble if we think in terms of our own race, proud if we think in terms of all mankind. Anthropology is the most general science dealing with man and I should like to read a statement issued by the American Anthropological Association: "(It) repudiates unscientific racialism and adheres to the following statement of facts. 1. Race involves the inheritance of similar physical variations by large groups of mankind, but its psychological and cultural connotations, if they exist, have not been ascertained by science. 2. The terms 'Aryan' and 'Semitic' have no racial significance whatever. They simply denote linguistic families. 3. Anthropology provides no scientific basis for discrimination against any people on the grounds of racial inferiority, religious affiliation, or linguistic heritage."

Go to your public library and get a few books on anthropology and you will find that these men and women who study man scientifically insist that when you come to the *quality* of human beings you have to judge on the basis of the individual and not the race to which he belongs. There are superior and inferior individuals in every race. We naturally like to think that the race to which we belong is inherently superior to others, but the facts do not bear this out. Every race has in it all the qualities of humanity; these qualities will be distributed in different fashion, one gifted with greater physical vitality, another with greater emotional stability or intellectual energy. But on the whole they balance one another pretty evenly and there is no group of people lacking the innate capacity to use civilization at its highest point.

We in this country are confronted with one of our most difficult problems in the relations between the white and the Negro. It is a problem which will tax all our understanding, our patience, our skill. For a variety of reasons the major responsibility rests on the white, though that in no wise minimizes the responsibility of the Negro. It may help us to deal with some of our prejudices and unfortunate emotional patterns if we fix in our minds what science has to say as the result of the studies that have been made of the two races.

First, the studies show conclusively that a large part of the inferior position of the Negro is due to the conditions the whites have forced upon him rather than to the inferior quality of the human material in him. Unless we have particularly had our attention called to it, it is hard for us to realize the vast difference which social and economic conditions make in the development of the human individual. Professor Garth, who has made a thorough study of the alleged superiority of white to Negro children in intelligence tests, comes to the conclusion that the difference is all to be explained by social environment and not to innate differences in mental capacity. Where the Negro children have equal educational advantages with the whites their intelligence quotient is as high as the whites.

The second result of these studies I should like to present in the words of the most famous of American anthropologists, Professor Franz Boas, now deceased. He was at one time President of the American Association for the Advancement of Science and had a worldwide reputation. His summary of the findings concerning the Negro is given in these words: "No inferiority of the Negro type is proven, except that it seems barely possible that perhaps the race could not produce quite so many men of the highest genius as other races; while there was nothing at all that could be interpreted as suggesting any material difference in the mental capacity of the bulk of the Negro population with the bulk of the white population."

The third result of the scientific studies is to demonstrate that race prejudices are not innate but learned, definitely planted in the minds of children or absorbed by them from the attitudes of their elders. Bruno Lasker, who made a study of racial attitudes of children in this country, found that while there might be some slight element of instinctive feeling in the antagonism, this is negligible when compared with the feeling that is socially induced and which we mistake for instinctive. Alas, scientific truth makes very slow headway against prejudice, but in the long run it does influence our attitudes.

Religion and science join hands in proclaiming the doctrine of the brotherhood of man. The great task confronting us is to make the principle more effective in our practice. There is not the slightest doubt in my mind that the path of progress is the path which leads to the fuller recognition and practice of the unity of mankind. It is a steep and rugged pathway and we cannot take it too quickly; but equally we dare not delay unnecessarily. Our science and our religion impel us to the fulfillment of Markham's fine lines:

> To this event the ages ran,
> Make way for brotherhood,
> Make way for man.

The Genie of the Jug

One of the most famous of the Arabian Nights' stories is that of the "Fisherman and the Genie." One day a poor fisherman cast his net into the sea and when he pulled it in found that he had caught a brass jug closed with a stopper of lead which bore the seal of King Solomon. He was delighted with his catch for he thought he could sell the jug for a handsome price. But first he took his knife and pried out the stopper to see what the jug contained. To his amazement nothing but smoke came out of it, but after a time the smoke gathered itself together and became an immense Genie whose head towered into the clouds, and whose feet were on the ground. It was dreadful to look upon. In a voice of thunder it cried out to the fisherman that he must prepare to die.

The fisherman was terrified but stalled for time while he looked around for a means of escape. He told the Genie that he had done him a great favor in setting him free and deserved rather to be rewarded than deprived of his life. The Genie replied that when, by enchantment, he had been confined in the jug he had vowed that to the man who released him he would give great riches, but when several hundred years went by and still he was not rescued he fell into a rage and vowed that if now any man let him out he would kill him. This penalty he was about to inflict on the luckless fisherman.

The fisherman, despite his humble position, was a man of intelligence and he said to himself: "I am a man to whom Allah has given reason. Shall I not use my reason to save my life?" Whereupon he asked the Genie, "How is it possible that you, big as you are, were ever able to enter that jug? Why, it wouldn't contain even your hand or foot. I shall never believe that you were in it unless I see you enter it again." "So you don't believe I was in it," said the Genie, "Well, I'll show you." Immediately he turned himself into smoke and began to enter the jug. The fisherman waited till the instant when the last of the Genie was inside and then quickly slipped the leaden stopper back into place, and though the Genie struggled with all his might the seal of King Solomon kept him from escaping.

Finding his efforts unavailing he began to plead with the fisherman to let him out; but no, the fisherman said he was going to throw the jug back into the sea and warn all men where it was located so that the evil Genie should be compelled to remain there for all time. Upon this the Genie made a solemn promise that if the fisherman would let him out he would do him no harm, but on the contrary enrich him forever. Finally the fisherman decided to take the risk; he released the Genie who kept his promise and rewarded him with great riches.

This ancient story provides us with a remarkably apt figure for the conditions in which we find ourselves today. Humanity is in the position of the fisherman who has drawn his jug from the sea and removed the stopper. Out of it there has emerged the great Genie of science who towers over our head and threatens to destroy us. At first there was in him the promise of greatly enriching mankind; but he has fallen into a rage, gotten out of hand and threatens to destroy us. There is desperate need for us to emulate the fisherman, saying, "I am a man to whom God has given reason. Shall I not use my reason to save my life?" Somehow we must persuade the Genie Science to get back into the jug so that we may win control over him and make him truly the servant of man.

The problem of what man will do with the enormous possibilities of power which science has put in his hands is the most vital and alarming problem of modern times. The inventions which flow in a steady stream from science are the most potent single factor in changing the character of our lives. Think, for instance, of how the automobile has changed our habits, causing a large portion of us to abandon our settled mode of living and to revert to a nomadic life, moving from place to place over the country. We are now being warned that the airplane is sure to aggravate this by vastly increasing the range over which we can wander. Every new invention has important repercussions in our lives and the cumulative effect is terrific. They put at our disposal the speed of electricity, the explosive might stored up in gasoline, and innumerable other substances. Power and ever more power is unleashed in our world today.

But power in itself is non-moral; it can be used equally well for beneficent purposes or for harmful ones, it can create and it can destroy. Just now, when we have so recently emerged from a war in which the destructive power of science has been used in unprecedented degree, particularly in the atomic bomb which unleashes the basic energy of the universe; now that we are confronted with the possibility of a further conflict in which this destructive power would mount to new heights of terror, we hear the voice of the Genie Science thundering to us to prepare to die. Is there no way in which we can subjugate him, no way in which we can make his power obedient to the requirements of morality, so that instead of destroying us it shall enrich and serve us?

There have been various proposals for dealing with this problem. Some men have said that the work of science is hostile to the best in our lives and that the only way to be rid of it is to get it back in the jug, warn all men away, and keep it there permanently; its gifts are only a delusion; the world would be better off without it. Others propose a remedy which is not so drastic. They say, let us put a stop to scientific invention for a period of ten years or longer and give ourselves a chance to assimilate the powers it has already put at our disposal, give ourselves a chance to develop the means of controlling it so that we can make it our servant instead of a Frankenstein bent on destroying us. The truth of the matter is that there is no possibility of our adopting either of these methods. Science is in our world to stay, and we may be very sure that it will go steadily onward in the process of putting new powers and new ways to use them into our hands. There is but one answer to this problem; it is that we shall devote as much of our energy, as much of our intelligence, to the invention of ways of controlling for desirable human ends the power which science has given us, as we have to the production of that power. Our best brains, our finest abilities have gone into the work of developing and exploiting the power that science has made available. Now the time has come when, under the compulsion of necessity, if we would survive we must turn those brains and those abilities to the task of humanizing our power, giving it the moral quality which it takes on when it ministers to the lives of men instead of destroying them.

This is preeminently the task of religion, for religion concerns itself with the values of life, the ends to which men shall direct their energies. The most effective way in which we can persuade the Genie Science back into his jug and wrest from him the promise to use his giant strength to enrich human life forever is to permeate all our enterprise with the spirit of religion. Unfortunately, however, while the organized institutions of religion continue to play an important part in human affairs, they have progressively lost their hold on the loyalty of a large portion of our population, particularly those men and women who are most intelligent and best informed. This is due to the fact that the churches have lagged behind the best thought of the secular world and have asked these men and women to accept in the name of religion beliefs that do violence to their reason. The loss is tragic because these progressive men and women are the very ones who could best help the churches adjust themselves to modern thought; tragic also because these men and women need in their lives the constant reminder of the values for which the churches stand.

It yet remains to be seen whether or not the churches can reinterpret the central truth of religion in such a manner as to renew the allegiance of those now alienated. To do so a drastic change will be required. Religion can no longer be thought of chiefly in terms of rescuing individual souls from this world and giving them eternal bliss in a world to come. It must concentrate its attention on this world, sure that if we do the best we can in the here and now we may safely leave any possible future world to take care of itself. Religion must give to men a vision of what we can make out of life on this earth when we set ourselves to the task of harnessing the powers which are ours to the progressive realization of our ideals; it must inspire in men a loyalty and devotion to that creative task, making them feel that they are partners in the most magnificent enterprise the mind of man can conceive; it must inspire them to develop all the methods, to invent all the means which are required to insure their steady progress toward the goal; it must encourage them to keep on despite all defeats and to surmount all obstacles; reward them by fulfilling their lives in the service of something vastly greater than themselves; it must be the marching song of humanity as it swings along the difficult trail to the promised land of fuller living toward which we are moving.

Such religion is already active in vitalizing the lives of men. It expresses itself in the patient, and ofttimes heroic, devotion of the doctor who brings the best results of his scientific training to bear not only on the task of restoring the sick to health but also in the creation of those conditions which promote the health of all of us. It expresses itself in the work of the school teacher to whom her position is not merely a means of earning a living but an opportunity to exercise all her art for the sake of making the maximum contribution to the enrichment of the lives of the boys and girls in her classroom; it expresses itself, this religion, in the program of the labor leader who looks beyond the immediate improvement in the economic status of his men to the way in which labor can contribute to the strength, stability, and progress of the entire community; it expresses itself in the enterprise of the merchant who looks not to his profits only but the creative quality of the relation which exists between him and the men and women who work with him, and to the service that together they are rendering to society; it expresses itself in the sacrifice which parents make in order that their children may have a better opportunity in life than they did.

But this religion is for the most part inarticulate. The people in whose lives it exists do not recognize it as religion; most of them are surprised and incredulous when you tell them they are religious. What we need is to dramatize the religion of the human enterprise, making every man, woman, and child aware of his share in it; aware of what he can do for it, and what it can do for him; aware of his partnership with others and with the creative powers of our world home; we are a mighty host engaged in the great adventure of seeing how fine a thing man can make of himself, how he can carry the evolutionary process which has brought him thus far to more sublime heights.

What the world needs is to subject the power of atomic energy and all of the other forces of nature which have been and yet shall be released by science, to the rule of the spirit which recognizes that all of us on this planet are members of one another and that the good life for any of us is dependent on our readiness to share the resources of our world home in a spirit of friendliness with all earth's children. Surely those resources are abundant for all our needs. The combination of science and religion, a religion of the open mind, the loving heart, the helping hand, such a combination would be irresistible. Are we not men of reason, and shall we not use our reason to save our lives? The crucial problem of our age is to win the Genie Science to the service of Humanity. Then we can march into the future confident of the fulfillment of the highest aspirations of our souls.

Reason and the Resurrection

On this Easter morning when throughout Christendom thousands upon thousands are celebrating with joy the central festival of their religion which has been built around the belief in the resurrection of Jesus, there comes into my mind a phrase by a friend long since dead. He said, "Let me reverence the reverences of others rather than what they revere." That accurately expresses my feelings in regard to the Easter celebration. I respect and reverence the sincere beliefs of the men and women who accept as true the ancient story that Jesus died and rose from the dead, and that all who believe in him as their savior will share his immortality. But I cannot share that belief myself. I know that the Easter faith brings joy and consolation to multitudes, and I rejoice for them that in this difficult world they can find such comfort. Yet I have no sense of loss that I must reject their faith and that their comfort is not for me. I have my own convictions, my own religion, which I am confident sustains me and meets my needs as fully as theirs does them.

Lincoln, after he had been elected President the second time, in expressing his satisfaction at the outcome of the election said that he regretted any pain which it might have caused his opponents, for he would not willingly plant a thorn in another man's flesh. Similarly, I would not needlessly cause pain to another by my rejection of his religious faith. Yet I feel it important and necessary that I give utterance to my own convictions because I know that I speak for many like-minded with myself and in this free country of ours it is our happy privilege to exercise the same right of expression which others enjoy. So I invite our attention to our subject, "Reason and the Resurrection."

One of the first things which we discover when we begin to inquire rationally into the story of the death and resurrection of Jesus is that it is by no means unique in the Christian religion, but that essentially the same tale has been told about numerous other dying and resurrected Gods. Let me transport you on the magic carpet of our imagination to the Oriental Museum at the University of Chicago. There in an alcove you will see the mummies of some Egyptian women who lived three, perhaps four, thousand years ago and which have been preserved in the sands of the Nile valley and brought over here by the famous Professor James Breastead, who participated in the discovery of the tomb of King Tutankhamen, "King Tut," as he was familiarly called by the American people.

Again using your imagination let us roll back the centuries and see one of these Egyptian women, not as she looks to us now, a mummy in a Chicago museum, but as she appeared as a living woman in the Egypt of long ago. It is the spring time and she with her companions is participating in a great religious festival which presents in dramatic form the death and the resurrection of the God Osiris. All the joyous worshippers proclaim their belief in Osiris as their savior and expect thereby to share his immortality. Professor Breastead, who had her mummy brought to Chicago, tells us in one of his books about the religion of these ancient Egyptians and I should like to give a brief summary.

We do not know whether or not there is a historical personage back of the God Osiris. There are some indications that in the dawn of Egyptian history there did live a great hero about whose figure have gathered the mythological elements I am about to relate. As he appeared in the Egyptian religion Osiris was a God; angels were present at his birth, and these were heard to announce that the savior of the whole world had arrived. He grew to manhood and became a great king who led the Egyptians out of barbarism into civilization. He developed agriculture in order that, instead of being cannibals, his compatriots might live from the vegetable life, and he carried the knowledge of agriculture throughout the world. But a conspiracy rose against him and he was cruelly put to death. His wife found his body and anointed it with oil. Then in answer to her prayers there took place the resurrection of the slain Osiris. Henceforth he ruled in the underworld where he was judge over the living and the dead. He presided in the great Hall of Truth and all who died came before him for trial. He weighed the heart in a balance and if he found that the deceased had lived a good life, that he had helped the fatherless, been as a husband to the widow, befriended those in need, earned his living in righteousness, then Osiris passed his soul on to the land of the blessed. If not, a great demon stood ready to devour him.

The Egyptian people identified their hope of immortality with the risen Osiris. He was the first of the immortals and by virtue of their faith in their oneness with him they, too, expected to enter upon immortal bliss. For millions and millions of Egyptians through a period of centuries longer than Christianity has been on earth, faith in the resurrection of the Lord Osiris was their anchor and hope. And at the spring of the year our little Egyptian woman, now lying in the museum in Chicago, awoke on a glad Easter morning, donned her new raiment in honor of the occasion, and joined the happy throngs in their shout, "Hail, the Lord Osiris is risen, he is risen indeed!"

The similarity of this story to the Christian Easter is very clear, and it is only one parallel among many which could be cited from the history of religion. Obviously we are dealing here with the same kind of material as we have in our own Easter celebration and it is much easier for us to be objective in examining the religious faith of someone long dead than it is to examine our own faith in that way. We have no trouble in seeing that the story of Osiris is what we call a myth. When we call something a myth we are not seeking to throw discredit on it. We do not mean that it was invented as a deliberate falsehood with the intention of deceiving. We have a much more charitable and sympathetic understanding of it than that. We know that myths grow up spontaneously out of the deep unconscious reaches of the human mind; they are a sort of poetry, a symbolical expression of truths toward which men are groping, of feelings which are crying for expression.

We now know that the Christian Easter story is a myth of the same order as that of Osiris. To be sure there are some differences; in certain respects the Christian story is not so crude in its mythological elements. Also it has at its core the splendid figure of Jesus about whom we know much more than we do about Osiris, and who is a much more appealing figure. None the less it is clear that both of them are myths and have in them essentially the same elements. Both of them are, in the first place, nature festivals. It is no accident that they were celebrated in the spring of the year; they grew out of man's rejoicing that the winter was gone and that life was springing up afresh. The very name "Easter," which is that of the Anglo-Saxon goddess of spring, is clear evidence of this; as is also the way the date of Easter jumps around the calendar, the 28th of March this year, the 17th of April next year.

The second element in the Easter festival grows out of man's concern for his own fate and that of his loved ones. "Death is the mother of philosophy," said Plato. Death must have inspired many fears and evoked many thoughts in the mind of early man. And it is not at all strange that when he began to formulate the idea of a life beyond death he should associate it by analogy with the death and rebirth which he saw take place in the vegetable world around him. "Except a grain of wheat fall into the earth and die." He saw great promise for his own future in the death and resurrection of nature. There are numerous other elements which have entered into the Easter festival; the students of religion have analyzed them with great care, but we cannot go into them here. Out of all of them combined there has grown as spontaneously as the tree grows in your yard the elaborate structure we know today.

When you have come to recognize that Easter is a myth you cannot, of course, continue to take it as the literal truth. But this does not mean that all its values are lost to you. What you do is to search out and retain the truths it contained. We can all continue to rejoice that at this season of the year the lilac leaves begin to open, the grass turns green, and that the surge of life renews itself in our hearts as it does in the outer world. There is, just now, particular need for us to renew our faith in the life that pulses in us. We have been going through a severe winter of revolution and war and spring does not yet appear in our human world. We need to have great faith that there are within us resources of intelligence, of courage, of will which shall yet break the bonds of winter, in which they are held, and put forth a fresh growth in a new human spring.

Nor is the hope of immortality dependent on the historicity of the alleged resurrection of Jesus. There are many intelligent men and women who cherish that hope, in whom it is not based at all on the truth or falsity of the story of the open tomb and the risen Jesus. They base it rather on the quality of human life, on the character of the universe, on their conviction that the great values of love and intelligence and devotion, the riches of personality, do not come into being simply to vanish into nothing, but are somehow perpetuated in the universe which has called them into being.

Others, equally intelligent, prefer to say with Lucretius, "Lives are mortal, life is immortal." That is, we as individuals are not immortal, but we must find our continued existence in our children and in the influence we exert in shaping the character of the community of which our lives are a part and which will continue to exist long centuries after we are dead. Both the good and the evil men do lives after them and it should be our deep concern to make sure that the character of our contribution to the unborn future is such that those who inherit the world from us may have reason to be grateful that we lived. This is the immortality which is celebrated in the magnificent lines of George Eliot's poem:

> Oh, may I join the choir invisible
> Of those immortal dead who live again
> In minds made better by their presence; live
> In pulses stirred to generosity,
> In deeds of daring rectitude, in scorn
> For miserable aims that end with self . . .

This leads me, finally, to speak a word about the place of Jesus in a rational conception of Easter. The true resurrection of that first Easter morning was not that Jesus had risen bodily from the tomb. The true resurrection took place in the minds and hearts of those who had been his followers. They had been prostrated by his death; now courage began to flow back in them. They discovered that what he had been to them had become so intimately a part of their lives that not even death could take it from them. The beauty and strength of his personality, the wisdom of his teaching, reasserted itself and impelled them to go forward with the work which he had to leave unfinished. Could that noble young Jewish teacher speak to us today he would say, "The true resurrection is not that you should cry unto me, 'Lord, Lord,' but that you should do the things which I said . . . love your neighbor as yourself, live in a spirit of mutuality and good-will with all men, toil for the creation on earth of that beloved community in which each human being shall have the fullest opportunity to reach the highest of which he is capable. This is the resurrection I ask of you."

Directed Evolution

In the mystical Gospel of John the author puts into the mouth of Jesus these words: "My Father worketh even unto now, and I work also." "My Father" refers, of course, to God, and while I am not at all sure what was in the mind of the man who penned the sentence it seems to me that we are justified in taking this conception of God as still being at work in the universe, and of man working with him in partnership as an intuitive anticipation of the theory of evolution. At least the statement suggests to me a picture of the universe still in the process of creation, and of man having a share in that process. "My Father worketh even unto now, and I work also."

We today are inclined to use the matter of fact language of science to describe the process, rather than that of mystical religion. We think of evolution in terms of the working of great impersonal forces which we describe as the Laws of Nature. We know that it has been going on for a very long time, indeed we cannot conceive of a time when it was not in process. We are confident that each new stage has grown out of the one which preceded it. The great fact of change, of development, seems universal, applying in the remotest reach of the starry heavens and to the events on our own earth. We ourselves are products of this evolution; we are fruit on the tree of life whose roots go down into the very stuff out of which the stars are made, and on whose branches appear the myriad other forms of life which are our kin.

Now, the most important thing about us, that which distinguishes us from all the rest of creation, as far as we know, is that in us this process has at length become conscious of itself. Electrons and atoms, suns and stars, crocus and cardinal, are pulsing with the universal energy; but only in us has there come into existence an awareness of the process; we alone are able to trace its long history and be aware of our own relation to it. To be sure, our knowledge of it is still a very fragmentary thing, and it ill behooves us to puff ourselves up with pride. None the less there is a great difference between ourselves and the rest of creation in this respect.

An inevitable consequence of our knowledge of the evolutionary process is that there should be born the daring idea that it is our destiny, at least so far as this little corner of the universe is concerned, to assume guidance of the future development of life. Again and again in the scientific works which I have read there is presented the thought that men have become the trustees of evolution; and that we now have the opportunity and the capacity to give conscious and intelligent direction to this process which heretofore has proceeded more or less automatically by the method of blind groping, of trial and error and success. The scientists challenge us to take advantage of our opportunity, seize control of this vital process and direct it to ends of our own choosing. Let me quote the words of the distinguished British scientist, Julian Huxley, who heads the United Nations organization for educational, scientific and cultural cooperation (UNESCO) among the peoples of earth. He says: "Let us not forget that we men are the trustees of evolution and that to refuse to face this problem is to betray the trust put into our hands by the powers of the universe."

As a matter of historic fact men have been doing this very thing for a long time; they have interfered with nature for their own purposes. They have sought to eliminate those animals which they have found a menace to their own lives and to preserve those which they have found useful. Men have even transformed the nature of some of these creatures that they might the better serve human ends. Consider the case of the cow which in her original state produced milk solely for the purpose of feeding her own young, but who has been transformed by man's selection into a constant source of milk with which to feed ourselves. In similar fashion men have been transforming the plant world for their own purposes. I have only to mention the name of Luther Burbank to suggest to you what has been accomplished in this direction. Our ability to do this has greatly increased in recent years by the development of the science known as genetics, which enables us to know how heredity operates and how to secure desired changes. We have made more progress in this respect in the past century than in all the preceding ages and the promise is for much greater progress in the future.

But far more important than what we do with the plant and animal world around us is what we do with ourselves. If we are indeed to become trustees of evolution and give it a direction of our own choosing, the chief work must be done in our own lives. There are two phases to this task, the one, biological and the other, social; the two are, however, so closely related that it is futile to try to separate them. The first is concerned chiefly with our heredity, the second with our environment. There has been a perennial argument as to which of these two is the more important; but as E.G. Conklin has pointed out in an article on "The Purposive Improvement of the Human Race" that argument has been largely beside the point because, to quote his words: "Heredity and environment are not competitors but cooperators in making or destroying breeds or civilizations."

Most of us, however, are prone to place the emphasis on the social to the neglect of the biological aspects of the problem, and it is wholesome for us to be brought back now and again to a realization of the importance of the biological quality of the men and women who make up our society. Professor Hooton, the Harvard anthropologist, in his provocative book, *Apes, Men, and Morons,* says: "The future of mankind does not depend on political or economic theory, nor yet upon measures of social amelioration, but upon the production of better minds in sounder bodies." This is an extreme statement yet a necessary reminder that it is imperative for us to take all possible measures to eliminate the defective strains from the human population and to perpetuate the race from the best that there is in it. This is a highly complex and difficult matter; there are overwhelming social reasons why we cannot breed men and women as we do animals; yet it is possible by education, by establishing a favorable social atmosphere, to do much to improve the human stock. We must remember that the principle of voluntary parenthood, "birth control" as it is popularly known, can be made a tremendously effective instrument to this end. To improve the human stock will be an immensely long and slow process, yet to do so must become an accepted part of our program of directed evolution.

When we turn to the other aspect of our program, that of improving the environment, there is more immediate prospect of progress. We know that the best strains of plants and animals require favorable conditions to produce the maximum results. No farmer wants to plant good seed in bad soil. The same is true in human life; we can get a lot more out of the material we already possess than we do. Some years ago there was a report published in one of the popular magazines of a study which had been made of the careers of some specially gifted children in California. They had been selected twenty years earlier by Professor Lewis Terman of Stanford University, who developed the intelligence tests which bear his name. These were the children who had rated above 150 in their intelligence quotients, which put them in the potential genius class. Now they were being studied to see how they had fulfilled those potentialities.

It turned out that one quarter of them had made a far greater success in life than the average of their generation; another 50%, one-half, had done moderately well; and the final 25% had done very badly. The investigators found that one of the important explanations lay in the home environment and the personality it produced in the child. In the top group, 57% had fathers who were professional men, able to earn enough money to give their children a stable and peaceful environment. The members of the bottom group often came from homes where there was insecurity, poverty and unhappiness. The conclusion to which the investigators came was that while high intelligence is chiefly the accident of birth, we can by proper training turn potential genius into an actual one, whose gifts are useful to mankind. The most important factors in bringing this about are: first, incentive -- living in a society that wants and appreciates great ability; and second, a sense of reassurance and security. Such studies are, of course, by no means conclusive. All of us can think at once of other factors that enter into the results, but they are important indicators of the lines along which we must move if we are to direct human evolution to the highest ends we can conceive.

Actually mankind has been at the business of shaping the physical and social environment so that it will produce the best possible results with the human material for a long, long time. But most of the endeavor has been haphazard; it has been on an unconscious level, groping and largely ineffective. We must now deliberately raise it to the conscious level and set ourselves to the task of using all the resources of our intelligence and skill to discover those conditions under which the human personality does thrive most vigorously, and then set about establishing and maintaining those conditions. We must envision clearly our goal and develop the techniques, the skill for bringing ourselves forward on the difficult path toward it.

We are under no illusion that it is going to be easy. If we look only at the obstacles we shall never even make a start. But we have behind us some record of achievements which should encourage us in the upward climb. I am thinking, for instance, of the remarkable success of the Folk High Schools in Denmark, before the recent World War. They were established under the leadership of a man by the name of Grundtvig who had a vision of how the lives of the farmers might be enriched if they had access to the culture and knowledge which is now available. Over sixty of these schools for adults were set up in a country less than half the size of Indiana. An American observer of the results has said that they made of the Danish farmer probably the most enlightened, cooperative, and prosperous in the world. Yes, we can do it and here and there we are doing it. By means of better educational methods, by the establishment of favorable governmental and social conditions, by bringing to bear on the problems of human life the same kind of intelligence and devotion which we lavish on our conquest of atoms, we can take hold of our own evolution on this planet and show ourselves worthy of the great trusteeship which has been placed in our hands.

I conclude with the words with which I began, "My Father worketh even unto now, and I work also." The vast cosmos itself is everywhere pulsing with energy, everywhere in the process of evolution. We are its children. A tiny portion of its creative energy has been caught up in us. We have become aware of the nature of the process that is going on about us and within us. We have discovered that it is in our power to win a measure of control over that process and give to evolution a direction of our own choosing. We are the trustees of evolution; into our hands has been committed its fate on this planet. "Know ye not that I must be about my Father's business." "My Father worketh even unto now, and I work also."

The Champaign
"Atheist" Trial

The Champaign "Atheist" Trial

In order that we may have the story straight let us review briefly the essential facts in the recent trial at Champaign, Illinois, which has aroused country-wide attention. Mrs. Vashti McCollum, wife of a professor at the University of Illinois, has filed suit against the Board of Education of Champaign to compel that body to prohibit the teaching of religion in the public schools by private teachers during school hours.

The situation against which her suit is a protest is this: In Champaign, members of some of the Protestant churches have obtained permission of the Board of Education to have disciples of the majority sects of the Protestant religion enter the classrooms of the public schools from the fourth to the eighth grades, and in each classroom, during regular school hours, conduct a course in religious instruction for a thirty-minute period each week. The Catholics are granted permission to use a classroom in the Junior High School for a fifty-minute period each week wherein a priest may teach the Catholic religion. A similar offer has been tendered the Jews. A pupil may leave the classroom during such periods of religious instruction if he so desires.

Mrs. McCollum has brought suit because she has a ten-year-old son, James Terry, who is a pupil in one of the schools. She says that she does not want her boy to take the religious instruction because she is a "rationalist" who does not believe in religion. The consequence is that Terry is the only pupil in his room who does not join in the class in religion. The fact that he is thus set apart from his fellows works a hardship on him; the other pupils tease him, fight with him, and he comes home crying. He says he wants to take the class in religion because he feels lonely when he is sent to the library or the music room to study by himself during that period. His mother, however, will not consent to his taking the instruction because, in addition to her personal rejection of religion, she has a strong conviction that the whole practice of teaching religion in the public schools is a violation of the American principle of the separation of church and state.

This is the major issue of the trial, but it has tended to be obscured because of the intrusion of certain sensational elements. Let us first dispose of these in order that we may consider the merits of her charge.

The first sensational element was that here is a woman who is an avowed atheist. The papers reported that "overawed spectators, most of them admitting that they wanted to see an atheist, jammed the little court room." This curiosity about, this horror of, the atheist is childish. Theoretical atheists are by no means rare among us. The Gallup poll on religion showed that 1% of those questioned definitely denied the existence of God. If the poll is a fair index it means that there are about 1,300,000 atheists in the country. Another 3%, which would mean nearly four million, consider themselves agnostics -- that is, they do not know whether or not there is a God.

There exists among the majority of persons an unwarranted, unreasoning, and emotionally prejudiced attitude toward the acknowledged atheist or agnostic. This indicates only how superficial is the understanding of those who harbor the prejudice, not how wicked the unbelievers are. Atheism in itself is neither good nor bad, just as belief in itself is neither good nor bad. Belief, or disbelief, is only one factor in a complex situation which determines whether or not the person who professes it is a desirable or an undesirable member of society. Some atheists are finer persons than many believers.

The second element of sensationalism in the trial was provided by the testimony of the Rev. Philip Schug, minister of the Unitarian Church in the neighboring town of Urbana, who appeared in support of Mrs. McCollum. This was why my phone was busy with people calling to inquire if Unitarians are atheists. The logic seemed to be, Mrs. McCollum is an avowed atheist; the Rev. Philip Schug supports her, therefore he must be an atheist; since he is a Unitarian minister, Unitarians must be atheists. The whole chain of reasoning is fallacious. (Here is the place to remind ourselves of Voltaire's famous saying: "I do not agree with a word you say, but I will defend to the death your right to say it." Many persons who do not share Mrs. McCollum's atheistic views are convinced that she has a just cause and want to support her in it.)

Unitarians are not atheists. The very name "Unitarian" is derived from the fact that the early Unitarians insisted on the *unity* of God, as opposed to the Trinitarians who taught that God is three persons in one. The majority of Unitarians continue to be Theists; that is, they believe in God as at once immanent in the world and yet transcending it, much as we feel ourselves to be present in every part of our bodies and yet at the same time more than the sum of all its parts. "Whose body Nature is, and God the soul."

But because of our basic principle of freedom, because we insist that each man shall arrive at his own belief in accordance with the dictates of his intelligence and his conscience, we have within our fellowship many who are not theists. We hold that religion is not to be identified with any particular belief, not even belief in God. The high-minded person who gives some other answer to the riddle of the universe may be genuinely religious. This is why Mrs. McCollum is able to send her three children to a Unitarian Sunday School.

The majority of those among us who are not theists would, however, reject the label "atheist." An atheist is one who *denies* the existence of God. Most of us in the Unitarian church who cannot accept the traditional theism do something which is much more significant than to deny. We go on to affirm a philosophy of religion which, as we believe, retains the chief values which were associated with the traditional belief in God, but puts them in a setting required by the new understanding of the universe which science has brought us in recent generations. We have arrived at a philosophy of life which avails itself of scientific insight without being coldly intellectual or crudely materialistic, but is warm and glowing with a feeling for the beauty and mystery and order of the universe, the wonder of human affection, good-will and love, the human yearning for the right and the just, human idealism and aspiration. All this you cannot put into the word "atheist." No, Unitarians are not atheists. Our emphasis is upon the positive values.

There was one passage in the report of a trial as it was given in our local press which brought great distress to many Unitarians. This was the statement that the Rev. Philip Schug had "likened the story of Jesus Christ to that of Santa Claus, stating that he regarded them both as folk tales." This provoked resentment among our people because they felt that it misrepresents our position. A close examination of the account, however, particularly in the fuller form given in the Chicago papers, discloses that it was not Mr. Schug who made this comparison, but the attorney for the School Board who asked him "if he felt the same reverence for Santa Claus that he did for Jesus Christ." The question is obviously "loaded," intended to discredit the witness. Mr. Schug made it clear in his reply that he believes Jesus to have been a historic personage, whereas Santa Claus exists only in the realm of fantasy.

Unitarians do reject the supernatural elements in the story of Jesus; we do not believe in the virgin birth, in the miracles, in the resurrection of the body. In that sense the New Testament story is a folk tale. For Jesus, the man, rather than the theological Christ, we have the highest reverence. We reverence him for his ethical and mystical insight, for his compassion and love of humanity, for the loyalty to conviction which carried him to a martyr's death. We are Christians, not in the theological sense, but in the human sense; in the sense that we seek to incorporate in our religion the poetry, the humanity of Jesus. But we refuse to use the word Christian in any narrow, sectarian sense which would exclude men of kindred spirit no matter what their historical tradition. The high-minded Jew, or Buddhist, or secularist belongs to our fellowship as well as the Christian. There are some among us who think the time has come when we should seek a larger name than Christian to designate that universal religion into which mankind is slowly but surely moving.

While Unitarians as a whole do not accept the particular views which Mrs. McCollum holds, we do think that she is rendering an important public service by challenging the right to teach sectarian religion in our public schools. Some persons have accused her of making a mountain out of a mole-hill, arguing that she is doing her son a great deal more harm by setting him apart from his

school-mates and by the trial than would be done him were he to take the class
in religion, for she could easily correct at home any mistaken ideas he might
acquire there. But this misses the whole point. Mrs. McCollum stated at the
trial that she knew she was doing harm to her son by bringing this suit, but that
even weighing the probable damage to him she feels compelled by loyalty to
her own ideals to carry it through. She believes in the complete separation of
church and state; she believes that such separation is a fundamental part of our
American way of life; she believes that what is going on in the schools of
Champaign is a violation of that American principle and that she is therefore
honor bound to try to stop it.

She is right! The teaching of religion, or as it would be more accurate to
say, the teaching of the doctrines of certain religious sects among us in the
public schools, is contrary to the long established American practice which has
grown out of our theory that church and state must be kept separate. To claim
that it is not the church but religion which it is proposed to put into the public
schools is a mere quibble, for if it were proposed to teach any form of religion
other than that in conformity with certain of the dominant churches there would
be an immediate protest from the very persons now pushing the program for
religious instruction in the public schools.

It is not only Terry McCollum who is the victim of the present situation.
The evidence at the trial showed that while he was the only one in his room not
taking the class in religious instruction, in the Champaign schools as a whole
twenty percent of the children up to the sixth grade do not take it, and in the
Junior High School eighty percent do not take it. These facts in themselves
condemn the whole program. I know from the parents who have come to me to
inquire about their children taking similar courses that it brings deep perplexity
and burning of heart because of the conflict between honest conviction and the
social pressure to which the children are subjected. This should not be, because
our public schools belong to all the children alike, whether they and their
parents are members of any church or none.

There has been a strong movement all over the country in recent years to
introduce the teaching of the Bible in the public schools. It has in large part
been a product of the war. The movement is sincerely and honestly motivated;
those responsible for it believe that the welfare of the nation depends on the
children of the land being brought up in the teachings of religion as they
understand it. They have been alarmed at the prevalence of juvenile
delinquency and have felt that the cure for it is the instruction of children in the
principles of religion. They know that the Sunday Schools are reaching only a
fraction of the children; between 1926 and 1936, Sunday school enrollment
decreased forty percent; so, naturally, they turn to the public schools to
accomplish their objectives. Their motives are of the highest but they are
terribly, disastrously mistaken in the method they are taking.

The movement has reached alarming proportions. An account of its extent is given in an article appearing in *The New Republic* of August 13, 1945, under the title "Church, State, and Schools." The immediate occasion for it is the Mead-Aiken Federal Aid to Education bill pending in Congress, which would allocated $300 million annually to the schools of the country, non-public as well as public, *including parochial schools of all religious denominations.* The article further states that in some instances "religious training is given in the public school buildings, the rooms bearing the crucifix and the teachers being nuns employed by the school board."

In other cases Protestant evangelists have gone right into the public schools with the avowed purpose of "winning all the young people of the community for Christ." The most widespread practice is that of the "Released Time" program which originated here in Indiana, at Gary. It provides that children may be dismissed at certain times during the week to go to their churches or elsewhere for religious instruction. This plan has been adopted by over a thousand communities in ten different states.

Already the "Released Time" program is revealing the weaknesses which those of us who opposed it from the start have predicted. The Public Education Association of the City of New York undertook to make an objective study of the results of the "Released Time" program in that city after three years of operation. The report was a vigorous condemnation of the whole plan. Only 28% of the pupils registered for this instruction -- 4% being Protestant, 1% Jews, 23% Catholic. The program seriously disrupted the routine of the school, for while this 28% was absent the other 72% had to mark time, much to the detriment of the morale of the classroom. "New evils began to make their appearance. Feuds between different religious groups are growing more and more. Where formerly the race issue was no problem on the public school campus, it is becoming so because the matter was discussed in religious education time. It has resulted in the attempt to use the schools as a means of enforcing attendance at religious centers . . . the whole school staff considers the program a waste of time, the benefit derived is disproportionate to the time involved, it encourages truancy and promotes delinquency."

Those who are advocating the teaching of religion in the public schools think that they are being very broad and are avoiding the sectarian spirit because they make provision for Protestant, Catholic, and Jew. But this cannot satisfy the innumerable minority groups among us. Furthermore, what they fail utterly to realize is that most, if not all, which is taught under the name of religion is sectarian to many of us. The plain truth of the matter is that most of the churches have lagged sadly behind the march of knowledge, and what they want to teach in the name of religion in the public schools is for many of us so tainted with error that we do not want our children to imbibe it. If the Bible were taught in accordance with the findings of modern scholars instead of in accordance with the dogma that it is the revealed "Word of God," those who now advocate the introduction of the Bible into the classroom would be the first ones to denounce it. Let us remember that today less than half the population of the country belongs to any church, less than 30% are active church members. This minority has no right to inject its interpretation of religion into the schools which belong to all of us.

Indeed, there are many churchmen who are opposed to this whole program because they recognize its dangers. There were two Congregational ministers who appeared at the Champaign trial in support of Mrs. McCollum, but because of the objections of the attorneys for the School Board their testimony was not made a matter of court record. One of the most vigorous opponents of the teaching of religion in the public schools is a Baptist clergyman, the Rev. Conrad Henry Moehlman, Professor of the History of Christianity at the Colgate-Rochester Divinity School where Baptist ministers are trained.

Professor Moehlman has written a book called *School and Church, the American Way*. In it he examines the history of the relation between school and church in this country and comes to the conclusion that those who are today advocating the introduction of religious teaching in the public schools are trying to abolish the first amendment to our national constitution which provides that "Congress shall make no law respecting an establishment of religion, or prohibiting the free exercise thereof." He says that they are trying to take us back to the condition which existed prior to 1791 when that amendment was adopted.

The founders of our nation deliberately entered upon the experiment of separating church and state. Because they saw the great evils of the union of the two they intentionally established a secular state, leaving the churches free to cultivate the religious life of the people. Our practice has not been entirely consistent with that principle, but on the whole we have been true to it and it has become woven into the warp and woof of our national life. It was freely predicted, when the experiment began, that it would be a failure, that a state could not exist on a secular basis. But those who so claimed have been proved false prophets by the course of our history, for we have grown great and powerful. One of the sources of our success has been the separation of church and state.

Under that policy we have developed a magnificent public school system. It has its defects as all human institutions do, but, by and large, it is the greatest single cultural achievement of our nation. It has done more to bring education to all the people than any other school system in the history of the world. It is one of the great bulwarks of our democracy.

The present attempt to inject the teaching of sectarian religion into the public schools is an insidious attack upon it, an unwarranted criticism of it. Professor Moehlman rightly denounces it as an encroachment of the church on the state, an attempt to renounce one of our most fundamental American principles. He says that it would be disastrous were it possible of achievement, but he does not believe that the sturdy common sense of the American people, convinced by a century and a half of the advantages of separation of church and state, can be induced to reverse the path they have taken. They will soon awaken to the danger of what is now being attempted and put a stop to it. We must make sure that they do.

There is a religion on which all of us are agreed -- the religion of America, of democracy, the religion of freedom, fair-play, unity undisturbed by differences of race, creed, or national background. Of that religion our public schools are our most effective ministers. Let us not hamper them by the introduction of elements that defeat their very purpose. Let us preserve their integrity by keeping them the schools for all the children of the land.

Forty Years
on the Frontier

The Religious Drama in Three Acts

During the summer, a group of exceptionally intelligent and well educated men and women were discussing the funeral service for Eduard Lindeman, the distinguished educator who had died a few weeks earlier. One of the women said that there was not anything religious about the service, that the Community Church of New York City where it was held is as cold and barren as a military barracks and that the men who conducted the service had not read the traditional comforting passages of scripture, nor had they said anything about immortality. She concluded her remarks by saying that perhaps all this was appropriate to the occasion because Mr. Lindeman had been a man without any religion. Other members of the group took issue with her.

The ensuing discussion pointed up the fact that there is no common agreement in the use of the words religion and religious. Some use the phrase, "He is very religious," in a derogatory sense, meaning by it that the individual is narrowly orthodox in belief and practice, cherishing outmoded dogmas and inclined to bigotry. Others use the same phrase as an accolade, meaning by it that the individual is dedicated to the service of truth and humanity and is the embodiment of virtues of the highest order. It is obvious that we are in need of a clarification of our words so that we are all talking about the same thing when we use them.

John Dewey maintained that there is no such thing as "religion"; there are only religions -- plural. There is much truth in this contention. Christianity itself is not one thing, but many; it was very different in the first century from what it was in the fifteenth, from what it is today. The contrast between the Roman Catholic Church and the Society of Friends, between the Seventh-day Adventists and the Unitarians is so great that it is hard to include them all in the same definition. Then when you include the non-Christian faiths, the religions of primitive peoples, those of the other great traditions, like Judaism, Buddhism, Islam, which likewise show great variety within themselves, the reason for Dewey's insistence that there is no such thing as religion -- but only religions, becomes crystal clear.

Yet somehow we are not content to leave it that way; our minds insist on trying to find some common element which unites them all. Perhaps there is no such thing as "Man," but only men in all their diversity; yet we do find it valuable to speak of them collectively and in doing so we are embodying an important truth, namely that all men do belong to the same order and that there is a degree of unity among them despite their diversity. The same is true of religions in all their variety; they do belong to the same order and they do have enough in common to require us to consider them together under a single, comprehensive name. If we can discover what that common element is it will help us to use the word more accurately, to void the confusion of those who were discussing Eduard Lindeman's funeral, and to do greater justice to those whose variety of religion does not fit into the particular pattern we have set up in our minds.

The best way in which we can do this is to view the whole area of religion in man's life from the historical perspective, letting our eyes sweep over the grand procession of the religions as they rise and fall in the course of the ages. Seen from this eminence the history of religions presents itself to me as a drama in three acts. I am aware that this is a great over-simplification which falsifies the story to a considerable extent. Yet it has the advantage that it enables us to disclose the plot of our drama, the great continuing theme, in the brief time at our disposal without getting bogged down in the incredibly complicated and rich details.

The first act begins in those remote times, a half million, a million years ago, we know not precisely when. Man was just emerging from his animal ancestry and becoming human. We will call it the religion of Dawn Man. This, of course, belongs to the period of pre-history. It had its own long development. We know something of what it was like because some of its relics have become embedded in the religion of a later era and so have been continued down to our day. We know it also from the fact that there are still some primitive peoples on the earth, peoples like the Indians of our own country, some of the tribes in the heart of Africa, the South Sea Islanders, and their religions are probably very close in character to that of the Dawn Man.

The Old Testament is replete with material which stems from a time much earlier than that actually reported. Consider, for example, the familiar story of Jacob's dream at Bethel as it is given in the 28th chapter of Genesis. You will recall that Jacob was on a journey and that when night came he lay down to sleep using one of the stones in which the place abounded as a pillow. He had a dream in which he saw a ladder reaching from earth to heaven and angels plying up and down it. And God stood by him and promised to give all that land to him and his seed after him. Awakening, Jacob took the stone on which he had laid his head, set it up as a pillar, poured oil on it, and called the place Bethel, that is, the House of God.

Scholars are agreed that this story was probably told to explain the fact that this particular spot had been considered holy time out of mind and that the Hebrews had taken it over as a sanctuary from the aboriginal inhabitants of Canaan when they conquered the land. The setting up and anointing the stone is reminiscent of the stone altars which the earlier inhabitants had established in high places. The belief that the gods reveal themselves to men in dreams, thus declaring their will, was widespread in antiquity. Here, as so often in the Old Testament, we get glimpses of the religion of the Dawn Man.

Another source of our knowledge of the religion of our early ancestors, as already indicated, is in the beliefs and practices of the primitive peoples who have survived into our own day. Malinowski, who lived among the Trobrianders of the South Sea Islands, gives an account of the way in which their religious practices are involved in the building of their canoes. In part they rely on their own skill as developed over the generations and in part on the rites and ceremonies intended to invoke the aid of unseen powers in securing the sea-worthiness of their craft. He points out that the religious element enters far more into the building of the big canoes intended for use in the open sea than in the construction of the small ones to be used only in the quiet waters of the lagoons. They feel a greater need of reliance on powers beyond their own when it comes to meeting the hazards of the great stretches of the ocean.

From various sources we get a fairly comprehensive picture of what transpired in the first act of our drama. When we do so we discover a truth of the utmost significance for our understanding of the whole course it takes, namely that religions grow out of the lives of men just as surely as the polar bear grows his heavy coat of fur that makes his survival possible in the rigors of the arctic. Dawn Man found himself in the midst of a world to which he had to adjust himself not merely on the basis of his animal instincts, but also on the level of his emerging intelligence. This gave a new dimension to his life and necessitated his trying to understand his world and make his understanding a means of serving his needs. His equipment for doing so was very meager at the start and we should not be surprised to find that some of his attempts took on forms that we regard as sheer superstition.

His imagination endowed the world around him with life akin to his own. The natural objects such as the storms, the streams, the sun and moon and stars, were personified, given spirits, purpose like his own. Some of the forces seemed friendly to him, others hostile. He tried to secure their favors and avoid their attacks. He developed rites which seemed to him means of compelling the spirits to do his will; we call this magic. He practiced ceremonies designed to give him success in the hunt, to make him victorious over his enemies. His imagination and fears were touched by the event of death and he established rites for dealing with the dead, rites that were compounded of his fears, his sorrows, his hopes, his ignorance.

He developed means of securing the solidarity of the group of which he was a member, rules of conduct governing his relations with the other members, sex standards, prohibition against murder, other basic moral requirements without which the group would not have survived. These, too, he early began to associate with the mysterious powers of the world around him. We cannot begin to enumerate the manifold ways in which the religion of

Dawn Man expressed itself, for truth to tell it permeated the whole of his life; it was not a thing apart as religion has tended to become with us, but entered intimately into all his doings. He made no distinction between the secular and the sacred; it was all of one tissue.

It is interesting to note the similarities and the differences in the religions on this primitive level in various parts of the world. As we would anticipate, the practices of the Eskimos differ markedly from those of the South Sea Islanders because their problems are radically different. Yet there is a remarkable similarity in the kind of answers they find. It is clear that men on the same level of culture tend to work out their problems in similar fashion. Their mentality works in the same way and the results are different because the circumstances of their lives are different.

All this vastly reinforces the general impression we gain that religions in their origin and development are not imposed on men from without but are spontaneous growths from within, springing out of their needs, their desires, their hopes and aspirations as well as their fears. We must understand that this process did not take place on the conscious level. Men did not say, "Go to, now, we will make ourselves gods to help us in the difficult business of living." No, religions in all their aspects grew Topsy-like out of the deeps of men's being. The element of reflection, or reason, was very meager at the outset; feeling, imagination, fantasy dominated.

The religion of the Dawn Man lasted a very long time, through the centuries and millenniums from the emergence of human beings down into the historic period. It had its own evolution; the practices changed as man's mode of life changed, when he shifted from hunting to agriculture, for example. The character of his gods altered as he learned more about his world. The moral content of his religion became clearer and more pronounced as experience pointed to better ways. Man climbed a very long way during the first act of his religious drama.

We of the western world are familiar with one striking example of this evolution of the religion of Dawn Man. It is recorded for us in the pages of the Old Testament. That literature is a meaningless jumble to us if we do not have this key to its understanding -- that it is a deposit of the evolution of religion representing it at every stage from low to high, from polytheism to monotheism, from worship at crude stone altars on the high places to the elaborate cult of the Temple at Jerusalem, from the savagery of "an eye for an eye" to the requirement to do justly and love mercy, from narrow tribalism to a splendid universalism. The culminating stage is so different from the beginnings as to seem almost of a different order.

A point to be particularly noted is that throughout this long evolution religion is oriented chiefly to this world. To be sure thoughts of a world beyond did play some part, but they were distinctly subordinate. The major purpose of religion was to enable man to feel at home in his world, secure, possessed of those values which his heart chiefly desired. It was, in the phrase Jesus used, "that they may have life, and have it abundantly." The terms in which the abundant life was conceived altered, the methods of obtaining it changed, but the purpose remained steadfast; man was seeking by whatever means available to him to make his life strong and secure and rich upon the earth.

Then there came a time about 2500 years ago, we will not attempt to date it too closely because it came about gradually, when men fell into despair of ever realizing their hope of achieving the good life on earth. They saw that they built up their civilizations only to have them crumble into ruin. They saw that a few men enjoy wealth and security but that the vast majority suffer poverty, hunger, injustice. They saw that their ideals were honored more in the breach than in the observance. They saw, alas, that there is but one goal for all men, rich and poor, wise and ignorant, exalted and humble -- all alike journey inexorably to the grave. "Dust thou art, to dust returnest."

A mood of despair overtook men. They grew weary of the struggle, the constant frustration and defeat. The cry, "Vanity of vanities, all is vanity!" rose to their lips. In their despair, they listened to the pessimists among them who argued that it is hopeless for men to try to win the good life they crave, that they are foredoomed to defeat on this earth. But there is, so the argument ran, a way of escape. Beyond this world there is another and better one in which all men have hoped for and been denied here is achieved. There is a way to make sure you will enter upon the bliss of that better world. Men listened and believed because of the hunger of their hearts.

Surely we of this generation can sympathize with them, enter into their despair and share their hunger, for we, too, know what it is to have our earthly hopes crushed. We have seen the fair promise of the age of science turn into the awful destruction of atomic bombs, we have seen our world rent with revolution and war. We have experienced the sense of helplessness and impending doom. Again in our day, spokesmen of religion have raised the cry that man of himself is powerless and that it is only as he turns to God that he can find the salvation for which he longs. Yes, we can sympathize with and understand those men of two millenniums and more ago with whom the religious drama entered upon its second act, the religion of Disillusioned Man, man in retreat from this world, taking refuge in the dream of a world beyond. "I'm a pilgrim and a stranger here; heaven is my home."

To be sure, Disillusioned Man inevitably took with him much that his predecessor, the Dawn Man, had accumulated in his many centuries. Men still tried to adjust themselves to the circumstances of this life, to make the most of it, but their hearts were not in the task because they knew it was hopeless; they were suffering from a failure of nerve. They still cherished many of the grand ideas at which they had arrived in their attempts to solve the riddle of the universe. They still tried to hold themselves to the moral requirements which had become embedded in religion. But this had now all become of secondary importance. There had been a shift of emphasis from this world to the next. The religion of Disillusioned Man became primarily a matter of making sure of obtaining the bliss of that other world which should more than compensate them for the ills they had had to suffer here. They were to be saved out of this world for the next one.

How did men seek to make sure of such a destiny? The ways were varying, differing in different parts of the world. In India, for example, it was by the absorption of the individual life into that of God. The great pyramids of Egypt are the symbols of another method. The mighty men, the kings and nobles of the Nile valley sought to guarantee their immortality by heaping stone on stone as though the sheer weight of matter which formed their place of burial could enable them to cheat death.

But the method with which we are chiefly concerned is that of the Savior God because this was the pattern which had the most influence in our western world, and indeed it is much a Savior God who constitutes the central figure of Christianity. Jesus, or Christ as he is more commonly called, is but one among a number of such deities. There was Mithra among the Persians, Osiris among the Egyptians, to name but two.

The mechanism of salvation was essentially the same in all of these cults. According to the story the god died, usually meeting a violent death. Then he rose from the dead to enter upon immortal bliss, thus setting the pattern for all who accepted him and ceremonies in which he identified himself with his savior and it all culminated in his having a sense of being reborn with the assurance that in the world to come he would share the joys of his lord. There was here a sort of refinement of the earlier magic by which primitive men sought to constrain the supernatural powers to give them what they wanted. Even so men were now resorting to magic means to gain the gift of heaven. They performed the proper rites, held the true faith, met the requirements of the Savior god, and the result was that they shared the destiny of the dying and resurrected deity.

Anyone familiar with the Christian plan of salvation in its orthodox form must recognize that it conforms to this pattern. It was one of the savior cults which were prevalent in the Mediterranean world 2000 years ago. It won out in competition with the others in part through certain inherent superiorities -- its connection with the monotheistic deity of Jewish religion and the sublimity of the figure of Jesus who was exalted to the status of a god. But it is clear that it was only because Christianity was able to meet its rivals on their own ground and offer to its adherents the machinery of a supernatural salvation that it was able to triumph. For multitudes then as now the appeal of the magic gift of eternal bliss was more powerful than the ethical idealism and human worth of Jesus.

There can be no doubt of the psychological power of these savior cults; they did operate powerfully to give men who were disillusioned a sense of new life and significance. But now we are living in the latter stages of this second act of the drama which is religion. Quite obviously the theory of the nature of the world on which it is based is invalidated by the progress of modern thought. We can see clearly that the Christian plan of salvation, no less than that of Mithra and its other competitors which fell by the way, belongs to the realm of mythology. True it has been very precious to men, they have believed in it implicitly and within its framework multitudes of beautiful and exalted lives have been lived. But not all the piety of the believers, not all the values it has created, can hide from us the fact that it is doomed by the march of knowledge.

This second act of our drama has continued the same motif, the same dominant motivation, as the first one -- namely to secure for men those things, those values which they needed in order to have a satisfying life. Only they transferred the scene of his satisfying life to another world because they despaired of this one. At its extreme this other worldliness is represented in a Saint Simeon Stylites who lived on top of a pillar, or in the monasteries where men lived in retirement from the world. It is represented in the emphasis on the importance of a "good death" rather than a "good life" which has been characteristic of one of the major forms of Christianity.

But let us not over-stress this otherworldliness of religion. After all, men did have to go on living in this world, and inevitably their religion had strong repercussions on this present life. Some of its influence was salutary, beneficent; some of it was noxious, evil. It is impossible to draw up a balance sheet. There is much evidence in these recent days that religion is turning more and more to the task of making this present world a fit place in which to live. The recent pronouncement of the General Board of the National Council of the Churches of Christ in the U.S.A. in connection with the annual observance of World Order Day which is to be celebrated two weeks hence is eloquent of this shift. It makes clear that it is the business of religion to see that the world puts its house to right.

This very emphasis, however, is one of the evidences that we are now living in the latter stages of the second act of our drama. This second act will doubtless be long continued. Religions do not die suddenly; the inertia of the past is strong upon them and this carries them far beyond the time when they can satisfy the best thoughts of men, meet their needs effectively. Just now we are experiencing a resurgence of orthodoxy, a fresh demand for a renewal of the traditional in religion. It is a product of the confusion, the tensions, the revolution through which the world is passing. It is bound to be of limited duration, for it is an effort to make water flow uphill; the stream of life flows on.

Already there are those among us who are preparing for the third act of our drama, writing its script, securing its properties, rehearsing its cast. We shall call it the Religion of Resurgent Man. The distinctive thing abut it is that once more religion concerns itself with this present world, rather than with a world to come. It returns to the scene with which the religion of the Dawn Man concerned itself, the making of life here and now as rich and satisfying as possible. But with this significant difference, it no longer relies on enlisting the aid of supernatural powers to secure its ends, for belief in such powers is fading into nothingness as we move on toward the noon day of science. It recognizes that man himself must win the values which in the past he has asked the gods to give him, that he will attain that degree of heaven which he himself creates.

There is a spiral movement in the history of religions. Modern man is returning to the same scene which occupied the Dawn Man, but on a much higher level. He has come back to the scene of this mundane struggle with renewed faith in what can be made of life here on earth. He is armed with new powers, a vastly increased understanding of the natural order of which he is a part, and a corresponding capacity to control it for his own purposes -- not by magic, not by calling upon the gods, but by the methods of science, by the development of his own skills. Yes, and he is beginning to get a better understanding of his own nature with the prospect that he may be able to harness his inner drives to the promotion of his dream of a better life, even as he uses the power that is in the lightning, the waterfall and the atom to serve himself.

He enters upon this third act with the lessons he has learned from the centuries that have gone before, for all was not loss in those millenniums of retreat. Good men and true did clarify the values of life, did seek the ways of establishing them and sharing them with others. We can appropriate these treasures from the past, build them into the new structure we are erecting.

To be sure, we are in the very early stages of the third act and have not yet learned the lines very well; it is only falteringly that we speak them. There is much nostalgia for the past, many predictions that the new is foredoomed to failure. This is to be expected and should not dismay us. Of course there will be disappointments and failures; of course there will be tremendous obstacles to overcome; of course we cannot be sure in advance how far we shall succeed. But we have set our feet in this path and we will not be deterred. We are determined to see what man can make of his life on this earth in the light of the scientific revolution which is upon us. It is high adventure and we propose to live it out to the full.

Such, then, are the three acts of the drama which is religion. The religion of the dawn in which man tried to constrain the mysterious powers to aid him in the business of living by such feeble means as were at his command; the religion of retreat in which weary and disillusioned man decided that the full life which he craved could not be attained here on earth and so postponed it to another world in which he should receive it as a gift at the hands of a savior god; and now the religion of return in which resurgent man again accepts this earth as the setting for the achievement of the values which give meaning to his being, returns with renewed hope because he comes with increased understanding, with new and more potent tools, with the clear and conscious purpose to push forward in the enduring quest for life more abundant.

That quest is what gives continuity to the whole drama, it is the thread running through all of it. Though there is no such thing as religion, but only religions, all of these different forms have been but so many diverse ways in which man has sought to attain his maximum. The motivation, the drive, throughout has been the yearning in man's own heart to surpass himself. That is what it must remain whatever forms religion may take in the future. At its best, it is the most inclusive of man's disciplines, comprehending all the rest, permeating his philosophy and his science, his politics and his economics, his art, and constraining them to its service. It enables him to "see life steadily and see it whole," to know where he would go and inspire and sustain him on his journey. Religion is that transcendent purpose welling up out of the heart of man bidding him marshall all his resources in the endless quest to make of his own life a thing of beauty and a joy forever.

The Pearl of Great Price

A recent issue of *Time* magazine carried a report on an address delivered by Nathan M. Pusey, the new president of Harvard University, at the convocation of the Harvard Divinity School. In his talk he took issue with his famous predecessor, Charles W. Eliot, on the subject of religion. Dr. Eliot had set forth his views in an address on "The Religion of the Future." In it he said: "The new religion will foster powerfully a virtue which is comparatively new in the world -- the love of truth and the passion for seeking it. And the truth will progressively make men free."

Dr. Pusey professes to find the rational, humanitarian faith of Dr. Eliot unacceptable, inadequate to the needs of today. He says, for instance, that he suspects President Eliot would have considered the doctrine that Christ came into the world to save sinners as "so much twaddle." This, the new president of Harvard avers, is where Dr. Eliot is wrong. Men need such "metaphysical" doctrines to feed the deep hungers of their souls which cannot be satisfied with the simple, rational faith that Dr. Eliot had advanced as the religion of the future.

This incident is a conspicuous example of that reactionary movement in religion which is sweeping our country today. It is understandable as a response to the fears and tensions of our time. Men are seeking to retreat to the spiritual dug-outs in which their forefathers sought refuge. But it is none the less a retreat and we are going to have to recover the lost ground; the only satisfying solution to the religious problem will, in the long run, be found in an advance.

Dr. Eliot would not have expressed his rejection of the dogma that Christ came into the world to save sinners in the phrase "so much twaddle"; his language would have been much more elegant though no less incisive. And he would have been right, for as we saw in the sermon of last Sunday, the doctrine of the dying and resurrected savior god was central to the second act of the religious drama which is now drawing to a close. In the light of our present knowledge we are constrained to recognize it as a myth, as a part of that elaborate theological machinery which men devised to enable them to escape their disillusionment and frustration.

When we characterize the doctrine that Christ came into the world to save sinners as myth we are not doing so in a hostile or derogatory spirit for we recognize that myth plays a very important role in the life of man. It becomes the embodiment of a whole system of precious values to those who do believe implicitly in it as the truth. Indeed, it may well turn out to be the case that centuries hence the doctrines which we today are beginning to substitute for the out-moded Christian theology will come to be considered as "myth" by our descendants. That is hard for us to conceive, particularly because we are persuaded that our present views have been arrived at by the use of the scientific method and hence have a greater objective truth than was true of the theological dogmas of the past. At least we may be sure that our present views will be greatly modified with the further advance of knowledge. But that does not make them less effective mediums for the carrying of our values; they are truth to us.

It will be worth our while to consider for a moment something of what the Christian myth did for those to whom it was the truth, those to whom it is still the truth. It confronted them with a vast cosmic drama which gave meaning and direction to their lives. More than that it assigned to each individual an important, a central role in that drama. According to the story, God, who created the universe, created also the human soul and made the destiny of that soul the major theme of the drama. This gave to every individual a vast importance; gods and demons struggled over him, his own decision was crucial in determining his immortal destiny.

Something of the significance of all this can be estimated from the passion for the saving of souls which it inspired. The story is told of Jesuit missionaries among the Indians of this country, in the early days of its settlement, that they would go on to the battle field and themselves mortally wounded would crawl from dying warrior to dying warrior baptizing them in their own blood to make sure that these heathen would go to heaven. I covet a comparable "passion for souls" in the religion which is now in the making. But it must take a very different form.

In the place of the cosmic drama of salvation which set the pattern for such action we must now substitute the drama to which we give the name evolution. It is just as vast in its proportions, just as marvelous in its mystery, just as capable of commanding our reverence and our awe as that which it is replacing. This is true even though it does not make the creation of souls and their immortal destiny its dominating purpose, and humbles man by making him realize his relative insignificance in the tremendous reaches of space and time.

It is not my intent to argue the case for evolution. I am going to take it for granted. The evidence for it is so overwhelming as to be convincing to the vast majority who come to its study with open minds and even to convert many whose minds have initially been possessed of contrary views. The theory of evolution has now reached that stage of respectability in which it has produced a crop of humorous poetry. Let me share with you a recent example:

Now Listen You Two

Three monkeys sat in a coconut tree
Discussing things as they're said to be.
Said one to the others: "Now listen, you two!
There's a certain rumor that can't be true,
That man descended from our noble race.
The very idea! It's a dire disgrace!
No monkey ever deserted his wife,
Starved his baby and ruined her life.
And another thing: you'll never see
A monk build a fence 'round a coconut tree,
And let the coconuts go to waste,
Forbidding all other monks to taste.
Why, if I'd put a fence 'round this tree,
Starvation would force you to steal from me.
Here's another thing a monk won't do --
Go out at night and get on a stew;
Or use a gun or club or knife

To take some other monkey's life.
Yes, man descended, the ornery cuss,
But brothers, he didn't descend from us! (author unknown)

This, of course, is but a sample of the way in which men use their laughter to protect themselves from truths in the presence of which they are not altogether comfortable. But there is a majestic aspect to this dynamic process of evolution. It seems to us to be the truth and it is within the framework of that truth that we must win for ourselves those values which are the essence of religion.

The theory of evolution confronts us with a doctrine of man. It is a doctrine derived from the evidence presented by the various sciences dealing with the origin and nature of man. An interpretation of this evidence indicates clearly that man in all that he is, his mind as well as his body, is a product of that tremendously long process in which there gradually emerged those qualities which are most distinctive of our humanity. That which we call "soul" is not an entity intruded from some external, supernatural source, but is itself the end product of the process itself. Soul is the name which we give to the mental aspect of man's life. We humbly acknowledge that as yet we have no adequate explanation of the relation between thought and brain, between ideals and the nervous system. But it seems highly probable that those aspects which we call "spiritual" are in some way a function of the physical organism rather than an intrusion from an alien realm. We are going to have to accept the full consequences of this conclusion.

There are obvious perils in doing so. We have been warned that it is dangerous to tell man how close he is to the brutes without at the same time reminding him how near he is to the angels. In other words, it is important that man shall think of himself and act not so much in terms of his origin as in terms of what he is and may become. It is true that there is in us an animal heritage some portions of which are in conflict with those reaches of our nature which we like to consider as distinctively human. Our problem is to subordinate that which is low in us to that which is high, but we express that problem in terms derived from our sciences rather than the theology of the past.

One of the dangers of the evolutionary view of man is to be seen clearly in an incident in the life of Stalin. This arch dictator of the Soviet Union had the reputation among us of being utterly ruthless and of disregarding the worth of the individual human life. The purges which were carried out under his orders certainly justify this estimate of him. Nonetheless, it seems that he placed a higher value on men than did some of his associates.

Early in his career he was in charge of a group of loggers who were riding a raft of logs down a river. In the course of their operations one of the men lost his life. Stalin was incensed by the indifference his companions showed, the little effort they made to save him. When Stalin protested, the men replied, "Why should we be concerned about men? We can always make men. But a mare, just try to make a mare." Stalin tried, without much success, to convince them that the most valuable capital the world possesses is people. His own later practice seems in direct contradiction to this.

Probably it is not just to charge the attitude of these men, their indifference toward human life, to the theory of evolution. It is likely that they had never heard of that theory, but their placing less value on a man than on a mare is typical of that low estimate of the worth of human life which is characteristic of large sections of the world and is said by the critics of the theory of evolution to be the logical and inevitable consequence of teaching men that they are descended from animals. Teach them that and they will act like animals, treat their fellows like animals. Something of this kind is doubtless behind the current protest that the only effective answer to Communism is religion which tells men that they are of divine origin.

But it is a mistake to assume that the inevitable outcome of the scientific view of man's origin is that cynicism and ruthlessness which have marked the practice of the totalitarian states. On the contrary, the evolutionary concept is wholly compatible with a high sense of the worth of human life, as is amply demonstrated in the lives of many of its advocates. "An individual man is the fruit which it cost all the foregoing ages to form and ripen." So wrote Emerson, and in that statement there is implicit a recognition of the surpassing worth of the individual man.

Whatever be the explanation of the origin of life, it is a marvel, a wondrous thing. Albert Schweitzer, who probably has as sure an insight as any living man, informs us that "reverence for life" is the essence of his religion. Surely human life is incomparably above all the other forms of which we have any knowledge and correspondingly more worthy of our reverence. In its capacities, its potentialities, it is magnificent.

To be sure it is subject to degradation and capable of colossal evil. But we will not succumb to the clamor of those who today are raising in the name of religion the ancient cry that man is in his essential nature a creature of depravity. The very essence of the new age of faith upon which we are entering is a robust, yet realistic faith in man. It recognizes that he is by no means as yet master in his own house and that in consequence he is often the victim of his own powers. But we do not accept this as final. We are persuaded that that process of development which began so long ago and has carried us to our present stature has not reached its conclusion. Under the guidance of our conscious intent and purpose, it will continue enabling our humanity to rise to yet greater heights.

But let us have done with theory and turn to the practical question. Is there within the framework of this evolutionary point of view the means of feeding the deep hungers of the human spirit as amply as they have been fed by the religion of the past? Can we today gratify men's desire to feel that their lives are significant and that they have a direction which gives them dignity and worth in any way comparable to the ancient myth which gave them a heroic role in the cosmic drama? The answer is an unhesitating and emphatic "Yes!"

This answer emerges from within the process itself. A clue to the nature of this answer is provided in a few lines of a poem by William Watson:

> Momentous to himself as I to me
>   Hath each man been that ever woman bore;
> Once in a lightning flash of sympathy,
>   I felt this truth an instant, and no more.

Each human being is important to himself. Each person who hears these words of mine carries around within himself his own world, and be it grand and expansive or petty and constrictive, it is suffused with the warmth and vitality which derives from the fact that it is intimate and personal. Everything which happens in that inner world is significant to us because it is our own, be it but a fleeting thought, a deep sorrow, a blessed friendship, a soaring ambition. That inner world includes our relations with other people, our home, our husband or wife, our business, our enemies, our friends -- all those various things and relations which have become part of ourselves. To each of us it is the most important thing in the world, our very life.

The superior man is he who intuitively recognizes this truth as it applies to others and governs his relations with them in the light of his sympathetic understanding that what is taking place in them is momentous to them. No person is so humble but what he has his own sensitivity, his integrity, his dignity and is entitled to be treated with respect. Here we have the reason why humanity spontaneously accords its highest veneration to the men of compassion, to those who are able by their sympathetic insight to project themselves into the lives of others, "even the least of these," identifying himself with them, treating them on the basis of the penetrating understanding that each man is momentous to himself.

It is in this simple fact that each man is important to himself that we find the directive for our religion in this new age. After all, it was just because the old time gospel of salvation was based on the recognition of this truth of human life that it appealed so powerfully to men and was so effective. Now the ancient appeal must be given a new form in keeping with the thinking of men today. If we substitute for the word "salvation" the word "fulfillment" we shall have a sign-post marking the road we must take.

Every human being has within himself certain capacities, certain potentialities; he has his drives, desires, his ability to feel, to think, to do. These differ widely in each of us; they occur in endless combinations. But in all of us there is the urge to exercise them to the utmost, to grow to our maximum. Despite this variety there is enough similarity between all of us, we have enough in common, so that it will be profitable for us to consider in general terms what it is we mean by fulfillment. What is it that we need to make our lives satisfying, significant, to give us the feeling "to this end was I born and for this cause came I into the world"?

> Man wants but little here below
>   Nor wants that little long
> 'Tis not with me exactly so
>   But 'tis so in the song.

So sang Oliver Goldsmith, and he spoke for most of us. The things that we want are legion, our desires are insatiable. We cannot expect to list them all, but there are a few basic hungers with which we may deal and consider them as representative of the whole wide range of values which we desire to achieve and which we feel as essential to our fulfillment.

First on our list of those things by which men live we would inevitably place love; we need to love and to be loved. Even the most self-sufficient of us come up against an ultimate loneliness which is unendurable. We need to transcend ourselves by effecting a union with others and the way whereby we do this is the way of love. It exists on many different levels, takes on a wide variety of forms in our lives. On its lowliest level, it may be little more than the biological urge of sex. Fortunately, we are beginning to learn that this powerful drive upon which we are dependent for the perpetuation of the race is not the evil thing for which men have aforetime mistaken it. To be sure, it requires control and direction, but it is one of our greatest resources, a primordial energy which enters far more than we are wont to realize into our highest achievement. It is to be revered and cherished.

At its best, it flowers into something which seems so lovely as to bear but little relation to the soil from which it springs. Ofttimes an apple tree in full bloom presents itself to me as an appropriate symbol of this transmutation. Those blossoms are a means whereby the tree seeks to perpetuate its kind; they are an expression of the drive of sex. Yet as we look upon the tree we think not so much of this utilitarian purpose as of the transcendent beauty that the tree has achieved and which we know in the background of our minds is the forerunner of that luscious fruit it is to bear.

Even so, the procreative drive in human beings flowers in the rare beauty of the love of mates, of parents for children, of children for their parents. How vividly there is still impressed upon my mind from my student days the picture of a little girl of perhaps three summers throwing her arms around her father's leg, looking up at him with ecstasy on her face and exclaiming, "Oh daddy, I love you so much." There was fulfillment for both father and daughter in that moment. This same power ramifies through all our lives seeking everywhere to bear its rich fruitage. It has been my observation that women are, on the whole, more sensitive to these values than men and that we need to learn from them that to love and to be loved is one of the chief values giving life its substance and its meaning.

Here we are confronted with the tragic fact that love does fail, holy writ to the contrary notwithstanding; love does "alter when it alteration finds." There are cruel blights that enter the blossoms on the apple tree and render them sterile, harsh frosts that nip them. Often the crop is meager, the apples gnarled, wormy, bitter. A major portion of the frustration, the heartache, the tragedy of human life has its source in love that has failed, that has been defeated, rendered sterile, ugly, by hatred, hostility, perversion. Fulfillment is denied.

This is a point where our religion needs to call on the ministry of those who are developing special skills and insights in this difficult field. There are those among us who are learning why love goes awry "leaving us nought but grief and pain for promised joy." They are learning what the conditions are for the normal and wholesome development of love. Yes, they are even learning to redirect the stream of love into more fruitful channels when it has gone astray. We shall have to acknowledge that as yet we are but in the feeble beginnings of this undertaking, but there is great promise in those beginnings and it is an urgent part of the business of religion to make that promise grow from more to more. There is a far greater degree of fulfillment available to men in love than we have as yet experienced.

Time constrains me to limit the presentation of our avenues of fulfillment to one further example. For that purpose I choose the area of work. We complain of the necessity we are under of earning our living by the sweat of our brow, yet we know well enough in our heart of hearts that it is good that it should be so. It gives us a channel in which to pour our energies, it enables us to exercise our skills, to develop and perfect them; it gives us the feeling that we are carrying our share of the load, helping maintain the fabric of the world. We are at our best when we are thus employed, when we are doing work which seems important to us and is so recognized by our fellows.

During the depression year of 1931 I was in London. One day when I was out walking I turned a corner and found myself in the presence of a vast concourse of men. I inquired what the occasion of the gathering was and learned that a factory in that street had run an ad in the paper offering work. Six men were needed; 6000 had responded. As I talked with some of the men who found themselves rejected, it was brought poignantly home to me that the tragedy of unemployment lies not alone in that the men are deprived of the opportunity to earn a living for themselves and their families, but more fundamentally that it strikes at their manhood, takes from them the sense that they are needed, that they are contributing their fair share to the common human enterprise, despoils them of the opportunity to expend themselves in their labor. The result is degradation, disintegration, the decay rather than the growth of souls.

Labor at its best brings to men a feeling of partnership in the creative process of the universe. George Eliot has expressed this truth in a memorable figure in the lines of her poem "Stradivarius." The elderly violin worker explains why he continues the arduous work of making his instruments:

> If my hand slacked
> I should rob God -- since he is fullest good --
> Leaving a blank instead of violins.
>   'Tis God gives skill
> But not without men's hands: he could not make
> Antonio Stradivari's violins
> Without Antonio.

There ought to be in all our work this sense of participation in the creative process. Somehow we should have imagination enough to redeem even the humblest task, transform the sheerest drudgery by our vision of the indispensable contribution it makes to the fabric of human life. Judged by this standard, it is obvious how much room there is for improvement in the way the world does it work.

How much such work there is to be done from sowing and reaping to organizing the community of nations for the purposes of peace! In every direction which we look the needs and the opportunities are boundless. There is enough to keep all of us busy as far ahead as we can see. The difficulties are immense in many areas but the rewards proportionate. When did ever men worthy the name ask for easy things to do. Mrs. Roosevelt reports a conversation with an American engineer who had been in charge of the construction of a canal in the Orient which had to take a devious route because of formidable natural barriers. She condoled with him over the tortuous path he had had to follow, and he replied that that was what made it so much fun. He did not want mere child's play, but found his fulfillment in a man-sized job.

Recently I had a letter from Arthur Morgan, formerly president of Antioch College, and head of TVA. It was in response to greetings to him on the occasion of the celebration of his 75th birthday. In the letter he tells of plans to leave for the Gold Coast of Africa on the 20th of this month to advise with the Gold Coast government on the Volta River project. He adds, "We may possibly go from there to Turkey to help plan a new university." Then he tells of a project for a new book.

There is one paragraph of the letter which I wish to share with you: "Life has been good to us. Personally I find the later years more satisfying, and with much less internal stress and strain, than were youth and middle age. Travelling through Europe several years ago, we observed that in the villages the old people kept busy and useful. When the days of heavy work were past, they would herd geese along the margins of the roads, and talk with passing friends. While traces of usefulness remain, we do not wish to waste them. So we are ready to herd geese, or to do anything else within our powers that may be worth while."

Yes, Arthur Morgan has appropriated in full measure those values of life which it is the purpose of religion to inspire men to achieve; he has found fulfillment. He is an exceptional man? Yes, but it is the aim and the resolve of religion come of age to produce more such men. The pattern is one which can be infinitely varied, but the locus of it is always a human character which has taken the raw materials of life up into itself, assimilated them, grown toward maturity in the process and given its own quality, its own stamp to the course of events.

I used as our readings this morning two passages which stand related in my mind. The one is that in which Jesus likened the kingdom of heaven to the merchant seeking goodly pearls who finds one pearl of great price and goes and sells all he has to buy that pearl. The other in which Spinoza tells how his search for supreme and unending happiness led him at length to the conclusion that the supreme good lies in that superior order of character which man sees as possible to himself. That is the pearl of great price, that is the kingdom of heaven. The natural impulse of our lives is to grow in the direction of that superior character even as it is the urge of the tree to grow straight and strong and symmetrical. But we need to marshall all our resources, all our science and all our art to the aid of that process, not forgetting that our own resolve is an indispensable ingredient. May the blessings of that heaven, the benediction of that supreme good, wax ever greater in all our hearts!

The Mind of Man Grows Broader

"My mind to me a kingdom is." This line from Edward Dyer, a contemporary of Shakespeare, may well serve us as a text. You will recall that last Sunday we said that in the religion which is now developing the major emphasis is on the fulfillment of life in individual men and women. Surely one of the chief areas in which that fulfillment is to be effected is in the life of the mind. "My mind to me a kingdom is." And a vast kingdom it is. Ours is the privilege of enjoying its reaches and its riches, of using its powers, of exploiting its resources.

We shall be better able to do this if we understand what the mind is. Notable progress has been made in recent years in enabling us to arrive at such an understanding. Seen in the light of the theory of evolution we now recognize that the mind is one of the instruments which life has devised in order to meet its needs, to serve its purposes. Just as the eye has been developed to enable animals to find their way around more effectively instead of groping forever in the dark, so the mind has been called into being to enable living things to solve a host of problems.

The mind of man has its antecedents in the other forms of life around us; we don't know just how far down the scale of living things to attribute mind. Some even think that plants have minds as well as animals. But in man, mind has attained a quality and a power incomparably greater than it has in the other creatures. This is particularly true of the power of reasoning, of taking conscious thought. But the difference is only one of degree, though such differences when they become great enough can produce a difference of kind, and we feel that such is the case when we compare the mind of a Plato with that of the most intelligent dog.

Yet for all the heights which mind achieves in us, its roots go deep down into the animal mentality. This has been made abundantly clear by the studies of recent years which have disclosed those reaches of our minds to which we give the name of the "unconsciousness." That is, a very large part of our mental activity goes on without our being aware of it. We live a large portion of our lives on the unconscious level in response to feelings, drives, impulses which surge spontaneously up out of the deeps of our being and it is only now and again that we "take thought" and resort to the conscious use of our intelligence.

That intelligence is the latest product in the evolution of the mind. It is not as yet very securely established; we do not use it nearly as effectively as we should. It is in need of much further development, much firmer establishment as the guide of our lives. Intelligence, reason is that which makes us most distinctively human.

There are those who deny this. You may remember how Hitler railed against reason and sang the praises of "blood," by which he meant the surge of the primitive forces which lie below the threshold of intelligence. Many who do not carry this attitude to the same extreme as the late unlamented Nazi Fuehrer are yet the victims of the same illusion. They decry the use of reason as dry and sterile; they insist that our reliance must be on deeper, more vital drives of life. A veritable cult of the irrational, of the anti-intellectual has sprung up among us.

This is, in my estimation, sheer tragedy. Intelligence is the most effective means we have for directing the forces of our lives. We cannot be too intelligent; too intellectual, yes -- with an arid, pedantic use of the rational powers; but too intelligent, no! We cannot think too clearly, too incisively; we cannot submit ourselves too fully to the direction of our intelligence. To be sure, the intelligent man will take into consideration the irrational forces of our nature, recognizing in them the sources of our power, but he will insist on subjecting them to the reins of the intelligence. Those who counsel to the contrary are like him who has only a candle to light him through the dark and blows out the candle. No one in our time has had a fuller understanding of the irrational in human life than Sigmund Freud. Yet it was he who announced that the ultimate hope of man is in his reason. It is very feeble, he said, but very persistent and in the long run the victory will lie with it.

The cult of the irrational reminds one of a passage in *Alice in Wonderland*. The Queen remarked to Alice: "Now I'll give you something to believe. I'm just one hundred and one, five months and a day." "I can't believe *that*!" said Alice. "Can't you?" the Queen said in a pitying tone. "Try again; draw a long breath, and shut your eyes." Alice laughed. "There's no use trying," she said: "One *can't* believe impossible things." "I dare say you haven't had much practice," said the Queen. "When I was your age, I always did it for half hour a day. Why, sometimes I believed as many as six impossible things before breakfast!"

While we have attempted an explanation of mind in terms of a natural process of development to meet the needs of living organisms we are wholly aware that our account is by no means complete. There is still much to be explained, but we are confident that we are on the right track. We know, also, that even in terms of our fullest account mind remains a mystery, a miracle; but it is a natural miracle, just as is a blade of grass. And we will not permit the gaps in our knowledge, the inadequacies of our explanations, to become a veil behind which we indulge in all manner of unwarranted fantasies of a world beyond our everyday experience.

More important, however, than our interpretation of the nature of mind and how it got here, is the use to which we put it. Therefore, let us proceed to tell of some of the ways in which we exploit the resources of this empire which is the mind.

We have already spoken of mind, particularly the intelligence, as the solver of problems, the guide in our daily affairs. It also has the function of the enjoyer; through it we appropriate the wonder, the beauty, the magnificence of our world. How beyond all description are the riches which it discloses to us and enables us to lay hold of as our own! They range all the way from the glory of the starry heavens by night which ravished the hearts of the ancient psalmist to the marvel of the structure of the atom as revealed by the modern scientist, and to loyalty in the heart of a man who lays down his life for a friend. How can anyone become bored with life to whom there is open the privilege of living with the illimitable mind!

I am not forgetting that our world has its horrifying aspects, that there open before the mind deep abysses of terror, the play of forces before which it shrinks in fear. I am not forgetting that ofttimes the mind itself becomes clouded, its light turns to darkness, its powers used perversely to frustrate and defeat rather than fulfill life. These, too, are realities with which we must come to grips, and we shall deal with them in due course.

There is a sheer joy in the exercise of our intelligence comparable to that of the athlete in the play of his muscles. The more we develop our skill in this direction the greater becomes our satisfaction. It is a delight to follow a closely reasoned argument; there are elements of beauty in the disciplined functioning of the intelligence. Einstein informs us that he derives a satisfaction from the solution of an abstruse problem in mathematics comparable to that which he takes in playing the violin.

Arnold Bennett has an essay on "The Pleasures of Life" in which he rates thinking at the top of the list. He argues that most of us never require our brains to carry their full load but allow them to stagnate. The result is that we deprive ourselves of a great deal of pleasure, the pleasure of disciplined thinking. The brain will respond to such discipline and if we would but give it as much time and attention as we do to acquiring skill, let us say, at golf or bridge, it would reward us immeasurably. Here is the greatest untapped resource of our lives.

There is one particular use to which men put their minds on which I wish to concentrate our attention. It is a use which is fraught with important emotional as well as intellectual values. We have a saying that every man is a philosopher. That is, every man finds himself under the necessity of trying to bring some kind of order and system into the world which his mind discloses to him. He wants to understand it and to tidy it up; thereby it is made safe and habitable for him. In much the same way that our bodies take in food, digest it, and build it into their structure, so our minds tend to take in material from the external world, assimilate it, build it into an organic system.

One of the major functions of the religions has been to meet the needs of the philosopher in each man. Religions have given their explanations of the origin and the nature of the world and of the relation which man bears to it. The answers which they have given to the riddle of the universe have varied widely depending on the stage of the particular culture out of which they have grown. In so far as these answers have met the intellectual and emotional needs of men they have contributed greatly to making men feel at home, secure in their world and thereby have rendered them more effective in their living.

The form of this enterprise with which we are most familiar is theology --
the science of God. From very early times men read into the world around
them a spirit akin to their own and attributed the things which happened to the
operations of a purpose and will like that of which they found themselves
possessed. This process culminated in the creation of the idea of a supreme
deity who was the maker and the sustainer of the universe. In childlike minds,
God was but a man writ large and projected into the sky. In more sophisticated
minds He became a being so utterly vast and mysterious as to be well nigh
incomprehensible to the ordinary mind. Yet He still bore the image of His
creator, and the theologians never wearied of describing in detail His qualities
and extolling His perfection.

God has been very precious to the hearts of men. He has been the
"Heavenly Father" who has cared for them as no earthly father could; He has
been the answer to their anxious questioning; He has been the bearer and
guarantor of their most beloved values. It is not strange that men have been
fiercely jealous for their gods and have denounced those who did not accept
them as stupid and dangerous. Ever and again the cry has been raised, "Believe
or die!" The lighted faggots in the midst of which Servetus met his death at the
stake just 400 years ago are eloquent of the intolerance which would not brook
any departure from the precise form in which those who wielded power held
the belief. No later than last week our press carried an article stating that a
local minister had charged that anyone who does not believe in the Fatherhood
of God is a traitor to his country and a fellow traveller of the communists!
Preposterous!

What is to be the future of this belief now that we are moving into the third
act of the religious drama? Does my exclamation mean that I conceive religion
in the future is to be atheistic? That word atheist is an ugly one, putting the
emphasis as it does on denial. It is perhaps justified in some instances where
men have stopped in negation and have not pressed beyond doubt, beyond
rejection of the traditional doctrine to a positive belief of their own. But it does
not do justice to the increasing number of thoughtful men in our day who
simply cannot accept the belief as it has come down to us from the past, but
who are just as deeply concerned for the values which God has symbolized as
are the most pious believers.

We will tread softly here out of sympathy for those whose feelings are
sensitive on the subject. A recent church survey in this country disclosed that
99% of the people interviewed believe that there is a God, and 79% of these
defined Him as "a loving Father who looks after us." We will not dogmatize. It
is possible, as many fine intelligences have held, that all forms of belief in
God, from the most naive to the most philosophical, are gropings after a reality
behind the natural order of the world which no human concept is adequate to

express. It may be that some form of this belief will constitute a permanent part of the equipment of a large portion of mankind in adjusting to the world.

Yet we must also take into account alternative beliefs. The tradition of the supernatural personified as God is by no means the only one in the history of human thought. There have been other strains as well. We remember the agnosticism of Buddha, the founder of one of the world's great religions, who advised men to avoid speculations about the existence of God and to concentrate on the practical problem of living wisely and well. We remember the materialism of Democritus, the "laughing philosopher" of ancient Greece, who thought that everything can be explained in terms of atoms in motion.

Both these strains, as well as the theological one, have persisted down the ages. In our own day, largely as a result of the impact of the various sciences, they have taken on new vitality and won many adherents. Consider, for instance, the implications of a recent statement by Dr. Azkoul of Lebanon: "For centuries when their children have died, our people have said: It is the will of God. When spared they have said: It is the grace of God. Now, if perhaps we showed them, by giving them proper food and medical care, that their children need not die, they would turn to their governments and insist that conditions be changed and that their children be given a chance to live in the future." In other words, he is proposing to substitute the providence of man for the providence of God.

Here we come face to face with one of the greatest obstacles to the traditional belief in God, an obstacle which can only be surmounted by blind faith which flies in the face of the facts. It is the problem of evil that is the rock on which theologies are shipwrecked. We cannot reconcile the existence of evil with the kind of God theology has described. It proves too much and makes God responsible for the existence of evil as well as good.

William Hudson, the naturalist, has given us an account of the feelings inspired in him as he became acquainted with the habits of the wasp which we commonly call the mud-dauber. This creature very cleverly stings other small insects in such a manner that they will be paralyzed but not killed. Then it packs them into its nest along with its eggs and seals it all up nicely so that the young when they hatch will have a living meal awaiting them to start them off in life. Hudson said that he found this cruel process, which he discovered was widespread in nature, revolted him if he had to attribute it to the deliberate intent of God, but was much easier for him to accept as the product of the working out of the impersonal forces of nature. His experience led him to abandon the religious faith in which he had been reared.

A few weeks ago I visited a friend of long standing. I had known him as a man of exceptional quality of mind and heart. Now he lay in bed unable to speak a word, unable to move; the victim of a succession of strokes over the past few years, and yet with no immediate prospect of relief from his suffering, from the burden he was carrying, the burden he knew he was inflicting on his loyal wife. You just cannot reconcile a situation like that with the providence of an all loving, all wise, all powerful deity.

This is the negative side; there is a positive one, namely that out of the various sciences there is building up a new understanding of the way in which the universe operates. These sciences, beginning with those which deal with matter, proceeding to those which are concerned with living forms, and including those whose field is human life, turn out to be all of one piece. They dovetail together to form a consistent whole; they give us a unified picture of our world. This picture is new; it is by no means complete; it is as yet by no means securely established in the minds and hearts of men. Only slowly is it replacing the one which has so long dominated over thinking. Yet it seems certain that such a picture will come into ever clearer focus as our knowledge progresses and that it will increasingly command the allegiance of men's minds and direct their actions.

The name which we give to this new interpretation of the universe, this new and yet very ancient philosophy, is "naturalism." By this we seek to convey that everything is in nature and that it is a mistake to try to look beyond nature to a supernatural power which manipulates nature. There is but one order -- not two, God and the world; ours is a genuine universe. Whatever it is that men have called God is in itself an aspect of nature which they have represented to themselves in terms of that magnificent concept. One of the foremost of contemporary theologians, Paul Tillich, has said that God is not *a* Being, but being. That, it seems to me, comes very close to saying that God and nature are one and the same.

We should make sure, however, that we understand that our naturalism is one which includes the highest reaches of the mind, of the spirit of man. All of our values, our urge to seek the truth, our response to beauty, our affections, loyalties, loves, our yearning for perfection are just as much a part of nature as are stars and stones. These intangibles are just as real as the tangibles. It may be hard to explain how we get from atoms to thought, from energy to love, and we do not profess to have all the answers. But we are increasingly confident that in this wondrous world such is actually the case. We anticipate that as our knowledge grows, we shall verify this supposition, even as the great brain physiologist is confident that he will some day learn the way in which impulses in the nervous system somehow become thought, a mystery he cannot now resolve.

This is but to hint at the picture of the universe which naturalism paints. It is by no means complete, but always in the making, subject to constant alteration, always being enriched and enlarged as our knowledge increases. We do not hold it dogmatically, but tentatively, yet none the less securely. We are aware of the limitations of our minds when confronted with so great an undertaking as that of encompassing the whole of being in a comprehensive system of thought. We humbly confess to a basic agnosticism, the realization that in any absolute sense we do not know. Yet there are areas in which we are confident that our knowledge is valid. Those areas are growing in extent, and they point to the validity of our naturalistic interpretation of our world.

We behold a system of nature which is self-contained. It is of inconceivable vastness of extension in time and in space. It has its orderly processes which we seek to describe in what we call its laws. It is dynamic, ever changing, evolving; the process of creation is unending. There is in nature, also, destruction, decay, devolution, death.

We ourselves are children of nature, products of the process of evolution as it has gone forward on this particular planet in one of the minor solar systems of the universe. Its energies are pulsing in us. We are subject to its laws. In consequence of this there is a degree of determinism in our lives; they proceed in accord with the laws of cause and effect, the working out of vast forces over which we have little or no control. Yet at the same time, we have a very real freedom, born of our ability to understand and to choose. Within limits it is possible for us to set a purpose for ourselves, fashioning it out of the materials at our disposal, working with all available resources for its fulfillment. We are not mere puppets dangling on the strings of an inexorable fate; to a degree we are self-determining agents, and it is within our power to increase the degree to which this is true.

This is a truth which is of the utmost importance to the new religion which is developing to fortify man's morale and inspire him to high achievement as he moves on into the act of his continuing drama that now begins to unfold. At long last the process of evolution which as far as we can see is largely mechanical, or at most guided only by an unconscious, groping purpose, below man has come into consciousness in him and is able to set an intelligent purpose for itself. In us the universe has acquired eyes with which to look upon itself; in us it has risen to mind with which it begins to know itself; in us it has developed an agent through which it can attain to a degree of self-direction.

We are the custodians of evolution on this planet, and if the expectations of the space-travel enthusiasts are fulfilled, we may yet extend that custodianship to other parts of the universe, though we certainly have enough unfinished business to occupy us here at home! How tremendous is the concept that the evolutionary process has achieved the possibility of intelligent guidance in humanity. At first thought, it may horrify us by the magnitude of the responsibility which it thrusts upon us. We draw back even as the people of this nation are inclined to draw back from the obligations of world leadership that have been thrust upon us. But when we have had time to assimilate the idea, when we have come to feel at home with it, we shall discover in it a great source of inspiration and strength. It will give us an objective, a goal for our efforts, and in the light of that purpose, our lives will take on new meaning and dignity. We will know why we are here and where we are going; we will have the lift, the morale of partners in a mighty enterprise.

Oh, I know full well that there are those who decry this and proclaim it to be the sheerest moonshine. Worse, they denounce it as man's supreme sin, his setting himself up as God. These charges do not unduly perturb me; there are always the pessimists around to assert that something can't be done, that it is impossible; and then we have gone on to prove how mistaken they are. And as for the sin of man setting himself up as God, the accusation leaves me cold. After all, what we are proposing is not incompatible with a due humility on our part, for we know full well that though we have risen to a position of responsible leadership, it is only through the mighty surge of the creative process which has brought us here and which continues to sustain us that we shall accomplish our purpose.

The criticisms have this value, however; they admonish us to be realistic in our application of the grand conception that we are the cutting edge of the tool of evolution. It were just as fatal for us to indulge in rosy dreams of what man may become at some distant date to the neglect of the immediate task as it was for men in the age of disillusionment to postpone the achievement of the good life till another world. The conviction that we are the trustees of the process of evolution will be validated only as we harness its drive to the immediate task, only as we learn in its light to take the next difficult step ahead in the long path which lies before humanity.

I am not thinking now in terms of man transcending himself, becoming superman, a new species, though the scientists tell us that that is not impossible in a million years or so. I am taking the shorter view, thinking in terms of the immediate years and centuries that are ahead, thinking in terms of that fulfillment of the individual life which we saw last Sunday to be the central and supreme purpose of religion, thinking in terms of those conditions which must frustrate that fulfillment, war, poverty, disease, ignorance, the selfishness that knows not itself. It is in these areas that the next steps in our evolution must take place and it is only as we gird ourselves to the task of bringing all our resources, all our powers to bear on the solution of such practical problems that our philosophy of naturalism, our religion of fulfillment will prove its worth.

Not long since I was talking with a grand old man now well along in his 80s. In his young manhood he was a minister in an orthodox denomination. Then he began to come into contact with the idea of evolution and it worked a revolution in his thinking. That poem of William Herbert Carruth "Each in His Own Tongue" with its lines, "Some call it Evolution, And others call it God," was a milestone on his journey. He found himself moving steadily into that naturalistic philosophy which we have here been expounding, and devoted his mature years to sharing it with others.

Out of his long experience and his deep wisdom he said to me: "I do profoundly believe in man and what he shall yet make of himself. I do believe in this earth home of ours as the true setting for man's fulfillment. I do believe, despite all the evil of which I am poignantly aware, that man is fundamentally sound and that he is headed for a magnificent destiny." My heart spoke a fervent "amen!" to his faith, as he quoted the familiar lines of Markham:

> We men of earth have here the stuff
> Of Paradise . . . we have enough!
> Here on the paths of every day, --
> Here on the common human way
> Is all the stuff the gods would take
> To build a Heaven, to mould and make
> New Edens. Ours the stuff sublime
> To build Eternity in time!

Born of Love

It has often been remarked that men of genius frequently arrive by a flash of intuitive insight at some truth which is only tardily confirmed by our slow moving rational processes of thought. A conspicuous example of this is provided by Shakespeare in a line of his Sonnet 151 where we read, "Conscience is born of love." The great poet there anticipates a truth which has only recently been proclaimed by our contemporary science. We have been discovering that conscience is almost literally born of love.

This is an insight of the utmost consequence for conscience is for good and ill one of the most potent forces operating in the lives of men. Shakespeare has other passages descriptive of the way in which conscience functions. Listen to these lines from *Richard the Third*:

> My conscience hath a several thousand tongues,
> And every tongue brings in a several tale;
> And every tale condemns me for a villain!

Or again, presenting the opposite aspect, in *Henry the Eighth*:

> A peace above all earthly dignities,
> A still and quiet conscience.

We are informed by scholars that there is no language on earth which does not have its word signifying conscience; eloquent testimony to the universality of the still small voice speaking within the innermost depths of men, making the distinction for them between right and wrong, good and evil, bidding them choose the right and avoid the wrong, punishing them with its condemnation when they violate its commands, rewarding them with a sense of inner quiet and well being when they have obeyed. Small wonder that men have stood in awe of this inward monitor and that they have come to the conclusion that it is the voice of God speaking in the soul of man.

A further development of this same interpretation of conscience is to be found in the way men have attributed to deity the authorship of the moral codes by which they have endeavored to rule their societies. The familiar story of Moses receiving the ten commandments at the hand of God is a case in point. It dramatizes the feeling very widespread among men that the moral laws must have their origin in a supernatural source. This feeling has operated powerfully to enforce those laws.

But now it is recognized among informed persons that the story of Moses on Mt.Sinai is but folklore, a tale devised to account for rules already existing and functioning powerfully among men. The same is true of similar stories among other peoples. It is to the credit of our modern sciences dealing with these aspects of our experience that they have been able to penetrate behind the folklore and give us a convincing account of the true nature of the forces which have been thus dramatized. They have written a natural history of conscience, of morality. Let us look at some of the evidence on which their account is based.

The first area from which the evidence comes is that of history. One of the most fascinating and significant books I have ever read is *The Dawn of Conscience*, the work of James Breasted, who was head of the Oriental Institute of the University of Chicago. His special field was Egyptian history. He was one of the men who participated in the discovery and opening of the tomb of King Tutankhamen.

Dr. Breasted points out that by the time man emerges into the light of history he is already far advanced in his moral life. He has become consciously aware of the distinctions between right and wrong. He no longer acts simply in obedience to the prompting of the immemorial ways which had been established among his forebearers in the incredibly long period of pre-history. The roots of his moral life do go back into the habits and the standards which have been practiced for so many generations that they have become automatic, second nature, as we say. But when he appears on the stage of history he has already reached the point where he makes conscious distinctions between right and wrong, where he chooses between the two. Conscience is already established in him. May I remind you that the word conscience is derived from two words, con, meaning with, and science, meaning knowledge; conscience is "with knowledge."

Breasted informs us that the earliest Egyptian records we have go back to about 3400 B.C. That is something over 5000 years ago and is much the earliest of any records that have been preserved for us. In them the very words which are used indicate that the origin of conscience lies in the realm of the emotions. They do not speak of right and wrong, or good and bad -- which are reflective terms. They tell of "him who does what is loved; him who does what is hated." Is that not significant?

The conclusion at which our historian arrives from the study of these ancient texts is a confirmation of Shakespeare's insight that conscience is born of love. Let me quote Breasted: "I have been not a little surprised to note how unmistakably they (the Pyramid Texts) disclose the family as the primary influence in the rise and development of moral ideas." "They furnish us with conclusive historical evidence that moral discernment had its roots in the life of the family." In ancient Egypt the individual's claim to worthy character was based on his spirit and conduct in relation to his own family. One of these texts reads in his wise: "I was one beloved of his father, praised of his mother, whom his brothers and sisters loved." The most common virtue discernable is filial piety.

According to this account, our ancestors literally created conscience in a world where it did not exist. It was a social creation, born of the relations of human beings to one another in that most intimate and fundamental of all societies, the family. "He who does that which is loved; he who does that which is hated," tells the story. The historian goes on to tell, out of the material which the ancient texts provides, how the range of conscience was gradually extended to include the wider community until at length as the result of the work of social prophets the moral ideal came to be enthroned above the king himself. It is the voice of human experience speaking out of the wisdom distilled from the centuries as to what is necessary if society is to be stable, if men are to live harmoniously and fruitfully with one another.

Another historian came independently to the same conclusion. Thomas Hill Green wrote: "No individual can make a conscience for himself. He always needs a society to make it for him." The social nature of conscience is clearly established.

When we turn to the anthropologists we find them telling us the same thing. Their study of primitive peoples has taught them that such peoples have their conscience and that in every instance it coincides with the standards of the social group. The clan, the tribe, has certain "taboos," acts which are strictly prohibited. It has other acts which are just as surely enjoined on all of the members. These commandments and prohibitions have grown out of the long history of the people. Some of them are rational and have a genuine basis in reality. Others are irrational, superstitious. But all alike are binding on the members of the group and contribute to its solidarity, its survival. So long as the individual conforms, his conscience is easy. If he violates them, his peace of mind is destroyed and his social fate is sealed.

Most conclusive of all the evidence advanced in support of Shakespeare's insight that "conscience is born of love" is that which comes from the science of psychology and the related practice of psychiatry. By virtue of the process known as psychoanalysis, it has become possible to beat back up the stream of life of an individual, as it were, and to discover with considerable accuracy how his conscience was established in him, why it has the particular content that it does.

What is learned in this manner is summed up in Brock Chisholm's definition of conscience as "the rules parents inflicted on us when we were too young to resist." This is a bit barbed and does not do full justice to parents, so let us elaborate a bit. A little child is completely dependent on those around him, in particular on his parents. He normally responds to them with love and they to him with love. This love is very precious to the child, indispensable to his physical survival, his emotional and intellectual development.

Although it is in part a free gift, he quickly discovers that in part he must earn it. There are some things which if he does will cause the sunshine of that love to be withdrawn from him, hidden behind the dark clouds of wrath. There are other things which he does which increase the measure of the love that is bestowed upon him. Inevitably these experiences build up in him a code for his guidance in avoiding the things that are hated and doing the things that are loved -- to revert to the language of the ancient Egyptians. This code is no formal thing; it is not consciously adopted, but is the spontaneous outgrowth of his experiences. It is established in the deep places of his mind below the level of consciousness. This adds to its effectiveness; when it speaks to him it does so with the voice of command, almost as though it were issued by someone outside himself. This is why he has sometimes taken it, in his mature years, for the voice of God. Actually it is the voice of his parents admonishing him to do the thing that is loved, avoid that which is hated.

We must understand that while conscience begins in this way, it is subsequently modified to a considerable extent. As the child moves out into the larger society beyond the family he discovers that there, too, there are things which if he does he will win love, and other things which will bring hate.These do not always coincide with what he has learned at home and in consequence his conscience is to some degree altered. Also as he matures, he begins to form his own judgments as to what is right and wrong. These, again, may differ to some extent from the standards he acquired from his parents. But always the abiding core of his conscience remains that pattern of emotional response which he acquired as a child. He may obey or disobey, but always his conscience is there to approve or rebuke.

We must understand, also, that conscience is by no means an infallible guide, a perfect instrument for distinguishing between right and wrong. Sometimes the standards of the parents are at fault and the child learns to love the wrong things; his sense of values is distorted. Sometimes the child sadly misinterprets his experiences and gives too strong an emotional tone to certain of the commands. There is such a thing as a diseased conscience, one that is over-weening and makes impossible demands on the individual with disastrous results in his life, making of him a sick soul.

But by and large it is a wondrous thing, an indispensable instrument in the development of human life. I have described it, most inadequately, in terms of its natural origin. But let that not obscure from us the marvel of it; we have here another of our "natural" miracles. It is redolent of the mystery that is life; the mystery that is love. "Conscience is born of love."

Such a natural history of conscience enables us to understand some of its aspects which are not to be explained on the theory that it is of supernatural origin. Why, if conscience is the voice of God, does it not issue the same commands universally? Why is it that conscience says one thing in America, another in China? Why is it that in our own country, there is what we term a "New England Conscience," which is much more rigid than that which exists in some other parts of the land? Why is it that different segments of the same community have different moral standards? All these questions become readily answerable when bearing in mind the fact that in each instance conscience has developed against a different background, that in each instance, it bears in itself the marks of the soil out of which it is grown.

Here also we have the origin of the modern insistence that all moral rules are relative and that it is a mistake to try to deal in moral absolutes, to lay down rules that are supposedly good for all times and all peoples. This ignores the truth contained in Lowell's lines:

> New occasions teach new duties,
> Time makes ancient good uncouth.

Life is constantly on the march; conditions are forever changing. When we reflect that virtue is not an arbitrary thing, but socially desirable conduct, we can readily see that as conditions change that which at one time was advantageous becomes dangerous and threatens the very existence of society, if in each instance we decide what is right and what is wrong, in the light of the particular conditions which have raised the question instead of trying to apply blanket rules, although, of course, we need the help of those generalizations in which men try to summarize the results of experience.

The recognition of the relativity of moral judgments is disconcerting to many and they are inclined to deny it vehemently. They say, if we can't tell people with absolute assurance this is good and that is bad, the case is hopeless. They retort to the lines from Lowell with other lines from the same poet:

> In vain we call old notions fudge,
>   And bend our conscience to our dealing;
> The ten commandments will not budge,
>   And stealing will continue stealing.

Because of the crucial nature of the problem with which we are here dealing, I propose that we consider it in the light of a specific example. For the purpose I have selected the controversy which has arisen over the publication by Dr. Alfred Kinsey and his associates of their study of *Sexual Behavior in the Human Female,* and the interpretation of the facts presented in this study as they have been given by Dr. Kinsey in his address before the Neuropsychiatric Association.

You are aware of the veritable flood of comment, pro and con, which the book has produced. It has been roundly denounced by religious leaders, Catholic, Protestant, Jewish. They have admonished Dr. Kinsey that just because a considerable percentage of men and women acknowledge that they have acted contrary to our traditional standards of sex conduct, does not make their actions right. The commandment against adultery will not budge. One of our local judges was equally emphatic in his condemnation of the book, indicating that he is convinced that its net result would be to encourage teenagers to act like monkeys.

On the other hand, the book has been acclaimed as pioneering in a vastly important field and bringing us invaluable knowledge, which will promote understanding and tolerance. A distinguished woman psychiatrist who specializes in marriage counselling says she welcomes the book and its companion volume on *Sexual Behavior in the Human Male* as indispensable tools in her efforts to enable married couples who are experiencing difficulties in their relations to make a success of their marriage. Dr. Herman Shibler, our Superintendent of Schools, does not agree with the judge and says that the findings of the book will doubtless trickle down into college and high school courses on home and family living and "become of tremendous benefit to students in general."

May I give briefly my own reactions? I shall have to acknowledge that as yet I have not read the book -- only extensive reviews. I do own the earlier volume and have studied it carefully. There is no area of human conduct in which there is so much hypocrisy as that of sex relations; nowhere else is the gulf that yawns between professed standards and actual practice so great. The whole area is one which has been clouded over with secrecy, myth, fears and misapprehension. The net result has been a terrific amount of frustration, anxiety, tragedy.

Anything that can bring the light of knowledge into this darkness, anything that can help blow the fog away and help us to deal with the whole subject sanely, openly, is to be welcomed. Dr. Kinsey's books are an important contribution to this end. That there is some danger attendant upon their publication I am aware; there will be those who misuse its information. But that danger always attends the advance of knowledge. The advantages, I am persuaded, far outweigh the disadvantages. Nor do I hold with those who contend that such information should be kept as the province of a few specialists. It vitally effects all of us and all of us should have access to it.

It does not follow from this that the Kinsey productions are beyond criticism; that is not to be expected in such pioneering work. What appears to me as probably the most valid criticism is that which has been advanced by Dr. Karl Menninger, namely that the study tries to isolate sex too much, to deal with it as a single factor when actually it can be properly viewed only as an integral part of the total personality. The Kinsey studies do not adequately relate sex to love, and when it is thus separated it is abnormal. But even when we have given such criticisms their due weight, the balance is heavily on the side of the constructive value of the studies.

Here we are concerned with one of the most powerful forces operative in the lives of men; used aright it is the source of some of our deepest and most substantial satisfactions; perverted, misdirected, it brings some of the sharpest pains, the sheerest tragedy to which human beings are subjected. The minister of religion is keenly aware of both these aspects because he is brought into intimate contact with them. He above all men ought to know the need for fullness of understanding and the discipline and skill which can come in the wake of that understanding.

Out of my years of observation and experience, I have come to certain conclusions. The first is that while there is need for letting the light of knowledge into this area, it is essential at the same time that we retain a sense of delicacy and reticence in dealing with it. After all, it involves the most intimate and precious of human relations and reverence toward it is an indispensable ingredient if it is to be at its best.

The second is that sex must be channelized, disciplined to flow in certain directions. No high civilization is possible without such discipline. The figure of the gasoline engine may be used to convey the idea. The volatile power locked up in the gasoline may be exploded in the open, harmlessly or with the wreaking of destruction. Our engines constrain the explosion to take place in a chamber where it can be harnessed to do our work. The engine which we have devised to harness the energy of sex is the monogamous marriage. The lifelong devotion of one man and one woman to each other. Confining its activities in this wise its surplus of power does much of the work of the world.

The engine is by no means perfect; there is much friction within it; bearings burn out; frequently it ends up in the ditch. But for all this, the monogamous marriage represents a valid ideal. This is true negatively because of the heartache and suffering entailed to the individuals involved when it is not adhered to, the irreparable damage which is done to children when it breaks down. It is true positively because the fullest riches in the relations between man and woman can be achieved only where there is a mutual consecration each to the other, because a home created by such a pair provides the atmosphere most congenial to the maturing of children. After all, the monogamous marriage does represent the simplest, least complicated of relations, the one which when it does function properly, functions most effectively. It is an ideal worth striving for.

My third conclusion is that at this particular juncture in the history of our culture we are going through drastic changes and that ideal is being put to very severe tests. A variety of factors have contributed to this; the mobility of our population which has come with the automobile; the ready availability of contraceptives; the altered position of women; the serious questioning of the accepted standards of the past. Men and women and young people are groping, experimenting, questing, seeking a satisfactory answer to the problems which are thrust so poignantly upon them amid the unstable conditions of today. This is the basic reason why studies such as that of Dr. Kinsey are of fundamental importance.

What the outcome of this ferment is to be there is no way of knowing with any certainty. Hope bids me believe that as our knowledge grows, as we clarify our understanding of the consequences in our lives and the lives of others of the patterns we follow in these vital matters, and more importantly as we develop greater skill in the educational process by which our lives are shaped, the old ideal of the lifelong consecration of one man and one woman will reassert itself on a higher level demonstrating its superiority as a way of life.

However that may be, this I do know, that the present is a time which calls for the utmost understanding and charity toward those who are the unhappy victims of our present chaotic condition. No later than this past week I united in marriage a young couple, both of whom had been previously married and divorced. They came to me because other ministers refused to marry them. I consented to do so not because of any looseness in my attitude toward marriage, but because I feel that such young people should not be debarred from trying to rectify in a new marriage the mistakes which resulted in the breakdown of their earlier attempts. My heart goes out to them. There is tremendous need of that insight and compassion which led one of old to say: "Neither do I condemn thee; go and sin no more."

But I dwell too long on this particular controversy. After all, it is only incidental to our whole discussion and I think that by and large an undue importance is attached to some of the transgressions of our traditional sex standards as though adherence to them were the one and only requisite of a moral life. I have dwelt on it simply because it is vividly present to our minds and in considering it, the general principles which I am concerned to present do emerge. Let us return to those general principles.

The first of these is contained in our definition of virtue as conduct which is socially desirable in its consequences. That is, good which contributes to the development of mature, wholesome, socially oriented personalities, that which contributes to the strength, stability, and progress of society. It is often very hard for us to decide what conduct is of this nature and we need to avail ourselves of such guidance as is to be found in the distilled wisdom of the ages. On the whole, the major moral commandments at which the great religions have arrived are of this nature. They represent the most enduring portion of our religious heritage.

The Golden Rule of doing unto others as you would have them do unto you, the commandment to love your neighbor as yourself, to do justly and to love mercy, the requirements to respect the personalities of others, to treat them as ends in themselves, rather than as means to your own ends, the injunction to know the truth, the insight that love is the fulfillment of the law -- these and much besides, have stood the test of time and it is imperative that we possess ourselves of them.

But quite obviously, they are not in themselves enough; if they were we should long since have arrived at the millennium. Where they fail is in providing us with the answer as to how we can fulfill their requirements. It does not make a man a moral hero to be able to recite the ten commandments and the Sermon on the Mount. Somehow he has to acquire the incentive, the motivation, the skill which shall enable him to put those moral principles into practice.

An illuminating example of this was provided in an experiment conducted a few years ago under the direction of a professor at the University of Michigan. It was decided to test certain groups of junior high school students for honesty; this was not a test of profession, but of practice. After the test, they were given an intensive training, using the best material available on the importance of honesty as a quality of character. Then they were again tested for honesty. The result was that all the groups turned out to be slightly more deceptive after they had had the training than they were before.

Must we then give up in despair? By no means! The significance of that experiment lies in the fact that it points out we have been relying too much on verbal instruction, on confronting people with splendid ideals. We shall have to learn to cut deeper. It is here that the insight that conscience is born of love is of such tremendous import. It points to the social nature of morality; it means that if we want our young people to be honest we shall have to build that quality into their lives by rearing them in homes where honesty is loved and dishonesty hated; we shall have to see to it that the larger society in which they move is likewise one which takes honesty for granted. We can build the desired qualities into the souls of men. It is an arduous task and we are only at the beginning. Man is still morally a child, but when we see him at his best, we know what he may yet become. At long last, we are acquiring the insights and the skills which shall help him come morally of age.

I need scarcely add, in conclusion, that the measure in which we succeed in doing this, is the measure in which we fulfill the purpose of religion, which is to minister life more abundant to men. Earth knows nothing so splendid as a human character shaped in the white light of sane ideals. There is a biblical phrase which captures the essence of the matter; it speaks of "The Beauty of Holiness." How better could we express the aesthetic demand of our hearts for that moral grandeur which is the finest flower of human nature, the beauty of the soul that has ascended by the way of personal affection for man to those sublime heights where it is wholly dedicated to the right and yet has mellowed with divine compassion, "The beauty of holiness."

The Furnace of Adversity

"Gold is tried in the fire, and
Acceptable men in the furnace of adversity."

In one of the previous addresses of this series, we said that the problem of evil is the rock on which theologies are wrecked, that it is impossible adequately to reconcile the existence of evil with the traditional conception of a loving Heavenly Father who cares for all his children and directs all things for their good. In order to resolve the difficulty men have denied the existence of evil, insisting that it is only seeming; they have said that God is using evil for the accomplishment of his purposes which are hidden from the sight of men; they have attributed it to an Adversary of God, the Evil One. But none of these attempted explanations is satisfactory. Evil remains evil in our experience.

Yet here is an aspect of existence with which we must come to grips, against which we must have some defense. This is a hard, hard world. Life is a perpetual battle against forces which threaten to overwhelm it. The blizzards of winter sweep down to take their dreadful toll; the blazing sun of summer scorches and burns; flood and wave and wind destroy in blind fury. Life feeds upon life; countless organisms are on the alert to thrive at our expense just as we prosper at the cost of countless others. "Man's inhumanity to man makes countless thousands mourn." Within the body of humanity war and ignorance and poverty lay their destructive taxes upon us. Friend betrays friend; we betray ourselves, choosing the low in preference to the high. Time takes its inevitable toll; finally the gulf of death receives us all alike.

We must have some spiritual fortress to protect us against the attacks of all this. Particularly at this present juncture of the world's history is this necessary, for the onslaught of the forces which threaten to overwhelm us is driving to a crescendo of intensity. Revolutionary forces have been unleashed round the globe; war, rebellion, social chaos are present in unprecedented degree. Many ancient safeguards have crumbled; multitudes find themselves disillusioned, cynical, without any sense of meaning and destiny in their lives. This is one of the most difficult eras in all the long saga of the human pilgrimage.

Under these circumstances, it is entirely natural that many should turn again to the time honored ways of softening the impact of the forces that beat upon them, that they should sing with renewed zeal, "A mighty fortress is our God, a bulwark never failing." The avidity with which multitudes are reading religious literature these days, particularly the kind which promises peace of mind, a way in which to satisfy the hunger of the heart for success, for power, for love, a way of escape from the clamor of the world that is too much with us, is a sure sign of the times. "Back to religion, back to God" is the cry.

One may have a full understanding of and a deep sympathy for the needs which have produced this reaction and still be convinced that it is a mistaken way to try to solve the problem. One may know that while the traditional answer is no longer intellectually tenable, it is still emotionally satisfying for those who can accept it, and yet question its value. Sometimes it seems to me that none of us have a right to peace of mind today, unless it be in a far deeper sense than is usually meant. Our world is in desperate straits; it needs the services of everyone of us even as the ship in a hurricane tossed sea requires the services of every member of the crew. This is no time for us to be absorbed in our individual peace of mind, our personal happiness and success, except insofar as that may be necessary to sustain us in pouring our energies into the common human cause. This is a time for us to forget ourselves in something bigger than we are, forget ourselves in action intelligently directed to the requirements of the world crisis in which we find ourselves, sustained by an ultimate confidence that the ship is sound, the crew equal to the emergency, and that we shall eventually emerge into quieter waters.

How, then, from the point of view of that naturalistic religion which we are here developing, are we to cope with the evils that we experience?

The first thing to note is that from this point of view evil ceases to be a theoretical problem for which we must find a solution and becomes simply a condition to be met as practically as we can. This is important; let us drive the point home.

If you do not start out with the assumption that the world is under the providence of a creator God who is responsible for everything which happens, but rather accept the fact that the universe is a self existent order which is evolving, developing in accordance with the play of its inherent forces, then evil is seen to be incidental to this process. Evil is relative to the individual who experiences it. It was not intended by some cosmic intelligence to accomplish an inscrutable purpose; it was not the work of some demonic power at odds with God. No, that which we call evil is that which affects us unfavorably, it is the product of forces which, for the most part, do not know our distinction between good and evil, but are amoral, producing their results blindly, unconsciously. This is what I mean when I say evil is not a theological problem to be solved but a practical situation to be met.

Some years ago, a man sought me out in my study and told me his tale of woe; a sorry tale it was indeed, rivaling that of Job himself. After he had detailed the tragedies he had suffered, the pain he had experienced, he exclaimed, "What have I done that God is punishing me in this fashion!" It seemed to me, as I sought to explain to him, that in addition to his very real burdens of sorrow, failure, disease, he was also carrying an entirely unreal and unnecessary burden in his sense of guilt, in his feeling that he was being punished for sins of which he was unaware. I did not succeed in relieving him of his obsession; it was too deeply ingrained to yield readily. But there was dramatized in him the Old Man of the Sea who has fastened himself on the back of humanity to his great detriment.

Do not misunderstand me. I know full well that we must ourselves accept the responsibility for many of the evils which befall us. They are the consequences of our own misdeeds, conscious and unconscious. But that is true of only part of them. There are many times in which we are the innocent victims of circumstances. You have only to remind yourself of those whose lives are crushed out in an earthquake or other such natural disaster, or the children who succumb to the invasion of polio to know that such is the case. It only hampers our effectiveness in dealing with evil when we fail to make this distinction.

What is required of us is not that we resolve a riddle, but that we look the evils of the world squarely in the face, determining as exactly as possible in each instance the nature of the evil and setting ourselves to the task of producing the appropriate remedy. To aid us in this process I propose that we consider briefly certain specific evils and the resources we have with which to combat them.

A large category of these evils is those which are inflicted on man by the processes of nature. Obviously they are not intended; they just happen. The recent drought which has severely affected large sections of our country with the resulting starvation of many cattle, the failure of crops, the economic ruin of farmers and cattlemen will serve as an example. Perhaps unsound agricultural practices had contributed to the disaster. If so, they need to be corrected and a long range program established to minimize the danger of a recurrence. But we know that in large measure the drought was the product of weather conditions over which we have little control. We have sought to alleviate the situation by rushing fodder from more favored regions to the stricken area. We know that the economic plight of the farmers is in considerable degree due to weaknesses in our overall economic system. There again we are seeking to minimize the loss by enabling them to draw on the resources of the whole country.

This entire situation and our response to it is symbolic of that human providence we are seeking to establish which shall operate to prevent, as far as possible, the evils which the unwitting forces of nature bring to man, and to alleviate the ills which we cannot avoid. There are many directions in which we are building up this human providence. Preventive and curative medicine is perhaps the most conspicuous single example of the way in which we marshall the resources of humanity to do battle with the enemies of the values that we cherish. It does not yet appear how far we can carry this effort to master the natural order around us for our own benefit. Obviously the opportunities are legion and we shall doubtless carry the measure of our victory much further than we can now envision. Here is a practical rather than a theoretical answer to the problem of evil.

Is there a limit to which we can carry this victory, a last enemy, death, that will not yield to our best endeavors? This is a crucial question for which religion in this third act of the continuing drama must have an adequate answer. You will remember that in the second act, religion was largely centered on another world beyond this present one in which men shall be compensated for all that they have to endure here. That is one of the attempted solutions of the problem of evil. It has never seemed valid to me, but rather to dodge the answer by putting it in an inaccessible realm. In a religion which takes as its motto, "One World at a Time!" and concentrates on making life here and now as satisfying as possible, is that answer excluded? Must we give a negative reply to the persistent question, "If a man die shall he live again?"

Let it be fully understood that I approach this question with all the sympathy and understanding born of the fact that over the years I have been called upon upwards of 1000 times to conduct the last rites over the dead, including members of my own family. Thus I have experienced the full impact of the grief, the yearning desire, the devastating frustration that ofttimes accompany it. I can understand the man who exclaimed, "If the individual is destroyed, the universe is a fake! I can understand the woman who wept bitterly because she wanted to believe that she would be reunited with her beloved child who had died, and she could not.

I know that belief is born of the demands of the heart, that it is a product of the urge of the life within us that will not be denied, that it is a response to the eagerness to carry on the adventure of life. I have a friend who is a scientist. He cries out: "I have to be immortal! I have started experiments which cannot be concluded for thousands of years, I must go on and know how they come out." Yes, I understand and I sympathize, but I am not convinced.

After all here is a matter of fact, and that cannot be decided on the basis of desire which ofttimes leads us astray. Socrates long ago confronted us with the alternatives when he said that either death is a sleep in which eternity is a single night, or it is a journey to another world where all the dead are. Then he acknowledged that we do not know which it is. Socrates inclined to the side of hope that it was the second alternative, but he was wise enough to know that there is no conclusive evidence.

We have not progressed beyond Socrates; we do not know. Have you not observed that often even those who profess the most certain faith in immortality are actually not as confident as they make out, else they would not be so disturbed when someone calls their faith in question. We don't get mad when someone announces that two plus two makes five; we laugh. Frederick Myers tells of a church warden whom he pressed for an answer to the question as to what he thought would happen to him after his death. Finally the man blurted out: "I suppose I shall enter into everlasting bliss, but I wish you wouldn't talk about such depressing subjects."

I have often wondered why it is that men of equal intelligence and equal integrity come to opposite conclusions in this matter. Is it a matter of temperament? I have recently reread an article written by Thomas Edison in his late years. Earlier he had denied the possibility of immortality, but in this article he wrote: "If there is any evidence of one side or the other, worthy of consideration by the scientific mind, it is in favor of the theory of immortality." And then within the week I came upon this statement by philosopher Will Durant: "I suspect that when I die I shall be dead. I would look upon endless existence as a curse. Death is life's greatest invention, perpetually replacing the worn with the new." There you have it; the truth of the matter is we don't know.

I have never observed that there is much difference in moral quality between believers and non-believers, not much difference in the courage with which they confront death in their own persons, the fortitude with which they bear the loss of their loved ones. If anything, in my experience, the advantage has been on the side of the skeptics. I do not generalize, however, because I am aware how limited my experience is.

What I have in mind is illustrated by an incident in the life of one of the noblest men it has ever been my privilege to know. He was a man of great distinction in his profession as an electrical engineer. A splendid daughter died in giving birth to a child. This man told me that his minister came to him in his grief offering him the conventional comfort, assuring him that his daughter yet lived and that he would be reunited with her in the world beyond. It left him cold because he simply could not believe.

Then he said he had reason to suspect that his daughter's death had been caused by inadequate facilities and care in the hospital where her baby had been born. He launched an investigation and despite vigorous opposition did not desist until the conditions were remedied. He harnessed his grief to a work which needed to be done, and found consolation in his sorrow in the thought that he had made his own tragedy the incentive for preventing a like calamity overtaking other families.

My own attitude is that of the agnostic who inclines to doubt. I do not close the door on the possibility of continued existence because I know full well that there are more things in heaven and earth than are dreamt of in my philosophy. But I have examined the arguments for immortality and they are unconvincing to my mind. I have reviewed the alleged evidence advanced in the field of psychic phenomena and find it very dubious. More weighty, on the negative side, is our growing knowledge of the inseparable relation between what we term the "spiritual" and the physical. As Sir Arthur Keith has put it, "The leading neurologists of the world are agreed that the brain is not a tenement inhabited by a spirit or a soul. The 'Spirit' or 'Soul' is but a name for the manifestation of the living brain. It was only when they abandoned the dual conception that they began to understand the disorders of man's minds and how to treat them. Modern science thus strikes at the very root of the Christian doctrine -- there can be no resurrection of the dead. Man has the seeds of immortality in him but the gift is for the race not for the individual."

Equally devastating is the analysis of the psychologists of the way in which the belief in life beyond the grave has been arrived at and how it is maintained. They hold that it is a very ancient error, born of a mistaken interpretation of the significance of certain natural phenomena of the mind and that it is perpetuated by the will to believe. The wish is the father of the thought. It is significant that James Leuba in an investigation of the religious beliefs of scientists a few years ago found that there were only three among the fifty leading psychologists who believe in the immortality of the soul. Such men do accept the biological immortality which we have in our children, the social immortality which comes from the fact that our lives are built, for good and for ill, into the ongoing structure of humanity, the immortality of influence so nobly sung in George Eliot's poem "The Choir Invisible." But it does not seem possible to them that the individual person survives the event of death.

It is, of course, possible that they may be mistaken. Scientists have been on numerous occasions. Perhaps I am misled in accepting their conclusions. If so, think of the delightful surprise I am in for when I wake up from that sleep which we call death and find myself immortal. Perhaps the adjective "delightful" is premature and the character of the surprise will depend on the destination at which I arrive. Some of my fellow ministers can tell you emphatically what that destination is to be.

I have never discovered that life loses any of its zest because I do not believe that it is to go on forever, any more than today is not worth living unless I can have the assurance that I will still be living five years hence. Indeed, I have sometimes felt that life gains in significance as importance is wrested from death. Let us do the best we can and leave any possible future to take care of itself. He who has been worthy of life need have no fear of death.

It is not being dead that is evil, for we will not know anything about it. It is the process of dying, the illness, the long drawn out suffering, the burden imposed on others. It is not death that is evil -- it is never to have lived in any full and adequate sense, to have been despoiled of life's opportunities and zest by untoward circumstances.

As medical science advances in its mastery of disease and pain, as we order the life of the world more successfully so that fewer go to the grave without ever having lived, the terrors of death fade. A life that has run its full course, has shared richly in the values of the earth, and then sinks naturally to its end, seems to us appropriate and beautiful. Here we have no sense of tragedy, but only the longed for repose of a life that draws to its close. "The day has been long, the road weary, and we gladly stop at the inn."

But we dwell too long on this portion of our subject. After all, there are many things which are worse than death. They are for the most part those which have in them the poison which comes from the fact that they are inflicted on us by our fellows, products of "man's inhumanity to man." Of this order are war, persecution, exploitation, all of the social diseases from which the body of humanity suffers. These are evil, but not beyond our power to cure; they must be socially resolved. Of this we shall have more to say later.

Among the most poignant of the ills from which we suffer are those which are inflicted on us in our most intimate relations with others and what as our greatest joy turns to gall and wormwood. A friend betrays the confidence we reposed in him and we suffer anguish which seems well-nigh intolerable. One we have loved rejects us or turns out to be unworthy and a numbing pain creeps over us, despoiling our days, torturing our nights. How shall we find surcease from our misery; how shall we regain our health of mind? There is no magic potion to do this for us, but we are not without our resources.

The first of these is in other human beings. As a little child when he has been hurt runs to mother for sympathy and help and finds quick relief, so we, on a different level, can turn to friends of insight and understanding. We have a saying that a sorrow shared is a sorrow halved. There is much truth in it. There is no strait so desperate that it does not help to have a friend who can make us know that we are not alone. It may be hard for us to bare our secret sorrow; we may feel that it is a confession to a weakness of which we are ashamed. But none of us is sufficient unto himself; all of us have our times when a hand slipped quietly into ours in understanding and encouragement is an indispensable fortification of our morale.

Sometimes the wound we have received is so grievous, the ill so deep seated, that our condition is beyond the power of a friend, even though he be ever so loyal and understanding, to be of much assistance. Then we need to avail ourselves of the services of one who has acquired special knowledge, exceptional skill in ministering to just such conditions. Fortunately we are beginning to produce these specialists, counselors, social workers with psychiatric training, ministers of religion oriented particularly to this service, and supremely the psychologists and psychiatrists who are pushing forward our knowledge and developing the essential skills for meeting these most urgent needs. Their numbers are yet small, their science still in its early stages. But already they have accomplished much and the promise for the future is encouraging.

Yet we must not expect too much of these specialists; they are not miracle workers. They can accomplish their results only with our cooperation; ofttimes their services are not available to us and we must be our own physicians, using such resources as are at our command. These are by no means negligible. Not long since a man told me the story of his darkest hour. He was in a foreign land, far from any friends, when he received word that the woman he was engaged to marry had rejected him for someone else. It was a staggering blow; at first he thought he could not endure it and was close to suicide.

Then he rallied his forces. He said to himself, two objects cannot occupy the same space at the same time. Perhaps that is also true in the mind and I can crowd this everlasting going over and over the same story out of my mind by concentrating on something else. He went out and bought a book and forced himself to read it, paying close attention to its thought. This was not easy; again and again he found his mind slipping away from the pages before him back into the emotional chasm that threatened to engulf him. He had deliberately to wrench himself round to his resolve. He persisted and in this manner was able to surmount his crisis.

There is a suggestion in this experience for all of us. When the woes of life overtake us, we need to remember that all about us there are resources which will take us out of ourselves if we will but avail ourselves of them. It may require a heroic effort on our part, but it is worth it. The whole realm of art is at our command; some will find surcease from their pain in music; others in the great works of imaginative literature which can relieve our tensions for a time and enable us to return refreshed to the struggle. We can subject ourselves to the calming influence of some majestic aspect of nature in the presence of which our personal problems shrivel to their true proportions. We can avail ourselves of the catharsis of humor, particularly learning to laugh at ourselves.

Actually the resource we have within ourselves for coping with the hardships, the evils of our lot, are far greater than we normally realize, or utilize. This is dramatized for us in such heroic tales as that recently published under the title "The Man Who Wouldn't Talk." It is the story of a British undercover man operating in France during the German occupation in the Second World War. He was disciplined to his part, inured to hardship and suffering so that not all the incredible horror of the torture inflicted on him by the Gestapo sufficed to break him and make him talk.

All of us need to cultivate in ourselves something of the Stoic, something of the spirit of the grand old Roman, Marcus Aurelius, who admonished himself to become as the promontory about which the proud waves are stilled and quieted. There is much evil in life which can be mastered only by enduring it. The potentialities for such endurance are in all of us; we were bred in a tough school. The fiber of generations that had to endure in order to survive is in us; it is for us to develop those potentialities.

More than endurance, however, is required if we are to exemplify the full reaches of our philosophy that evil is not a theoretical problem to be solved, but a practical situation to be met. "Acceptable men are tried in the furnace of adversity." The implication of that statement is that it is within our power to make of the ills of our lot, the sorrows which inflict us, the tragedies we experience, a fire which purges away our dross and from which we emerge purified and strengthened. The subtle alchemy of the human spirit is so potent that it can transmute the evil which comes to it into the means of an otherwise impossible good. We can grow in the understanding heart because of our own sorrows; we can increase in wisdom because of our failures; we can rise refreshed and strengthened from our defeats. Here we truly exercise the creative power that is in us.

There is inspiration to this end in the career of Beethoven, who has been called the grandest and best friend of those who suffer and struggle. His lot was tragic beyond that of most, yet he was able to master his tragedy and make it the means of his greatness. "Sorrow personified, to whom the world refused joy, created joy himself to give to the world. He forged it from his own misery . . . and indeed it was the motto of his whole heroic soul: joy through suffering." (Romain Rolland) He used to go to a mother in grief, and, without uttering a word, console her with his music which was born of his own suffering and his mastery of it in the innermost recesses of his soul. How magnificently he ministered to the world by that transmutation.

To rise to these heights is not easy; we do it hardly, if at all. But ours is not a religion of ease and compensation; it does not draw a soft veil of illusion over the harsh aspects of life. It asks hard things of men, confident that they can respond. It seeks to strengthen the sinews of the soul to the point where it can stand this world of ours and even use its malign aspects to rise superior to the forces which would crush it.

During the past week, one of Indiana's most distinguished scientists stopped in at my study for a visit on his way to the annual meetings of the Academy of Sciences at Richmond. It chances that we were boyhood friends, and we fell to discussing a mutual acquaintance who has recently suffered the loss of a beloved grandchild. My friend expressed surprise that this man is so badly broken up by this death, for, he said, that is the kind of thing a mature man takes in his stride. He was not callous, for he is a man of sensitivity. He was speaking out of his own maturity.

The attitude he expressed spontaneously coincides with that which the religion upon which mankind is now entering seeks to establish. It demands that we become mature, intellectually, emotionally, morally; that we stand on our own feet, not kept erect by others; that we face the realities of life and master them in the might of our own spirits. It is ready to help when we are stricken and laid low, but only that it may return us as quickly and fully as possible to manhood's posture. It lays high commands upon us, but when did ever men and women worthy the name refuse to respond to such a summons?

There is a magnificent apostrophe to man in the work of Norwegian writer Johan Bojer which is conceived in the spirit of this religion. I cannot do better in conclusion than to share it with you:

> Even the happiest must die. In his own home he is but on a visit. He never knows but that he may be gone tomorrow. And yet man smiles and laughs in the face of his tragic fate. In the midst of his thraldom he has created the beautiful on earth; in the midst of his torments he has had so much energy of soul that he has sent it radiating into the cold depths of space and warmed them with God. "Honor to thee, O spirit of man. Thou givest a soul to the world, thou settest it a goal, thou art the hymn that lifts it into harmony; therefore turn back into thyself, lift high thy head and meet proudly the evil that comes to thee. Adversity can crush thee, death can blot thee out, yet art thou still unconquerable and eternal."

Of One Blood

"God hath made of one blood all nations of men." This sentence from Paul's famous speech to the Athenians will serve us well as a starting point for the vastly important question with which we are to deal this morning. It came to my mind last summer as I read the accounts of the unhappy squabble which marred the conquest of Mt. Everest.

You will recall that during the period of the festivities leading up to the coronation of Queen Elizabeth, one of the presents made her Majesty was the success of the expedition under the leadership of the Australian, Hilary, who, with the native guide Tenzing, were the first men to scale this highest mountain peak on earth and return to tell the tale. Then in the midst of the universal rejoicing over this well-nigh incredible feat of human courage, stamina and ingenuity, there broke out a fierce controversy over the question as to who was chiefly responsible for the victory.

Tenzing's compatriots claimed that the credit should go to this seasoned native guide, that he was actually the first man to reach the top and had had to pull Hilary up the last difficult height. Fuel was fed the fire by a tactless remark on the part of one of the British leaders of the expedition who minimized the value of Tenzing's contribution. The principals themselves denied that it was possible to apportion the credit, that it had been a cooperative achievement and each was indispensable to the other.

The incident itself might seem trivial were it not for the fact that it is an indication of the volcanic fires which are seething in our world, flaring up at innumerable points and constantly threatening to explode with destructive violence. They are the fires engendered of racial antagonisms and hatreds, of racial exploitations and assumptions of superiority. In this particular instance it is possible that the fires were stirred up by Communists who are quick to avail themselves of such tensions for their own purposes, but they could not succeed were not the cauldron boiling fiercely.

In these conditions which are today planetwide we have one of the most formidable obstacles to the progress of that religion of fulfillment toward which humanity has set its face. We cannot achieve the good life in a good world so long as the body of humanity is rent with these fierce hatreds. There are, of course, other antagonisms which contribute to our frustration and we shall deal with some of them in due course. But none of them is more basic than the racial conflicts to which we shall confine our attention this morning.

The historic religions at their best have long since laid upon men the commandment of brotherly love unlimited by race or creed, universal in its scope. The genius of the great religious founders has given them sure insight into the underlying unity of all men. We find Confucius in China in the 6th century B.C. saying: "The good man loves all men. He loves to speak of the good of others. All within the four seas are his brothers. Love of man is chief of all the virtues. The mean man sows that himself and his friends may reap; the love of the perfect man is universal."

In India at the same time, Buddha was saying: "Let boundless love, as of a mother for her only child, be spread abroad among all men." Within the Jewish-Christian tradition the same recognition of universal brotherhood was achieved. It came to expression in the outpourings of the remarkable poet whose lines are embedded in the book of Isaiah. He proclaims that what God desires is the salvation of the whole world and that Israel is the chosen people only in the sense that it has the unique privilege of being a spear point in implementing the forces of justice, compassion, and holiness, thereby redeeming the world.

Jesus was heir to this universalism, though he seems only gradually to have entered into it. At the outset of his mission he felt that it was only to his own people, the Jews; but as he progressed he broadened his conception of the Kingdom of God to include all peoples. One of the most important points of his parable of the Good Samaritan is that the hero of the story is a member of a race which the Jews hated and with which they would have no dealings. Paul was called the Apostle to the Gentiles because he deliberately broke with the narrower views of some of the early followers of Jesus so that he might carry the message to the larger, non-Jewish world. His recognition of the universal brotherhood of man is expressed in the words of our text: "God hath made of one blood all the nations of men."

Even Islam, which we of the west usually think of as fanatical in its attitude toward all outsiders, proclaims in the Koran: "Mankind was but one people." It is true that the Muslims have for the most part been bitterly hostile to those who did not share their own faith. But within the circle of that faith they have transcended the usual racial antagonisms. This has given them a decided advantage over Christianity, for example, in reaching the peoples of Africa with their gospel.

But while we recognize that religion at its best, as it was represented in Mahatma Gandhi, has insisted that men of all races are brothers and should be treated accordingly, we are constrained to recognize that the followers of the major historic religions have seldom risen to that best. On the contrary, they have often fostered racial antagonism. For all the fine words of Confucius many of his devotees have looked upon all outsiders as barbarians, to be despised. We know full well that a large portion of the Old Testament breathes a bitter spirit of hostility toward all other peoples.

There is no more tragic chapter in the history of Christianity than that which tells of the persecution of the Jews. A Catholic scholar has recently published an account of anti-Semitism within Christianity. He does not spare his own church. Sorry reading it makes, this story of how in the name of the gentle Jesus, the officials of the church which he is alleged to have founded, have deliberately fostered the most cruel persecution of the very people from whom their founder was sprung. Ghettos, pogroms, genocide! What an incredibly terrible fate has been that of the Jews at the hands of Christians. The Catholics are not the only ones who have been guilty, nor is anti-Semitism by any means entirely a thing of the past. It continues to raise its ugly head among us even in enlightened circles where you would least expect it.

How about it? Is the insight of religion at what we have called its best a valid one? Is it true that all men are brothers and that we can achieve satisfying relations with other men, men of all races, only as we conform our attitudes and our actions to that truth, only as we include them within the circle of our good-will and love? Or is this mere sentimentalism, the vagary of a few idealists and dreamers, not true to the facts and undesirable in practice? There are plenty to reply that such is the case. Some years ago when William Howard Taft was the Governor of the Philippine Islands, he spoke of the inhabitants as our little brown brothers. To which an American publicist responded: "He may be a brother to big Bill Taft, but he ain't no brother of mine." That represents the attitude of multitudes.

But something exciting is happening in our world, namely science is confirming the validity of the insight of the religious seers, discovering that truth is on the side of the dreamers and idealists who have been proclaiming the universal brotherhood of man. I trust that all of you are acquainted with the pronouncement on this subject issued by UNESCO on July 18, 1950. Aware of the gravity of the issues involved, this organ of the United Nations set up a committee of experts on race problems. Eight distinguished scientists in the field of anthropology, drawn from such diverse areas as India, New Zealand, Brazil, France, the United States, cooperated in the preparation of a statement embodying the main conclusions of their science. This was then submitted to a further list of distinguished scientists in related fields -- biology, genetics, sociology, etc. After further revisions, the conclusions were finally released by the original committee. It is as authoritative a statement as the scientists are able to produce at this stage of our knowledge.

Let me give a condensed version of those articles which are most pertinent to our present purpose. The documents begins with the statement that "Scientists have reached general agreement in recognizing that mankind is one." It goes on to say that all men are probably derived from the same common stock. Such differences as exist between the different groups of mankind are due to the operation of evolutionary factors of differentiation, such as isolation. In other words, we all have essentially the same heritage and the differences between us are due to the particular history of the group to which we belong.

There are hereditary differences between the different groups of mankind, but they are minor; the likenesses among men are much greater than their differences. The evidence indicates that the range of mental capacities in all the different groups is much the same, that in character and personality all of the groups are equally rich. "The one trait which above all others has been at a premium in the evolution of man's mental character has been educability, plasticity. This is a trait which all human beings possess."

These anthropologists propose that we shall eliminate the word "race" from our vocabulary because the unscientific views which have produced the "myth" of race have done an enormous amount of damage, human and social, and that they still prevent the normal development of millions of men and women, still deprive civilization of the effective cooperation of productive minds. "The unity of mankind from the biological and social viewpoints is the main thing. To recognize this and act accordingly is the first requirement of modern man."

They state that the mixture of ethnic groups, the phrase they would substitute for "race," has been going on from earliest times. "There is no evidence it produces biologically bad effects." There is no biological justification for the prohibition of intermarriage. They do not mean by this necessarily to give the green light to intermarriage, because even though there may be no biological justification for prohibiting it, there are many times social reasons which may make it highly undesirable.

The document concludes with the pronouncement that "biological studies lend support to the ethic of universal brotherhood; for man is born with drives toward cooperation, and unless these drives are satisfied, men and nations alike fall. Man is born a social being who can reach his fullest development only through interaction with his fellows. The denial at any point of this social bond between man and man brings with it disintegration. In this sense, every man is his brother's keeper. For every man is a piece of the continent, a part of the main, because he is involved in mankind."

Do you feel the terrific impact of this declaration? Here are the words, not of visionary sentimentalists, but of scientists disciplined to deal with the facts and to arrive at objective conclusions from those facts; here are men whose supreme loyalty is to the truth. In the light of their dictum what becomes of our prejudices of race and clan? They are seen to be what they are, errors, "myths," the products of our ignorance, our narrowness, our hostilities, our fears; perhaps inevitable products of our history, but nonetheless, to be outgrown, transcended, left behind us. What a mighty reinforcement the conclusions of the scientists give to the religious doctrine of the brotherhood of man. That doctrine is now seen more clearly than before to be in conformity with the deepest strain of our common humanity. What a powerful stimulus is here to the hope that we may yet indeed "Make way for brotherhood, make way for man!"

Yet sober second thought makes us realize that despite the prestige of the scientists today, such a declaration on their part is not going to resolve our problems. The truths they are enunciating have long been known to many men; they have been embodied in great religious systems. They have not been entirely impotent; they have won some measure of acceptance, produced some degree of conformity with their requirements. Yet, on the whole, how ineffective they have been. How much more is needed before we can even begin to approximate the ideal which the seers of religion have envisioned in that term brotherhood.

In my youth, there was a cartoon which attained wide popularity. It portrayed two small boys who had been fighting and were separated by a kindly lady. She inquired why they were fighting and back came the response: "Cause we're brothers!" There you have it; the fact of brotherhood does not eliminate strife and produce cooperation. It may even intensify the hostility. The question of how we can implement the drives toward cooperation, which the anthropologists assure us are present in men, is crucial.

What are we to do, for example, when we are confronted with a situation like that which obtains in South Africa at the present time? The conditions so poignantly portrayed in Alan Paton's *Cry the Beloved Country* has been further aggravated by the triumph of the reactionary forces under the leadership of Premier Malan. The result is that we have there one of the vicious caste systems based on color, one of the most potentially explosive areas of the entire globe. And all this has been done in the name of religion, for the Premier is a devout churchman!

One of the tragic aspects of what has happened in South Africa is that a few years ago, under the enlightened leadership of Premier Jan Smuts, genuine progress was made in the area of race relations. A sociological study had been made of the problems involved, an educational campaign carried on resulting in considerable improvement. Now that has been wiped out, the color lines sharpened, the injustices deepened, and strenuous efforts are being made to fix this pattern permanently on the land. It is disheartening. Yet if the anthropologists are right, as I am convinced they are, the deep lying drives toward brotherhood will not be denied. Their triumph may be delayed, the cost of correction sharply raised, but the awakening forces in the submerged peoples of earth will push relentlessly on until these problems are solved on the level of justice and humanity.

What is happening in South Africa is but a particularly nasty instance of what is taking place in various guises in all parts of the globe. Indeed we do not have to travel to distant lands in order to find the problem in acute form; it is in our own midst. Part of my early boyhood was spent in Alton, Illinois, where there is a monument to the abolitionist martyr, Lovejoy. One of the most vivid recollections of those years is that of a battle royal between Negroes and whites which was precipitated by a fight between one of my playmates and a Negro boy. If it had been a white boy who had licked my companion, the father would not have interfered, wielding a baseball bat, as he did. That early experience, which is seared on my memory, has doubtless contributed to my sensitivity to the racial antagonisms which appear in so many forms in our American scene.

Shortly after I came to Indianapolis, one of the businessmen of our city told me that he realized that had he been living at the time of the Civil War, his sympathies would have been with the South, for he regards the Negroes as an inferior race who need to be kept in their place by the use of force if need be. Only this past summer a group of the members of this church on their way to our conference in Wisconsin were denied service in a restaurant in Kankakee, Illinois, because one of their number was a Negro. Are your sympathies keen enough so that you can feel what it must mean to a sensitive person to be thus rejected, not because of anything for which he is personally responsible, not because of any individual viciousness, but simply because of the ethnic group into which he happens to be born?

If we are to eliminate such incidents, if we are to correct the attitudes out of which they spring we must understand why it is that people react as they do; we must understand the sources of race prejudice and antagonism. There is a mistaken notion widely held that these feelings are instinctive, that they are inborn. The verdict which emerges from the scientific examination of the evidence on this point is clear. It announces that while there is a modicum of instinctive reaction of fear and hence of hostility to that which is different, racial antagonisms are predominantly the products of conditioning; they are not inherent, but learned. They are the outgrowths of particular social and economic conditions.

Children do not share these attitudes save insofar as they are inculcated in them by their elders, save as they imbibe them from the social pattern into which they must fit. Another of my early recollections is that of a little white girl and a little Negro girl walking home from school together, each with an arm around the other, sharing an all-day sucker as they went. The mother of the white girl, coming upon them unexpectedly, was horrified and yanked her child away. It is not hard to imagine the consequences in the feelings of both children.

If we are to correct such patterns of reaction, we shall have to get at their roots. Education can be a factor in accomplishing this. It is important that a knowledge of such conclusions as those contained in the statement issued by the experts of UNESCO should be universally disseminated among men. It is important that the religious ideal of the brotherhood of man shall be inculcated in all peoples. But obviously, this is not enough; it must be supplemented by other means.

It is only reluctantly that I have come to this conclusion, for I was reared in the school of thought which held that if only we relied on the gradual process of social evolution, the inherent impulses to justice and brotherhood, the increasing effectiveness of education, the lessons taught by experience, would in the course of time take care of the problems. I was averse to the resort to coercion in any form, the use of laws as a means of changing the social pattern. Now I am convinced that I was mistaken and that it is necessary to supplement the educational processes by these other methods, that indeed social compulsion has proved to be an effective means of promoting the educational process. I still have some reservations about this, but tentatively I am accepting it.

That which has brought about my changed opinion has been the degree of success achieved through the use of such social machinery. Numerous accounts have appeared of the relative ease with which the color bars have been abolished in the armed services. The men have accepted each other far more easily than was deemed possible. A story appeared in the newspaper only last week telling of a southern port where the color line had traditionally been sharply drawn and yet a naval vessel with mixed crew which docked there experienced no difficulty over the race issue.

Similar results seem to have been achieved in the District of Columbia when a local ordinance went into effect forbidding restaurants to discriminate on the basis of color. While the change was not effected without some unpleasant incidents, and while the law has by no means accomplished its full purpose, it has not provoked the calamities predicted. Much the same has happened in the public housing projects where discrimination has been banned. True there have been some outbursts of violence, but on the whole, white and black have discovered when they do live together in this close proximity that the fears and hostilities are diminished and tend to disappear.

The experience under the Fair Employment Practices legislation adopted by a number of states and some cities confirm this. The laws prohibit discrimination in hiring, firing, compensation or promotion on the basis of color or religion. They apply also to labor unions in regard to their membership policies. To be sure the experiment has only been under way for a period of eight years, which is not long enough to assess its value properly. Yet the results in that brief period are encouraging. An article on the subject appeared in the *Annals of the American Academy of Political and Social Science* a few months ago. Its conclusion was that these laws make fair employment practice a concern of the entire community, not merely a relatively private affair between the discriminator and his victim. They have justified the community's and the legislators' faith in their efficacy. The enforcement agencies have moved carefully, stressing the educational rather than the coercive provisions of the laws. They have eliminated discriminatory practices in a great many instances, and there have been few unfavorable repercussions.

How this operates is perhaps well illustrated by an incident out of local experience. The head of a department in one of the state agencies decided to add a Negro secretary, who had applied for the position and was well qualified, to the staff. The other members of the staff were informed of this and their cooperation asked. Two of the women rebelled and said that if the Negro was employed they would resign. The head of the department was firm, however, and the Negro secretary went to work. The other women did not resign and some months later went to the department head and apologized for their previous attitude, stating that they now realized that they had been acting on unreasoning prejudice and that actually they had enjoyed working with the new member of their team.

The *New York Times* for July 26th of this year carried a story indicative of the fact that this method is effective on a much larger scale. It told of the efforts of a group in Oregon to make inoperative an act passed by the state legislature which gave "all persons within the jurisdiction of this state full and equal accommodations, advantages, facilities and privileges of any place of public accommodations, resort or amusement, without any distinction, discrimination or restriction on account of race, religion, color or national origin." The effort to nullify the act fell by the way when the opposition found itself unable to secure even half the necessary number of signatures to their referendum petition.

The *Portland Oregonian,* commenting editorially on this failure, said that it is evidence that Oregon public opinion has made great strides in the past few years with respect to race relations. "The natural inference from the failure of the referendum attempts is that a substantial majority of Oregonians has become convinced that racial and religious minorities should be assured by law equal treatment in places of public accommodation. One reason for this obvious shift in sentiment has been the success of the Fair Employment Practices Law, which has demonstrated the education value of civil rights legislation."

Such legislation is by no means the only social machinery which must be devised in order to implement the principle of brotherhood. It is but indicative of a whole area in which we must exercise our talents. Most fundamental is the discovery, the invention, in the light of our increasing knowledge of how emotional patterns are established in human beings, of ways and means to make spontaneous and powerful those reactions which are favorable to the requirements of the fact that we are "of one blood."

The most knotty problem with which we are here confronted is that presented by intermarriage; it is here that prejudice and passion flare most violently. We saw in the statement issued by the anthropologists that there is no justification on biological grounds for prohibiting intermarriage. It has been going on for a very long time and the human species is the most hybrid of animals. The objections are social; they do not exist where such intermarriage is commonly accepted and widely approved. They do exist in intense form in a society like our own where it is definitely disapproved.

It is easy to exaggerate the extent and the urgency of this problem. For the most part, the members of the different ethnic groups will naturally and normally mate with those like themselves. Certainly the facts do not warrant the attitude of those who immediately respond to any suggestion of inter-racial association with the query: "Do you want your daughter to marry a Negro?" Only they are prone to use a far less polite term. Yet we must not blink the fact that inter-marriage does take place and that probably it will do so with increasing frequency as we move on toward more amicable relations between the different races. I heard one anthropologist predict that in 5000 years the intermixture will have gone so far that all round the earth it will be impossible to distinguish between the divisions that we now differentiate. But our pressing concern is with the immediate scene.

A woman came to me to discuss her daughter's impending marriage to a Negro. She was proud of the girl's independence of mind, her readiness to follow the dictates of her love, her courage in defying the judgment of public opinion. She felt that her daughter was pioneering the difficult road humanity is taking. Yet at the same time, her heart bled for her daughter as she thought of the probable social consequences to her, to her husband, and their children -- the inevitable severing of the ties of friendship, the restrictions, the ostracism to which they would be subjected. There are a few centers in our country where such marriages are accepted and have a fair chance of success, but the prejudices against them are terrifically powerful and yield only with glacial slowness. About all I could do for this woman was to extend to her my sympathetic understanding and suggest that she do everything possible to keep her daughter's trust, that she stand by her in her decision which was irrevocable and continue through whatever happened to be her loyal and loving mother. This she had already resolved in her own heart.

During the past week I turned back to the pages of that monumental study of race relations in this country which bears the title *An American Dilemma*. It is the work of Gunnar Myrdal, who was brought here by the Carnegie Corporation because they felt that while we have competent scientists at home, the whole question is so emotionally involved that more objective results would be achieved by importing an outsider. Gunnar Myrdal was a professor at the University of Stockholm; he has an international reputation as a social economist, was economic adviser to the Swedish government and a member of the Swedish Senate. Incidentally, he is one of the scientists who produced the declaration on race problems issued by UNESCO.

At the conclusion of his book he says that the treatment of the Negro is America's greatest and most conspicuous scandal but at the same time our greatest opportunity. The eyes of the colored population of the world, which outnumbers the white two to one, are upon us and our scandal is salt in their wounds. They are judging us by it. Yet if we are true to the deepest vein in our own national life, which is the principles of liberty and equality, we shall conquer the color caste system we have established and in so doing immediately increase our power, our prestige, and our leadership in the world at this critical time.

The Swedish scientist announces that the problem is essentially a white problem rather than a Negro problem; the responsibility for the existing conditions rests upon the majority rather than on the minority. The responsibility for correcting them also lies with the majority. We should take that point to heart and never forget it. Yet it does not absolve the minority from assuming its share in moving on toward a solution. Every fine achievement, ever bit of self-discipline, every acquisition of skill on the part of the members of the minority contributes by so much to the triumph of our common cause.

The ideal of the brotherhood of man is clear and sure. It has a religious motivation and is fortified by scientific findings. It is based on the fact that we are most literally "of one blood," that we all share in the common human nature. It demands of us that we shall so conduct ourselves in our relations with our brothers that all of us alike shall have the fullest possible opportunity to mount to the greatest heights of manhood of which we are capable.

Gunnar Myrdal concludes on an optimistic note, expressing his personal confidence in the improvability of man and society. I share that confidence. We began this discussion with reference to the conquest of Mt. Everest. Let us come full circle and recur to it. Tenzing and Hilary, who reached the summit, and their companions who made the feat possible, were not supermen. Probably as individuals they were in no wise superior to the men who had tried innumerable times before and failed. But they availed themselves of the experiences of previous expeditions, they provided themselves with the best proved equipment, they used the latest developments such as the oxygen tanks which gave relief to their tortured lungs. It all added up to victory.

Herein is a symbol, a portent of our ultimate conquest of that other formidable peak which bears the name of Mt. Brotherhood. Its precipitous cliffs, its yawning crevasses are the prejudices and ignorance in the heart and mind of man. Its fierce storms, its avalanches, its killing cold, its rare atmosphere, are the passions, the cruelties, the selfishness that yet reside within us. Yes, and the very loftiness of the ideal that challenges us. Many have sought in vain to scale that mountain; many have died in the attempt; many have turned back awed by the difficulties of the way. But we do not despair. Again and again we return to the attack with the courage and determination of men who refuse to recognize the impossible. We learn from the experience, the successes and failures of the past; we avail ourselves of new equipment, invent fresh means of enabling us to press on to our goal. We shall persist until we have planted the banner of humanity on the summit of Mt. Brotherhood.

The Beloved Community

"Of a truth, men are mystically united; a mysterious bond of brotherhood makes all men one." So spoke Thomas Carlyle. His words point us to another aspect of that same great truth which we dwelt upon last Sunday, that the brotherhood of man stems from the fact that we all are in strict literalness "of one blood." There is a biological basis for our brotherhood. But there are other bonds than those of blood which unite us; they are the bonds of community, the ties which develop because we live together in close association.

"Man is born a social being who can reach his fullest development only through interaction with his fellows." This sentence from the statement on race issued by UNESCO is a recognition on the part of the scientists responsible for it of the existence of that "mysterious bond" of which Carlyle speaks; it is the social bond, the bond of community. We shall devote ourselves this morning to making this more explicit, for here we come to the very heart of religion.

From the earliest time we have known about men they have lived in communities. Indeed the communal life doubtless antedates humanity for we know that our closest relatives, the apes, lived in communities. The original form of these communities was the family, father, mother and children. In some respects, the mother's role was more important than that of the father because the children were more dependent on her, and it was her response to their needs which was the cohesive force. The makeup of the family has varied considerably, perhaps beginning with a single male who claimed a number of females and their offspring as his own, and evolving slowly toward the monogamous family which is not as yet securely established.

The ties which held the members of these original communities together were those of their mutual need of each other and the natural affection which springs out of such close association. It has long been recognized that the family has played a tremendously important role in the development of civilization. It has been the seed plot of the social virtues. There the members have learned the distinction between good and bad; there they have learned cooperation and loyalty; there they have learned a variety of skills which in turn they have passed on to others. It has been rightly observed that "civilization resides not in our blood but in our society." Were it not for the way in which the communal life preserves the achievements of men, each new generation would have to start from scratch with very meager equipment and civilization would not be possible. The insights achieved by modern psychology confirm and reinforce our understanding of the vast importance of the family in making human beings out of the little animals which we are at the outset of life.

The family is, of course, but one form of community life and long before the historic period it had merged into the large organization of the clan or tribe, family uniting with family in their common interest. There has been a reciprocal relation between the family and the larger social units which they have formed. The character of the family, the nature of the relations between the individuals who comprise it has varied considerably with the particular social setting in which it has been found. You have only to contrast the Chinese family as it is described by Nora Waln in *The House of Exile* with the family as we are familiar with it in the American scene to be made keenly aware of these differences.

Again, it is in the face to face relations of the community that the essential social virtues are acquired, that men learn the importance of honesty and neighborliness, of cooperation and loyalty, of respect for the integrity and rights of others. The roots of democracy, the roots of moral qualities which have been demanded by all of the great religions go down into the community life. This is why they are as stable, as secure as they are. They are not artificial, imposed on men from without, but grow out of the necessities and possibilities of our common life.

Man is a social being, born in and for society. Through the long millenniums of his existence he has lived in communities and continues to do so today. Three quarters of the world's population are still villagers. The farmers of the world, with the notable exception of the American farmer, live in villages. The dwellers in towns and cities seek community. Ofttimes they do not find it with their neighbors so much as they do with others who have common interests, in church or club, in business or fraternal organization. The isolated individual, the man who is denied community, has difficulty in keeping normal. We need each other.

But not all has been on the credit side in the community. Because it has been important to preserve and pass on the skills and knowledge that have been acquired, the social gains, the community has put a premium on conformity, on doing things as they have been done, on adhering to tradition. It has laid a destructive tax on innovation, change. The result has been that often the community has become rigid, incapable of adjusting itself to new conditions. There are always those who do not recognize that circumstances have changed; they demand that we must get back to the good old ways of doing things. When their reading of the scene is mistaken, the result is disastrous.

Ofttimes the community has sacrificed freedom for the sake of group safety. In order to achieve a close-knit order, an effective defensive solidarity, the community has insisted upon conformity in belief and action. This has been true of churches; it has been true of states. We are currently confronted with a blatant example of this propensity to sacrifice freedom for safety, right here in our own community. Indianapolis has had the spotlight of national publicity thrown upon it because of the action of the officials of the War Memorial in refusing the use of its auditorium, at the behest of the American Legion, for an organizational meeting of the American Civil Liberties Union. The Legion regards the Civil Liberties Union as a subversive organization, pro-Communist, despite the fact that it has been given a clean bill of health by investigating agencies and has won the praise of President Eisenhower himself. In the name of safety, the Legion would, apparently, prohibit if it could, the meeting and organization of this group which has constituted itself the watchdog of our civil liberties.

Fortunately a Roman Catholic Church came to the rescue, to its credit be it said, and the meeting was held in the social hall at St. Mary's Church. That is a curious commentary on our present state of mind -- that the Catholic Church should have to be the one to come to the defense of our traditional American principle of freedom. May I add that *this* church (All Souls Unitarian) was prepared to offer its facilities, were none other available.

A further weakness which community has manifested in the past, and which is still with us, has been the narrowness of its outlook. The sense of identity of interests, and therefore the readiness to apply the virtues of the community, has been confined to relatively small groups, to one's own clan, or class, or nation. The breadth of sympathy has been sharply restricted and men have readily regarded all outsiders as enemies. This is entirely understandable because the community in which our sympathies have been schooled has for the most part been a narrow one, and we have had ample reason to distrust and fear outsiders, even as they have feared and distrusted us. Any genuine world view of community has scarcely existed in the past.

But conditions are radically changed in the world today and it has become imperative that we free the community from the shortcomings it has manifested. We need to reaffirm the great tradition of community, which is common to all mankind; reaffirm its neighborliness, its goodwill and mutual regard, its cooperation and mutual aid. Then to these traditional virtues we must add the modern values of tolerance and freedom, of the open mind, flexibility, and the spirit of progress, and finally, the community must be conceived as a worldwide brotherhood. Its very survival depends on its ability to adjust to the new conditions which have developed.

This adjustment must take place on different levels. The place to begin is where we are, in our own communities, be they small villages or great cities. The emphasis should be on quality rather than on size. It should not be the desire of a small town to grow into a city so much as it should be to make its own life so vital, so well rounded that its citizens will bear in themselves the marks of their community; they shall have a democratic simplicity, neighborliness, sincerity and self discipline, the unassuming confidence of people who feel that they belong, that they are secure and at the same time have vital relations with the world.

Even on a small scale, the establishment of such a community is no easy achievement. It calls for much intelligent planning, a comprehensive grasp of the needs and opportunities of the community as a whole, provision for a healthy economic, social, political and cultural life, and for the establishment of wholesome contacts with the outside world. To envision such a community and work out its requirements in cooperation with our neighbors can be adventure of the highest order. It should appeal to young men and women of parts and help stem the tides that are constantly draining off the most adventurous young people from our small communities to the big cities. The strength of nations in the past, and it is probably true in the present, has lain in the human material that has been developed in the intimate relations of small but vigorous communities. It is there that the qualities of character are produced which give backbone and leadership to the nation. It is a notorious fact that vast cities do not maintain themselves either in population or leadership and have to be recruited continually from the small communities.

This does not mean, of course, that large cities do not have certain advantages and alllurements. Obviously they do or they would not continue to exist. But we are beginning to suspect that perhaps these advantages are outweighed by the disadvantages and that a considerable measure of decentralization would serve our best interests. While there is much that can be done in the vast aggregations of population which constitute our big cities to develop a sense of citizenship and civic pride, for the most part the purposes of community have to be served in a different way. This is by the lines of interest which are largely unrelated to geography and proximity but which bring together people of like interests, whether they be economic, professional, cultural, political or religious. This has the clear disadvantage of narrowness and does not promote that sense of belonging to an organic whole which is characteristic of community at its best.

One of my own great teachers was sociologist Charles Horton Cooley. In his book, *Human Nature and the Social Order,* he says, "The central fact of history is the gradual enlargement of social feeling, social consciousness, and rational cooperation." This describes succinctly the expansion of community which begins with one's immediate companions and develops until in its ripest form it includes the whole of humanity, not only those who are alive at a particular time, but humanity as it moves across the ages past, present and to come. Pascal expressed this by saying, "The whole succession of men during the ages should be considered as One Man, ever living and always learning."

This is a somewhat mystical expression and yet it contains an essential objective truth. There has clearly been a historical process by which community has widened; clan has united with clan to form tribes, which in turn have united to form nations, and nations have been merged to form empires, and at length there is clearly present to our minds the possibility, the necessity of the United Nations, a single community around the globe.

But just as clearly, this historical process has reached different levels in different parts of the world, and in the minds and hearts of different individuals in all parts of the earth. At the present time there is a strong resurgence of the nationalistic spirit. This is particularly true in large sections of Asia where the revolt of colonial peoples expresses itself largely in the form of intense nationalism. The same impulses are manifest elsewhere; they constitute a formidable obstacle to the achievement of a United States of Europe which is so obviously needed. They are powerfully operative in our own country in resistance to the further involvement of our nation in international affairs.

Most conspicuous of the cleavages in the body of humanity at the present time is, of course, that between the Communist world and our own, with a large group of nations outside both camps insisting that they will not be party to our quarrel. But despite all such tragic conflicts which set man against man, people against people, the forces of human life which have been bringing us into ever closer community are operative today as they have been in the past. Indeed they have been greatly intensified in our time as the result of the technological advances which have brought all sections of the earth so near together. What chance is there for "splendid isolation" in a world of radio and jet airplanes with twice the speed of sound? It becomes increasingly certain that our very survival may depend on our carrying this historical process to its logical conclusion in the establishment of a single unified community round the globe.

It has been the glory of the religious genius of mankind that it has glimpsed this truth and sought to lead men toward its realization. Lin Yutang in his book, *The Importance of Living,* reproduces for us the passage from the Confucian writings which was the first lesson which the children learned in school. It is a description of the way in which "clear moral harmony" is to be achieved in the world. The same vision of universal moral harmony has ravished the hearts of religious prophets in many lands. It has been variously named. Jesus called it "The Kingdom of God." His thought of it was that of the family at its best extended to include all people within its circle of goodwill and cooperation.

The name which most commends itself to me is that of "The Beloved Community," which was coined by one of the foremost American philosophers, Josiah Royce. "The Beloved Community." How descriptive it is at once of the ideal and the devotion it inspires in our hearts! Royce was wont to say that religion in its highest form consists of loyalty to the Beloved Community. Another contemporary philosopher says essentially the same thing. John Macmurray, of England, states that the religious attitude is best expressed in the terms fellowship, communion. "The religious attitude of mind is that for which our relations to other people are central. The task of religion is the maintenance of the human community. Religion is the only means by which this can be achieved."

It was under the influence of such teaching and out of my own experience that as a young man I wrote the responsive reading which we used this morning which I entitled, "The Beloved Community." That was 35 years ago, but the truths I sought to express, the feelings and attitudes it was designed to convey, still seem fresh and vital to me today, still are the living heart of my religion.

There is this difference. The years have brought me a heightened sense of the importance of implementing the vision in our daily life, the necessity of working out the practical implications at every level of society, developing the essential skills and social machinery required to give the spirit of the Beloved Community the means of becoming embodied in the affairs of every day. Often I have been accused of having no religion but only a social philosophy. It does not disturb me because I know that social idealism has constituted the core of all high religion and that it is particularly so with that religion of human fulfillment upon which we are entering.

It is way beyond the scope of this address to attempt anything like a full description of the process whereby the word is to be made flesh. We shall have to confine ourselves to a brief consideration of a single example. For the purpose, I select the area of our political life. Here in this country we have the firmly established tradition of the separation of church and state. That is grand; may we ever adhere to it. But it does not mean that there is no connection between religion and government. Our government should be permeated throughout with the religious spirit, not in any sectarian sense, but rather in the sense that it is only to the degree that government is an agency for the promotion of the Beloved Community that it can fulfill its legitimate functions. That is what government is -- a means of establishing truer community among men.

It is here that the importance of democracy makes itself felt. Democracy is an ideal which keeps the relation between the individual and the community in proper balance. It recognizes that life is lived in persons and that therefore the well-being of the individuals is the supreme concern of society. The community exists only in and for the persons who comprise it. But democracy also recognizes that it is only in and through the community that the individual can survive and grow towards the fullest human stature. The state is only our effort to organize the common life so that it will serve this end.

The contrast here with Communism is great. I hesitate so much as to utter that dread word lest I shall be relegated to the category of Robin Hood! It cannot have escaped you how close the word community is to Communism.

The relation between the two is obvious. The Communist has laid hold of a great truth but he has carried that truth to an extreme where it becomes invalidated. A Communist is one for whom the community has become an end in itself and the individual is demeaned as an instrument to serve that end.

The opposite extreme is "rugged individualism" which tends to ignore the importance of community. Actually, individual and community cannot be properly considered apart from each other; they are the two sides of the same coin. This is the truth which the rugged individualist is prone to ignore or deny. We do so at our peril. Men need to feel their identity with the community; they respond to its appeal. It is able to elicit from them their highest. We have only to remember that men have regretted that they have only one life to lay down for their country to have this truth brought forcefully home to us. This is the source of much of the appeal of the totalitarian governments and the reason why they are able to command the fanatical loyalty of vast numbers of men. It is difficult for men to keep the right balance between individual and community; we tend to swing from one extreme to the other.

Lincoln was right in his pronouncement that democracy is "the last best hope of men." Democracy is the form of government which best succeeds in keeping this balance. It integrates the individual into the community but at the same time makes the well-being, the development of the individual its purpose. It preserves for him the essential freedom and undertakes to provide for him the conditions which enable him to be his best self. It is a difficult way to take, but judged by its fruits it is the superior way and it would seem that however many setbacks it may experience, it is destined in one form or another to become the way an ever larger portion of mankind will take.

At the same time we congratulate ourselves on the superiority of democracy we need to remind ourselves that our own brand of it is very imperfect and stands in constant need of improvement. It confronts us with many difficult dilemmas. How can we combine liberty and authority in such wise that we maintain order and at the same time promote justice and make freedom secure? How can we adjust our democracy to the changing demands of the world in which we find ourselves -- especially how can we keep the military mind subordinate to the civilian in a period that demands a vast expansion of military power? How can we make sure that a majority will not use the political machinery to legislate democracy out of existence? How can we extend the democratic principles to other areas of life than the political, and make sure that our people have democratic experiences in these areas? Simply to raise these questions is indication enough of the gigantic problems which confront us. They are religious problems for they concern the vitality of the Beloved Community which is the matrix within which all of us are seeking to fulfill our lives.

With these considerations in mind, let us return to Charles Horton Cooley's statement that "The central fact of history is the gradual enlargement of social feeling, social consciousness, and rational cooperation." Clearly we have now reached that stage in the gradual enlargement of social feeling where it is planetwide in its scope. We have become definitely conscious that the Beloved Community must include all men.

It is no accident that our era produced both the ill-fated League of Nations and the present United Nations. Whatever their defects, these organizations have been attempts to give expression to the fact of the interrelatedness of human life, to the truth that "above all nations stands humanity," to use Mazzini's phrase. They have grown out of our need, out of our awareness that a global community is coming into being and that it is imperative that we shall give it an organized form just as we do any of the communities which are lesser in scope.

It has been argued with some plausibility that a true internationalism is out of the range of human possibilities, that it involves too great an extension of the community to be encompassed by the feelings of men in a manner necessary to give it unity. We are told that the nation-state is and must remain "the widest organization which has the common experience necessary to form a common life." It seems to me that such a dictum is entirely premature. Granted that most of us are parochial in our point of view and our sympathies, we are getting educated willy-nilly in the larger point of view, our sympathies being stretched, Procrustes-wise, to fit the bed upon which we must presently lie. There are certain areas in which a genuine internationalism has already been achieved and to which many of us have adjusted our feelings.

The realm of art is one of these. Who but the most narrow type of patriot asks of a great picture, a splendid poem, a magnificent musical composition, a masterly novel, whether it be the creation of an American, a German, a Japanese? Of course we are interested to know the part of the world from which the artist comes, and we recognize that there are certain characteristics of his work that are born of his immediate environment. But so far as he has succeeded in embodying truth and beauty in his work it belongs to all humanity, takes place in that country of which all men who are lovers of truth and beauty are the citizens. The Taj Mahal, a statue by Praxiteles, a play by Shakespeare, an opus by Mozart, a novel by Tolstoi, a picture by Rembrandt, these are the property of the world, the heritage of us all because we are human beings.

In like manner the products of the scientific advance in knowledge and technique go into a common pool for the benefit of all mankind. Pasteur and Mendel, Darwin and Einstein, Edison and Burbank, belong to the world. There are no boundary lines against truth. The Japanese doctor, Noguchi, laying down his life in research into the causes of a disease that devastates the population of Africa is a fitting symbol of the internationalism of science. It is concerned with us, not as Americans and Turks and Chinese, but as human beings. And it has brought us all into such close proximity in time and space that we are inescapably neighbors of all the peoples of the earth.

How obvious it is that the economic life of the world cuts across all national boundaries. A depression in America would make itself felt to the ends of the earth with devastating effect. The distinguished British economist, J.A. Hobson, wrote a book entitled *Economics and Ethics*. In it is a chapter on "The Ethics of Economic Internationalism," in which he says that none of the graver problems of human welfare is capable of a sound solution on a purely national scale, that peace and prosperity and the other essentials of civilization are quite unattainable unless we abandon exclusive national economic policies and undertake the stupendous task of organizing the economic life of the world on an international basis. The truth of his contention has become increasingly clear in the years which have passed since his book was written.

All this, and much besides, adds up to the fact that we can no longer escape the necessity of organizing the political life of mankind on the international level, achieving a genuine United States of the world. It means further, and this is more fundamental, that internationalism must cease to be an idea cherished by a relatively few minds, but must be made to permeate the entire population of the globe, sinking down to those deeper levels of our nature where lie the springs of conduct. We must cultivate a loyalty, an enthusiasm for humanity which shall be capable of moving men as powerfully as patriotism now does. We must *feel* ourselves to be members of the Beloved Community.

It has ever been the function of religion to take the individual up and merge his life in a larger whole, not to the defeat of his self, but to its fulfillment. The boundaries of his being are expanded, the narrow limits of self broken up, and he feels he has become identical with the universal. This is the meaning of the mystical phrase in the Gospel of John, "I and my Father are one." This is the identification which religion must enable men to achieve today by means of their membership in the Beloved Community.

There is a passage in the writings of Romain Rolland in which he says: "For the finer spirits of the world there are two dwelling places: our earthly fatherland, and that other City of God. Of the one, we are the guests, of the other, the builders. To the one, let us give our lives and our faithful hearts; but neither family, friend, nor fatherland has power over the spirit. The spirit is the light. It is our duty to lift it above the tempests, and thrust aside the clouds which threaten to obscure it, to build higher and stronger, dominating the injustice and hatred of nations, the walls of that city wherein the souls of the whole world may assemble." Such is the summons of the Beloved Community of which we are at once the children and the builders.

The Fourth Revolution

We are all poignantly aware of the revolutionary character of our times because it makes our own lives so difficult. We commonly think of that revolution in terms of what has happened, first in Russia and then in China, with the establishment of Communist regimes. We know that the revolt of colonial peoples is also a factor in it. But what we do not usually take into sufficient account is the fact these political upheavals and rebellions which have produced the tensions and wars with which we are inflicted, are themselves the results of a more fundamental revolution, namely the changes wrought in our way of life by the development of the sciences.

I have called it the Fourth Revolution because some historians tell us that it has been preceded by three similarly basic changes in the way of human living. The first of these came with the use of fire. It took place so long ago that its beginnings are lost in the mists of prehistory. It meant, among other things, a radical change in the diet of man because he used fire for the purposes of cooking and thus was enabled to avail himself of a wide variety of foods which he had not before been able to use.

The second revolution came with the invention of agriculture. Then men ceased to be merely collectors of food which they found ready at hand, but deliberately set about to raise food. This took place, by slow degrees, some 10 to 15 thousand years ago, recently enough for us to know considerable about it. A great change took place in the mode of men's lives with the advent of agriculture. They ceased roving about from place to place in quest of food and settled down to the life of the farmer. The more abundant food supply resulted in a large increase in population.

The third revolution was that of the establishment of urban life. This happened simultaneously about 6000 years ago in a number of different parts of earth. Men began to gather together in larger communities, to establish cities. The populations of these cities were supported by the agriculture of surrounding areas. This gave some men release from the constant pressure of having to earn their living from the soil. Their energies were free to flow into other channels, and the resulting product was what we call civilization. The word itself is an indication that civilization is an order of society that develops in cities.

The fourth revolution is of relatively recent date. It is that resulting from man's progress in science. To be sure there were foregleams of science in antiquity. The Chaldeans were able to predict eclipses with considerable accuracy nearly 4000 years ago, and the Greek, Pythagoras, 500 B.C., pictured the earth as a sphere enclosed on all sides by air, and suspended without tangible support in the center of the universe. But science as we know it today is not much over 300 years old. Its beginnings are associated with such names as Copernicus and Galileo, both of whom lived after Columbus discovered America. Actually the scientific revolution did not swing into full force until the great industrial changes which stemmed from it began to take place in Britain only about a century ago.

The scientific revolution is still in its early stages. We have not as yet begun to feel its full impact. There is every reason to anticipate that it will continue with accelerating influence on the lives of men for a very long time to come. Already it has altered our living in a great many different ways, conferring on us great new powers and at the same time raising a host of perplexing problems. In all probability it will change the course of human existence as much as, if not more than, all of the preceding revolutions. Let us have a brief look at two of the major ways in which it has exerted its influence.

Most fundamental is the way in which it has altered the character of our thinking. Our usual thoughts are largely colored by our feelings; we think in terms of our own interests. The story is told of a young research scientist who successfully completed a study in the field of nutrition and reported this to his wife. She at once exclaimed: "Good! and what does it mean in terms of honor for you? And what shall I feed the baby?" This is, of course, an exaggerated example, but it does illustrate the subjective quality of most of our thinking.

Set over against this the letter which Thomas Huxley wrote in reply to Charles Kingsley, who had written him in condolence on the death of a son. Huxley began by saying: "My convictions, positive and negative, on all the matters of which you speak are of long and slow growth and are firmly rooted. I have searched over the grounds of my belief, and if wife and child and name and fame were all to be lost to me one after the other as the penalty, still I will not lie." And a little further along he writes: "The longer I live, the more obvious it is to me that the sacred act of a man's life is to say and to feel, 'I believe such and such to be true.' All the greatest rewards and all the heaviest penalties of existence cling about that act."

There speaks the scientist. Huxley had been disciplined in that method of thinking which is the major tool which the scientists use to secure their results. He defines that method in one of his Lay Sermons: "Every great advance in natural knowledge has involved the absolute rejection of authority, the cherishing of the keenest skepticism, the annihilation of the spirit of blind faith. And the most ardent votary of science holds his firmest convictions, not because the men he most venerates hold them; not because their verity is testified by portents and wonders; but because his experience teaches him that whenever he chooses to bring those convictions into contact with their primary sources, Nature -- whenever he thinks fit to test them by appealing to experiment and observation -- will confirm them. The man of science has learned to believe in justification, not by faith, but by verification."

The scientific temper of mind, involving as it does a respect for the facts, a disciplined method of ascertaining those facts, the effort to explain the facts in general theories or laws, the open-minded readiness to change those theories in the light of new knowledge or better interpretation, is exceedingly difficult to achieve and maintain. It requires special training, the cultivation of certain moral as well as intellectual skills. Even in the great scientist, it is often confined to the area of his own specialty and outside that he may be anything but objective. It is one of the supreme achievements of the human spirit, and as Huxley further said, "the scientific spirit is of more value than its products."

Let us, however, consider some of those products, for though they may be of less value than the scientific spirit itself they do exert a vast influence in our world. One of the most conspicuous of these results is our changed conception of the nature of the universe and man's place in it which has come as a result of the progress of scientific knowledge. It is only necessary to contrast the account of creation as given in the early chapters of the Bible with that which is advanced by modern scientists to become sharply aware of what has happened.

Take the time factor as an example. The famous Archbishop Usher figured from the Biblical data that the world was created in the year 4004 B.C. -- a mere 6000 years ago. Put over against that the estimate given by Dr. Kirk der Haar, the distinguished scientist who a few years ago was a Visiting Professor of Physics at Purdue University. He places the age of the earth -- not the whole universe, mind you -- at somewhere around 3 billion years, a figure which has begun to be comprehensible to us recently because of the size of our national debt -- or has it? Three billion! That is 500,000 times as much as the Biblical 6000 years. A whole series of methods of measuring the duration of the earth has been developed, including the recent one of radioactive decay, which are far more reliable than the ancient guess. Incidentally, it is interesting to note that the ancient Hindus did a much better job than Archbishop Usher. They estimated the age of the earth as just short of two billion years.

When we think in terms of extent instead of time, the contrast is much the same. The universe which is revealed by the giant 200 inch telescope on Mt. Palomar is so much vaster than the tidy little universe which excited the admiration and the awe of those ancient Hebrew poets who have given us the Psalms as to seem almost to be of a different order. Perhaps the quality of reverence which it stirs in us is no different but our understanding of the nature and the reaches of cosmos is immensely increased.

Even more significant is the fact that the sciences offer us an alternative to the traditional religious interpretation of the observed facts. It substitutes what we call the laws of nature for the workings of divine providence. That is, it advances a natural explanation for what happens in our world in place of the supernatural in which men generally believed before the advent of the scientific revolution. I find a contemporary scientist saying that one of the chief principles of the scientific method is "the belief that every occurrence, no matter how mysterious, has a natural and understandable cause and that with sufficient observation and work we can understand that cause." This applies not only to the laws by which the stars are steered, but also to what happens in a blade of grass, in the mind of man. All is the working out of natural forces inherent in the universe.

Here we are on debatable ground and some scientists themselves warn us against the dangers involved in trying to make a philosophy or a religion out of their feelings. Mills College in California celebrated its 100th anniversary a short time ago by presenting a popular symposium on evolution. Its purpose was to have authorities in a number of sciences tell of the present status of the theory of evolution in their respective fields. The symposium was introduced by Richard B. Goldschmidt, Professor Emeritus of Zoology at the University of California. He said: "For a hundred years, the doctrine of evolution has been the center of the biological sciences, as well as of much of the progressive thought in all other sciences, from chemistry to anthropology, to medicine and jurisprudence, to psychology and philosophy."

But he goes on to warn against the danger of introducing metaphysical ideas into a field which belongs to the naturalist. He instances Bergson and Lecomte du Nouy as examples of what he has in mind. They have enjoyed great success with the laymen, but, says Professor Goldschmidt, they have never helped science to make the smallest step forward into unknown territory. "They have never done anything but replace temporary ignorance by an appeal to unknown, supernatural forces or agents, and lure untrained minds into the self-deception of mistaking cleverly circumscribed confessions of ignorance for a deep insight and explanation."

The warning is salutary, yet it seems to me inevitable that men should try to take the results of scientific investigation and weave them into a coherent philosophy. It seems to be a necessity of our minds to try to bring order into our whole experience, and science is today such an important part of our experience that no attempted interpretation of our world which does not incorporate the findings of science can long command the assent of our minds. It seems to me incontestable that science has already progressed far in remaking the picture we draw of our universe and that it is destined to continue this process at an accelerated rate.

We must not make the mistake of assuming that there is anything absolute, final about this picture. Science, for all its wonders, is simply one of the creations of the mind of man. It has proved itself a particularly useful way of looking at the world and manipulating it for our benefit. We must remember that there are other ways of looking at the world which are also fruitful. There is the way of art, of aesthetic appreciation. The immediate experience of beauty tells us important things about our world and ourselves. There is the way of love, the way of ethical and religious experience. Science has important things to tell us about all these realms, but it is no substitute for them. They equally with it must contribute to that picture which the artist in us is striving to draw.

There is a fine recognition at once of the possibilities and the limitations of science in providing us with a philosophy in an article in the current *Scientific Monthly* (Nov. 1953), by Ludwig von Bertalanffy. At its conclusion he says that science is "one of those symbolic worlds that man has created for mastering the great enigma of the universe, the creation of which is part of his uniqueness . . . However, none of the worlds of symbols, the sum total of which is called human culture, is a full presentation of reality . . . What science can do is to symbolize reality in its way, knowing, as its great masters always did, that this is but a humble way to redraw a few traces of the great blueprint of Creation." Yes, science has magnificent contributions to make to our understanding of the world. We will avail ourselves of them to the full, but at the same time keep science in its place as just one of the disciplines which helps us make ourselves at home in our world.

To the man in the street, the woman in the home, the more obvious effects of science are not the ways in which it has modified our picture of the world, but the ways in which they experience its impact in their own lives through the inventions which have flowed from it. To multitudes science means primarily gadgets; it means autos and airplanes, vacuum sweepers and electric mixers; it means radio and TV; it means miracle drugs and preventive medicine; it means atomic and hydrogen bombs. All this affects them much more directly and powerfully than do the intellectual consequences of science.

Do the ten league boots that men have thus acquired, does the increased control over the forces of nature which we have won actually serve the purpose of religion which is to bring life abundant, fulfillment, to men? Are we any happier, more content, secure, wiser as a consequence of this fourth revolution which is upon us? The questions are highly debatable. There are gains and there are losses; it is exceedingly difficult to weigh the one against the other and come to a decision as to where the balance lies.

There are some things which seem clear gains. The increase in the world's food supply as a result of the development of scientific agriculture is a case in point. We know, for example, that the wheat yield in this country was increased more than 25% per acre in a half century as a result of the application of science to the farmer's problems. There are still areas of the world where thousands die of famine, but we are confident that with the further spread of modern practices of agriculture and with improvement in distribution we shall be able to provide the necessary sustenance for the peoples of earth.

One of the most striking contrasts between the old and the new is afforded by the methods taken to assure a good crop. Here is an incantation used by the priests of the Orthodox Church of Russia in years gone by to protect the growing grain from pests: "Worms and grasshoppers! Mice and rats! Ants, moles and reptiles! Flies and horseflies and hornets! and all flying things that wreak destruction: I forbid you in the name of the Savior come to earth to suffer for men. I forbid you in the name of the all-seeing cherubim and seraphim which fly around the heavenly throne. I forbid you in the name of the angels and the millions of heavenly spirits standing in the glory of God. I forbid you to touch any tree, fruitful for unfruitful, or leaf or plant or flower. I forbid you to bring any woe upon the fields of these people!" Comment would be superfluous. Pray versus spray!

But science has consequences which are not foreseen; some of them are advantageous to men, others definitely harmful. Consider this matter of increased food supply; combined with the progress which medical science has made in keeping people alive who would otherwise die, it has resulted simply in giving the problem of population pressure a new and even more acute form. The increase in population has more than kept pace with the increased food supply; there are more and more mouths to feed and we are confronted with the very difficult problem of population control on which we are making little if any progress.

The difficulties which the advance of science brings with it are seen in quintessence in the problem posed by the advent of the atomic bomb. Man's supreme achievement in unleashing the primary energy of the universe threatens him with his own destruction. He is in the situation of the fisherman in the Arabian Nights who drew a jug out of the sea and when he extracted the stopper a genie emerged and announced that he was going to kill him. The fisherman was astute enough to get the genie back in the jug and would not release him until he had extracted a promise that the genie would be his servant. Are we going to be equally clever in making the science, which threatens to destroy us, our servant?

Our greatest hope of so doing lies in the fact that at long last, science has begun to turn its attention to man himself. At the start, it concerned itself with things remote from man -- the movement of the stars. Then it came down to earth and dealt with matter and the sciences of chemistry and physics developed. Following that it turned its attention to living things. Last of all, man has come to himself, and is only just beginning to direct his science to the study of his mental and social life. I have a book in my library entitled *The Development of the Sciences*. It was published no longer ago than 1923, yet it contains no mention of psychology, sociology, or the other sciences dealing with man. Indeed, even now these newer sciences are looked at askance by the older ones and many times denied the name of science.

To be sure, we cannot make any very great claims for the sciences which deal with man. They are frankly in their early stages, yet significant progress has been made in the past half century. The methods which have been so successful in the older sciences are, as far as they are applicable, being used in the study of man. The result is that we now have a considerable body of scientific data about ourselves and are developing some skills in using our knowledge and insights to direct our own energies to desirable ends. This is notably the case with psychology, where the knowledge acquired is proving an important adjunct to the practice of medicine, is applicable to the educational process and to a great many social problems.

We need to remember that the older sciences had their long periods of apprenticeship and only slowly demonstrated their practical value. The social sciences are just beginning to develop the necessary techniques and instruments to do their work properly. It is true that they are dealing with immensely complicated materials, with intangibles and obscurities. Nonetheless, they have already achieved some modest success in predicting movements within society and giving direction to those movements. It is entirely possible than when they are come of age they will give us a measure of control over our own lives, individually and socially, which, if not comparable to that of chemistry in its field, will yet be immensely useful to us in guiding the destiny of man. Certainly we will be well advised to push the development of the human sciences as we have the physical and biological sciences.

It is the sciences which are chiefly responsible for the complexities of our modern social life. It is they which have brought the world so close together that we now constitute a single neighborhood. It is they which have produced the high standard of living characteristic of the most advanced peoples, and have produced the machines which speed up the tempo of our lives. It is their results which have inspired in the non-industrial peoples of earth the desire and the determination to share in the good things that the rest of us enjoy. This whole process is a cumulative one; there does not seem to be any prospect that we will declare a moratorium on scientific progress. For good and for ill that progress will continue as will the problems which accompany it.

The scientists themselves are displaying an increasing sense of responsibility for the consequences of their discoveries and inventions. The ivory tower science which could disregard what happened when it turned the fruits of its labor over to society is becoming a thing of the past. Scientists are recognizing that they are citizens as well as scientists and that as such they share with the rest of us the responsibility for the end results of their labors. The menace of the atomic bomb has accelerated their awareness of this by shocking them into the realization that they have come perilously close to creating a Frankenstein's monster which may destroy us all.

The scientists, particularly the social scientists, can do much to help us resolve the difficulties which have been thus created. But they cannot do it all; indeed they can do little save as the rest of us make it possible, and insist upon it. This confronts us with the necessity of integrating science and religion, for it is in religion that we must find the motivation to undertake the heroic task of making sure that science is in truth the servant of human life and not its destroyer. You will remember that we are here defining religion as the continuing urge in the minds and hearts of men to achieve the highest of which they are capable.

It is one of the tragic aspects of our present situation that there is this present conflict between science and religion in its organized forms. It would be more accurate to speak of the conflict between science and theology, for it is not the humanitarian purposes of religion that science is opposed to, but to the theology with which these purposes are associated. There are, of course, scientists who feel that they can reconcile their science with the traditional theology, but the great majority of them are convinced that the conclusions of theology are not relevant to the world they are exploring. This means that their personal support is lost to organized religion. Beyond this, it means that large and increasing numbers of men and women whose minds have been shaped by advancing scientific knowledge are alienated from the churches which refuse to bring the intellectual content of their teachings into conformity with that knowledge.

Is there any possibility that this situation will be corrected, the churches revising their position, assimilating the contributions of science and winning renewed allegiance of the scientists and their like-minded fellow citizens? It must be confessed that at the present time the outlook for such a consummation is very dubious. Under the impact of the fears and tensions of our present world the tendency of the leaders in the churches is rather to turn back to traditional forms of thought and to blame our present predicament on the inroads that science has made on those traditional forms. This is understandable, but deeply to be deplored, for there is no solution to our problems in that direction.

The ideal is clear. It is that science should carry forward its activities within a society dedicated to the achievement of the highest human good, such a society as we sought to describe under the designation of the Beloved Community. It is the business of religion to create such a society. Within its compass the uses to which science would be put would be constructive, creative rather than destructive. Then we should not have to fear that men's ability to split the atom would be used to annihilate us, that the insights of psychology would be used to mislead the multitudes. Then we could be confident that these triumphs would contribute to the prosperity and peace of men.

Perhaps the historical approach will enable us to see better what is needed to achieve this desirable end. There was a time in our western culture when religion as embodied in the church presided over practically all the phases of men's lives. She made and unmade kings and emperors; she provided education and administered charity; she set the rules by which businessmen carried out their transactions; the arts were devoted to her service, painters illustrated her sacred story, sculptors adorned her temples, musicians the wonders of her message into their harmonious strains. At this period, such science as there was also served at the altar of religion and interpreted the world in terms prescribed by the "queen of the sciences," theology.

But a great change took place at the time of the renaissance. the church lost her preeminence, her power to command the services of all these disciplines. One by one they established their independence.There was gain in this emancipation because the church had become a constricting influence, hampering the free play, the full development, of her subordinates. On the whole, we are better educated, better ministered to in our need, our business life is more vigorous, our arts are broader in their scope, and above all, science has made tremendous strides forward, as a result of the emancipation from the all encompassing power of the church.

Yet there has been distinct loss as well as gain. No overall integrating and directing agency has arisen to take the place of religion with the result that the energies of men are not directed to a great common objective. Ofttimes, indeed, those energies are prostituted and perverted to base purposes. Education becomes propaganda, business becomes exploitation, and science is diverted to the destruction of civilization. There is a profound and genuine need for some means of coordinating and guiding the activities of men in the light of a transcendent purpose which shall enable us to avoid the disorder and abuses of the present and bring all our resources to bear on the fulfillment of a divine objective which calls forth the best effort of which we are capable.

In the absence of any such over-arching agency, the state is in some instances, as in Russia, undertaking to fill the vacuum. But this is of doubtful validity because the state is doing it on the basis of compulsion which is sure to produce the same crop of restrictions and evils which led to the revolt against the authority of the church. Furthermore the ideal, the objective of the state is too limited, too low, to satisfy the requirements of what is best in men.

It is my conviction that we must again look to religion as the natural, the inevitable source of the overall guidance and the motivation which we need to make our lives as effective and satisfying as they should be. But this time it must not be religion organized into an institution which seeks to impose its will on the world, resorting to the methods of authority and compulsion. Rather it must be religion which permeates our lives and works through the methods of persuasion and cooperation. It must be religion which conceives its relation to such disciplines as education, art, business, science, on a more mature level than it has in the past. They are now like children grown up. Religion can no longer compel them to its service; it can win them.

It can win them by itself providing a unique and indispensable service, namely that of providing the vision in the light of which all these others can alone be at their best. Religion can "see life steadily and see it whole"; it can make men conscious of the quest for a good life which has endured through the ages; it can make each man aware how in his particular station he can promote that common quest; it can inspire him to do so. Religion is the marching song, the victory morale of humanity as it tramps across the centuries; it is the glimpse of the distant goal we seek, it is the way we must take, the sustaining power that upholds us and drives us forward.

We are here particularly concerned with the role of science in this partnership. It is for religion to set the goals toward which we strive. Science can provide important and effective means to enable us to accomplish the ends of religion. It does this not alone by its specific achievements in adding to our mastery over our environment, but also by the contributions which it makes to our understanding of the nature of the world and our place in it. Most significant of all is its dedication to the truth, its development of methods for arriving at the truth and its strict adherence to those methods. There is a religious quality to all this. No religion can adequately meet the needs of modern men which does not avail itself of the gifts which science brings to its altar.

There is no ugly fatality which is driving us inexorably over the brink of destruction into the abyss of an atomic war. That possibility is terribly, frighteningly present, but it need not come to pass if we do not resign ourselves to it, if we make every effort to avert it. We have a powerful deterrent in our common fear of it, in our common knowledge of how destructive it would be to all of us. We know that there would be no such thing as a victor in an atomic war. We have powerful incentives to resolve the difficulties, the conflicts which threaten to hurl us over the precipice, in the common desires and hopes of men to live out their lives in peace and mutual security, in the common knowledge of what a full and satisfying existence we could work out for ourselves if we would but direct all our energies, all our resources to that end.

Let no man think that what he does, or does not do, makes no difference in determining whether our fears or our hopes are to be fulfilled. This is a war in which all of us are enlisted for the duration. It has now reached a crucial stage. Our attitudes, our convictions contribute to the outcome. We are not impotent. Ofttimes one valiant soldier can turn the tide of battle. Let us dedicate ourselves afresh to that vision which refuses to die in the human heart, the dream of a world shaped more nearly in the image of the ideal. Let us hold high the banner of that central and enduring cause of humanity across the ages, and rally to it the hosts of men and women who with religious dedication are ready to serve it by directing the new forces released by the fourth revolution, the revolution that science has brought upon us, to the creative ends of which they are capable.

Thou Shalt Think!

"The one trait which above all others has been at a premium in the evolution of men's mental character has been educability, plasticity. This is a trait which all human beings possess. It is, indeed, a species characteristic of *Homo Sapiens.*"

These sentences appear in the UNESCO statement on race to which we have previously referred. The fact to which they point, that man is educable, affords the sure ground for the great hope which lies at the heart of religion as it is taking form today, the hope that men shall yet win to a much larger measure of fulfillment than is now possible. The material of which our mental character is made is not rigid, fixed for all time; it is plastic, capable of being progressively fashioned into finer form. There are perhaps limits within which this process must be carried on, limits imposed by the given qualities of human nature. But most certainly we have not begun to reach those limits; we have barely made a start at exploiting the possibilities of our nature.

The major tool which we have for the accomplishment of this purpose, our chief means for bringing us forward toward the ends our religion envisions, is education. When we use that word education, however, we do so in the broadest sense and do not confine it to the formal instruction which takes place in our schools. We must recognize that the plastic substance of our mental lives is constantly being molded by numerous agencies. Education is a constant and life long process. It involves not alone our intellectual development, but our total personality.

The first school in which we are enrolled is the family into which we are born. It has now become a commonplace among us that this is the most important school we are ever to attend. We enter it bearing within ourselves a definite equipment which has been bestowed upon us by our biological heritage, because of the particular parents we have. This initial endowment does make a difference, opening up some possibilities, closing others or making them more difficult. We do not know in advance what these are. But more important in determining what we are to become is the influence which is brought to bear on us in the home during those early years which are the most plastic ones. I covet for all little children the inestimable boon of a wholesome, happy home. I covet for all parents of young children a wise understanding of how potent is the influence of the home which they create in shaping the future of their children.

It is in this school that the emotions are chiefly educated. Only recently have we become aware that the emotions are in need of being educated as well as the intelligence. To be sure we have been educating the emotions as long as man has been man, but it has been done on the unconscious level. Now we have become aware of what we are doing. We know that what our children will love and what they will hate, what their prejudices will be, the value judgments they will pass are in very large measure determined by their experiences in the home, by the example of their parents.

Recently, I saw a copy of a speech a small girl of eight gave in her class at school. It was on the subject of [Sen. Joseph] McCarthy; in very forthright language she told how she hated him, including among other things, the statement that she would split in his face. Her mother's comment was that the speech shows how a child reflects the conversation at the dinner table. While I have a very considerable measure of sympathy with the value of judgment of McCarthy, I could not but feel that the tone of the dinner table conversation in that home is in need of definite modification in the interest of the child's future.

There is a valuable discussion of what we mean by the education of the emotions in John McMurray's book, *Reason and Emotion*. He says that the purpose of the education of the emotions is to make them rational. That sounds like a contradiction in terms for we usually think of the emotions as being essentially irrational. What he means is that our emotions should be in conformity with the objective situation. There are true and false feelings just as there are true and false beliefs. The touchstone of rational belief is that it corresponds to the facts. The same is true of the emotions; our feelings are rational when they are appropriate to the situation.

An extreme example will clarify this. Some years ago I was asked to help in a family situation where the wife was inordinately jealous of her husband. Her attitude had necessitated their moving from city to city because she said that there was a certain blonde who was pursuing her husband and that he was having an affair with her. A careful investigation into the facts, including an interview with the detective the wife had employed to keep watch on her husband, convinced me that the blonde existed only in the wife's diseased mind. Her feelings were not in keeping with the actual situation. Her's, poor woman, was a pathological case; but such extremes are only exaggerated instances of normal tendencies. All of us are in need of disciplining our emotions so that they are geared to reality, so that they are rational.

Such discipline is difficult; this only adds to the importance of the early schooling our emotions receive in the home. Fortunate indeed is the individual who is reared in a family where he gets a good start in establishing a normal, wholesome emotional life so that he spontaneously desires to be and do those things which are required by his situation. We are much concerned these days with the problem of freedom. The most basic form of that problem is emotional freedom. He cannot be free who is entangled in the chains of his own hostilities and fears, the pattern of whose emotional life is such that his energies are turned inward upon himself and expend themselves in civil war, which leaves him frustrated and defeated, instead of being directed outward in creative endeavor. Emotional freedom is a primary requisite of that fulfillment which is our aim; it can be won only as our emotions are disciplined to the requirements of reality. The school where the groundwork for this discipline is laid is the home.

The early years are crucial, but nature has arranged to give us a second chance. This comes at adolescence when the child is being transformed into an adult. Then a new plasticity is achieved; the earlier emotional patterns are made malleable in the fires generated by the efforts of the child to assert himself as an individual and achieve the status of adulthood. It is proverbially a period of difficulty for both child and parents, but at the same time it provides an opportunity to carry the process of emotional education to new levels of independence and freedom. Fortunate indeed is the individual who successfully consummates this and can truly say, "When I became a man, I put away childish things."

There are other aspects to the education which the child receives in the home. In addition to the establishment of his fundamental emotional pattern he also requires the rudiments of certain practical skills and a considerable body of knowledge, some of which is true, and some of it, alas, is false, and will have to be corrected or it will remain a handicap to him and a source of difficulty to his fellows. All told, in its intellectual and emotional aspects and its practical skills, the education which the individual receives in his home is incomparably more significant than any other portion of it. And he often educates his parents quite as much as they educate him.

We would be hard put to it to conceive and establish an adequate substitute for the family as an instrument for fashioning the plastic substance of human nature into the likeness of those fairer forms which we see as possible to it. Our homes vary widely in the quality of the educational job they do; some sadly warp the material they are working with. The majority do a passable job; a few are extraordinarily successful. With the increasing insights which modern knowledge is bringing as to the nature of the task it ought to be possible for us to raise considerably the average level of achievement to the great advantage of the individuals involved and to the health of society.

Obviously the home is by no means the only agency which participates in the education of the young. The family in its turn is vitally influenced by the whole culture of which it is a part. Actually everything which happens in the child's world has its repercussions in his life. In ways that sometimes are direct and crude, sometimes indirect and elusive, it helps to shape his life. He is not wholly passive, but to some extent accepts or rejects in accordance with his own nature and his previous training. We should never lose sight of the organic character of the social process, the interrelations of its parts. The character of the business life of a community, the quality of its newspapers, the standards of citizenship it establishes, the character of the people it regards as important -- all this is part of the education the child is receiving.

Of course, the formal schooling children and youth receive is a vital part of the process, but much of its success or failure is determined by the character of the society in which it has its setting. I am recalling how a high school principal complained to me that his school was criticized because of the unruly conduct of some of the pupils, but that he felt powerless to do much about it because of the standards which prevailed in the rest of the community. First, let them put their own houses in order and then he could see his way to putting his school in order.

Observers of primitive peoples tell us that though they may have no schools they do educate their young by having them participate in the life of the community as far as their capacities permit. In this way they absorb the knowledge, the skills, the traditions, the attitudes of their elders. We are informed, for instance, that in some of the remote regions of Africa where the people are devoid of anything which we would call civilization, the young men do yet acquire an adeptness in the way of life in forest and jungle which could not possibly be duplicated by an intelligent young man from our own community in four years of intensive training. They are educated for and by their particular setting.

We have to educate our young people in the ways of our setting. That setting is our democratic society. From the early days of our republic there has been a recognition of the close relation which exists between the success of our experiment in popular government and the quality of our education. In 1786 Thomas Jefferson wrote to George Washington: "It is an axiom in my mind that our liberty can never be safe but in the hands of the people themselves, and that, too, of the people with a certain degree of instruction." The American public schools have been the outgrowth of this recognition on the part of our people.

To me the schools of this land, all the way from the kindergartens through the universities, are just as truly temples of the religion which is developing among us as are the churches; indeed, in many instances they are truer to the genius of that religion than are many of the churches. This being the case, let us have a look at the functions which the schools exist to perform. They are at once individual and social.

The schools are among the most effective means we have devised for the purpose of assisting each child and youth to grow toward his maximum. We need always to bear in mind that life is lived in persons and that in so far as the individual child is given the opportunity for rich experience in the school, experience that is geared to the stage of his development and helpful to him in his further growth, it is fulfilling the purpose of religion.

Because we differ markedly in our needs and capacities the schools have to make provision as far as possible for these differences and not attempt to fit all our children to the same pattern. There are those whose rate of development is slower than that of most of their fellows, but who ultimately may go as far or farther. There are those who have a special aptitude for working with intellectual tools, while others are more gifted with manual dexterity. Such differences pose difficult problems for educators. It is part of their task to help the individual student discover where his special capacities lie and to provide him with the opportunity to cultivate his particular gifts.

This is the basis for the different kind of schools that have been springing up among us -- those which aim to produce vocational competence rather than prepare their students for the traditional "learned professions." This variation is valid and desirable within limits. It is well that the traditional college curriculum no longer dominates our high schools to the extent it formerly did. It is well that an increasing proportion of our educational system is being shaped to the needs of the vast numbers who will find their life work within the structure of our increasingly industrialized civilization.

But this vocational education has its dangers. Chief among them is that an unfortunate cleavage shall develop between those who follow this line and those who pursue the traditional academic lines. We ought to avoid as we would the plague class distinctions based on educational qualifications. This brings us to a consideration of the social purposes of education. We maintain schools not only to help the individuals grow toward the fulfillment of their lives, but also that we may strengthen the structure of our society.

In a democracy this requires that all the children and youth share to a very considerable extent the same experiences; this is indispensable to the maintenance of our unity. It requires that our schools shall be a major means of imparting to all our children the principles and traditions of our way of life in order that they may understand it, be loyal to it, maintain it. What happens in our schools is of crucial importance to the future health of our democratic society. They have a major responsibility in cultivating those attitudes, developing those skills, which are the lifeblood and the sinews of democracy. Only as we have an informed public, capable of intelligent judgment, imbued with the principles of liberty and equality, can we meet the requirements of the critical period ahead of us as a nation.

James Bryant Conant, formerly president of Harvard University, and now High Commissioner to Germany, in an address delivered at the University of Virginia in February of 1952 made the following statement: "Those youth today are really fortunate who can attend a local high school where boys and girls with a variety of religious and economic backgrounds study and play together. The majority of young Americans are now enjoying these advantages.

That this is so is the principle reason that I for one have confidence in the future of this nation."

Yes, it was a sound policy which our forebearers established of maintaining public schools which all the children and young people should attend. The reasons for it are sociological quite as much as pedagogical. We see this in the way the public schools have helped us as a nation assimilate the children of the millions of immigrants who have come to us from other lands. The need for them to exercise their unifying influence is a continuing one.

It was a recognition of this which led Dr. Conant in that same address to deplore the tendency manifest among us today to set up rivals to the public schools. He acknowledged the right of citizens to establish private schools and conceded that to a limited extent they have a function to perform in offering a challenge to our public schools. He acknowledged the legal right of people to establish schools under religious auspices. But he deplored both these movements, insofar as they are a genuine threat to the pattern of education which has grown up in this country to meet the particular needs of our democracy. Anything that attempts to set up a system of schools parallel to our public schools is a threat to our unity. This is particularly true when those rival schools are conceived on an authoritarian pattern which is the direct contradiction of democratic principles.

Dr. Conant's statement was, of course, denounced as an attack on religion. I should rather acclaim it as a defense of democracy. Indeed, it was a defense of religion itself in the only sense in which I can use that word, for, as Dr. Conant insisted, the pubic schools "have had as a great and continuing purpose the development of moral and spiritual values." It is only when you identify religion with certain theological doctrines, with certain church requirements, that you fail to recognize this. I quite concur with Dr. L.P. Jacks that wherever there is good teaching in the classroom, there religion is being taught. It is not something that must be added to the rest of the teaching, but a spirit which should permeate it all.

There are numerous forces in this country which are seeking to capture the public schools, or make use of them for their own purposes. Some of these speak in the name of sectarian religion, others in the name of an intense nationalism, still others in the voice of a thinly disguised fascism. It is imperative that we be on the alert to guard the integrity of the public schools from all such encroachments. They belong to all of us, they have too important functions to perform in the interest of our common life for us to permit them to be diverted from their purposes. "As go the schools, so goes America."

I am recalling what happened in Russia. After the revolution a new educational system was established under the leadership of Lenin. It drew heavily on the principles of progressive education which are associated with the name of John Dewey. But when Lenin died and Stalin seized the helm, all vestiges of this liberalism were eliminated and the schools converted into propaganda machines to promote Stalin's version of communism.The Hindu poet and educator, Rabindranath Tagore, visited Russia and criticized its schools severely on these grounds. We must not permit anything comparable to happen in this country, but must keep our schools true to the principles of freedom, flexibility, growth which are the genius of our society.

Our schools, said Jefferson, exist to do two things for us: to provide all the people with that degree of instruction which is essential to safeguard our liberties, and to provide us with that natural aristocracy of intelligence and virtue which shall give us the leadership we need in our national life. How far have our schools succeeded in fulfilling these purposes?

According to some qualified critics their greater degree of failure has been registered in the second item of providing leadership. Of course, Jefferson conceived his "natural aristocracy" not as one of privilege, but of service. We are informed that our nation is deprived of the service of a great deal of its potential leadership because there is a wealth of natural ability which never has the opportunity to develop because of economic obstacles. There are numerous young men and women distributed throughout our population who have exceptional ability but are debarred from going to college because their families cannot afford it. Furthermore, our colleges and universities, their atmosphere vitiated as it is by the many who go to enjoy themselves rather than to get an education, are not as productive as they should be and therefore capable of providing us the leadership we should have.

How is it in regard to the other function of providing that degree of instruction for the people generally that is required for the preservation of our liberties? Clearly much more is required in this respect than was the case in Jefferson's time, because of the greater complexity of the conditions under which we live. Are our public schools proving adequate to the occasion? Educators themselves are the first to point out the defects and the shortcomings of the institutions in which they labor. They know full well that the schools do not measure up to our needs, and they are struggling heroically to overcome those defects, many of which must be laid at the door of the community, rather than the schools.

The army of teachers and administrators who man our schools are human beings like the rest of us; they vary widely in ability and training with the result that there is a corresponding variance in the schools. Yet on the whole it seems to me that our schools are doing the best job they have ever done. They are availing themselves increasingly of the insights provided by modern knowledge of the ways in which we learn, and are developing the necessary tools and skills with which to put those insights to work. Likewise the teachers are availing themselves of the new insights into the need of educating the total personality, not just the intelligence, but the emotions as well. They have a broader, more comprehensive understanding of what constitutes education and how it is to be accomplished. The possibilities for improvement are, of course, infinite all along the line. But we are making progress.

The debate over the merits of "Progressive Education" continues. The *Atlantic Monthly* carried an article last April by Albert Lynd under the title, "Who Wants Progressive Education?" He denounced it scathingly as a menace to the basic values of our civilization. This was answered in the May issue of the same magazine by Frederic Ernest, Deputy Superintendent of the New York Public Schools, in an article entitled "How Dangerous is John Dewey?" whose name is almost synonymous with Progressive Education.

As between the two, my sympathies and my convictions are wholly on the side of the proponent of Progressive Education. To be sure, some grievous sins have been committed in its name, and much of its success depends on the understanding and skill of the teacher, but on the whole, it represents a most significant advance. I remember the story which Sidney Hook tells of how experience compelled him to discover and utilize the principles of Progressive Education for himself. His first teaching position was in a slum area of New York City where he was given a class of young toughs who were over-age, and simply sitting out the time they were required by law to be in school. The principal told Mr. Hook that he did not expect him to teach the youngsters anything, but that he did expect him to keep them quiet -- a difficult assignment!

Mr. Hook soon discovered that the only way he could solve the disciplining problem was to teach them, and to do so he had to reach them through their own interests. He learned that they lived very largely in baseball; it was their religion. So he taught them their mathematics by getting them to figure out the averages of all the players in the major leagues; this they were eager to do. He taught them the geography of the United States by having them follow the journeys of the teams to the various cities where they played. It was not difficult to interest them in learning something about these cities, and indeed they found themselves interested in many things which previously had seemed academic and remote. Mr. Hook's comment is that in all his subsequent teaching he never had any problem with discipline when he could enlist the interest of his pupils by relating the subjects they were studying vitally to their own lives.

In announcing this sermon I made the statement that the supreme goal of the schools is to enable men to fulfill the commandment, "Thou Shalt Think." That statement needs a bit of elucidation. What I mean is that the purpose of education is not to stuff a certain amount of knowledge into the minds of the scholars, nor even to develop certain fundamental skills such as reading, writing, and arithmetic, though these are important. Its major purpose is to help people to deal effectively with their environment.

Children are not taught to think by admonishing them to do so; they may knit their brows to give the impression that they are laboring mightily to bring forth a thought, but going through the motions doesn't constitute thinking. John Dewey has some important things to tell us on this subject in his book *How We Think*. The essence of it is that we think only when we are confronted with the necessity of making a choice, when we are puzzled, when we have a problem to solve. I have long been grateful to my father because one time when I was a lad and had a difficult practical problem to contend with, he did not solve it for me as he very easily could have, but instead said to me: "Use your head, boy! use your head!" The lesson sank home and I am sure it would qualify under the caption of "The best advice I ever had."

Certainly the world at this present hour confronts us with plenty of problems to constrain us to use our heads. They are the best, the only adequate instruments we have for arriving at a solution of those problems. Independent, downright thinking is one of the most powerful forces in the world. It has its dangers; it is not respectful of established ways; it can be as explosive as an atomic bomb, but like atomic energy it can be harnessed to creative uses. A new world is struggling to be born out of the agonies and confusion of our time. It is the world in which our children and their children for many generations to come must live. All of us must think for that world, live for it, help it to pass through these throes to a happier time.

I have spoken of education chiefly as it effects the earlier years in the family and in the school. But I would not for a moment have you think I believe it is confined to those years. On the contrary, it is sheer tragedy when we stop growing mentally. To be sure, there are unfortunate circumstances when the deterioration of the physical organism may lead to mental decline. But all too often the failure to keep mentally alert and growing is not a necessity, but due rather to our own attitude, due to the fact that we have settled down in the position already won and have let the world pass us by.

We would do well to pattern ourselves after the example of the great Greek lawgiver Solon. You will recall that he was regarded as one of the wisest men of antiquity; it was he who was responsible for the motto inscribed in the Temple of Apollo at Delphi, "Know Thyself." Plutarch says of him that he was very desirous of knowledge, and he himself used to say frequently in the late years of his life: "I grow old learning still." Yes, that plastic, educable mystery which is the mind of man can maintain these qualities through the advancing years and when we keep it so, it confers upon us the nearest thing to perpetual youth which it is within our power to attain. "I grow old learning still."

The Handiwork of Their Craft

"These maintain the fabric of the world and in the handiwork of their craft is their prayer." That splendid passage in praise of workmen from the book of Ecclesiasticus is a recognition of the religious significance of workmanship. Does not this stir a responsive chord in our hearts? It is in our work that we find a large measure of our fulfillment. It is in our work that we have partnership in the unending process of creation.

I know this from my own experience. The hours I spend in the preparation of Sunday morning addresses flit by with amazing speed; they are deeply satisfying. And the few moments during which I share the results with you bring me the feeling that I can only express in the Biblical phrase, "To this end was I born and for this cause came I into the world." Carlyle is right when he speaks of the "sanctity of work," when he says "man perfects himself in working." I know it from watching the spectacle of the world's work on the farm and in the factory, in the market and the office, in the home, the laboratory and the studio.

Work has the immediate practical purpose of earning a living, of sustaining ourselves. But how much beyond this! It enables us to adorn and enrich the world, to assert ourselves as "Man, the master of things," to function as man, the artist, the creator. There flash on my inner eye certain pictures. One is of a small boy of less than three seated on the floor of the kitchen, his little fingers fumbling at the pods of the peas he was attempting to shell. He was absorbed in his task; he was helping mother get dinner, and he radiated a sense of achievement.

Another picture is that of a young woman I visited in the hospital after the arrival of her first baby. She was transformed; she was radiant and gave me the feeling that in this miracle she had wrought of bringing a new life to birth she had achieved an understanding of what the world is all about. She looked upon her work, and beheld it was very good!

Yet another picture is that of a man in the prime of life who was the head engineer for a great manufacturing concern. He told me that the firm paid him only a modest salary, that he could have secured much more elsewhere. But it placed at his disposal all of the equipment he needed to carry out his experiments and complete his projects. Money was as small dust in the balance to him when weighed against the maximum opportunity to fulfil himself in his inventions. Yes, man is a working animal; this restless, teeming energy within us demands to be harnessed to creative labor.

Oh, yes, we gripe about our work, complain that it rides us, that we have too much to do. We look forward to the time when we can retire and take it easy. And then we stagnate, deteriorate and long for something significant to do. Only recently a man who had sold his business so that he could enjoy his leisure told me that he found himself restless, no longer felt important, and he wished he were back in the harness again. I have myself been warned by one of the wisest physicians of my experience that now my own "retirement" is at hand. I must, in the interests of my health of body as well as of mind, find something which will occupy my energies. I know he is right.

To be sure we can overdo this matter of work; we need to establish a rhythm; rest, repose, recreation alternate with our labor. It is this truth which is written into the commandment to observe the Sabbath as a day of rest. We are in all the more need of such a day of rest in the midst of our tense and hard driven industrial civilization than was the case in the much more leisurely agricultural life in which the commandment was originally devised. We in America, particularly, have much to learn in regard to the importance of leisure and its right uses. I rejoice that we begin to show signs of approximating the wisdom of older cultures in this matter.

There is, of course, a lot of work in the world which is sheer drudgery and by its excess is deadening. One thinks of the lines in Markham's poem, "The Man With the Hoe":

> Bowed by the weight of centuries, he leans
> Upon his hoe and gazes at the ground,
> The emptiness of ages in his face
> And on his back the burden of the world.

Anyone who has shocked wheat long hours, day after day, under the pitiless sun of our western prairies, anyone who has tended a machine where his whole function was to repeat some mechanical operation over and over endlessly will appreciate the significance of the poet's thought. Fortunately we are increasingly consigning such drudgery to the machines themselves and releasing the energies of men for more rewarding and congenial efforts. It is, perhaps, a question as to whether or not we have as yet succeeded in using those released energies more fruitfully; but we will learn so to do.

There are certain conditions which must be met if our work is to be satisfying to us. The first of these is that it must seem important to us. It must not be just made work to keep us employed and give us a wage after the manner of much of the work which was offered to men during the depression years. That was better than nothing, but it was obviously makeshift and did not bring the psychological satisfactions to those who did it which are essential if work is to fulfill its purpose in our lives. It must seem important to those who do it, must be so recognized by the community, and bring the recognition and the rewards which are its due.

The second condition is that our work must have about it something of the same spontaneous quality which is characteristic of play. This is essential if our energies are to flow freely and effectively. During the summer I watched a litter of three half grown kittens at play. They would race around the room, dodge, fling themselves into the air in a veritable frenzy of expended energy. It was marvelous to behold. I thought how fine it is when we can capture some of that same zest and harness it to our work. It is not always easy or even possible, but more often than not a little exercise of the imagination will disclose to us ways in which we can derive unexpected enjoyment from our tasks with resulting ease and improved quality of accomplishment.

A third condition for making our work satisfactory and rewarding is that it shall, as far as possible, engage our whole personality and not just a fragment of it. How well I remember a few sentences from a speech I heard Eugene Debs make many years ago. It was during my theological school days. He came to Meadville, Pa., where the school was located and spoke in the opera house to an audience that packed the place. They were mostly working men. I shall never forget the earnestness with which he besought them not to be just "hands" but men who put their minds into their work as well as their physical labor.

He was right, of course; our work should enlist our total personality. It is profitable for both us and our work when it does so. This is an ideal that is confessedly difficult of attainment. There are a few lines of endeavor which make such varied demands on those engaged in them that they call for the exercise of all our powers. But particularly in this age of specialization it becomes necessary for most of us to find fulfillment for some facets of our personality in activities outside the field which we regard as our work. The opportunities are endless. I have often thought that the reverse of Debs' advice is valid and that some of us need to be admonished not to be just minds but to work with our hands as well that we may acquire the wisdom that comes through such labor.

The consideration of the conditions of satisfying work brings me to certain reflections on the special problems that confront us in our industrialized world. More and more of the world's work is done by machines. They have invaded the farms and we now even talk of "factories in the field." It is not necessary to dwell on the obvious advantages which this development has brought. But we need to consider some of the difficulties which are also its products.

They are mostly in the social realm. In times past, mankind has had a variety of rulers; sometimes it has been the successful warrior who has established his authority over his fellows and perhaps started a dynasty that has maintained its power for centuries. Sometimes it has been the priest who has ruled, even making and unmaking kings and emperors; often the two have ruled jointly. During the feudal centuries it was the landowners who ruled over the people. But with the rise of capitalism, with the development of an industrial civilization, the seat of power has shifted to another class of people. A new aristocracy has arisen; it consists of the industrialist, the financier, the businessman. We express this in our saying, "Business is king." Robert M. Hutchins, formerly president of the University of Chicago, in a recent article in the *Saturday Review* makes the statement: "I admit this is a business civilization."

How well does business use its dominance to achieve those conditions which truly make for life abundant among men? It is always with some reluctance and trepidation that I raise this question because bitter experience has taught me that any critical judgment immediately arouses the hostility of those in the seats of economic power and those who identify themselves with that power. "The king can do no wrong!" and is quick to punish any who suggest that he not only can, but does. The dangerous heresies in our day are not those of theology, but those of economic and social policy. I recall the time when a trustee of a church I was serving called me on the phone one day and said: "Backus, lay off this social action stuff and just give us spiritual entertainment!" "Spiritual entertainment" for sooth; that is to degrade the function of the minister to the lowest possible level.

I have been loathe to speak critically of our business civilization not only because of the resentment it arouses but also because I recognize that I am myself a beneficiary of its regime. I have been as reluctant to speak critically of it as I am to point out what I believe to be the errors of our national policies, for it is my country; as I am to speak critically of members of my own family. Yet I know at the same time that vigorous criticism, conceived in a constructive spirit, is an essential ingredient of a healthy society. It has always been the function of religion at its best to provide such criticism. Witness the passage from Amos we read this morning; it is typical of the prophetic spirit which impels men to criticize things as they are in the interest of things as they might be. Our own Unitarian tradition has raised up such men as Channing, Parker, Starr King, and in our own day John Haynes Holmes, who above all were prophets of a better social order.

It is too much to expect that the businessmen, with rare exceptions, will contribute this essential ingredient to our civilization. They are too busy with practical affairs to indulge in critical thinking and are inclined to be scornful of it. They are too prone to identify their own interests with things as they are and hence to be opposed to change. The criticism must come from other sources, and come it does.

Much of it comes from other spokesmen than those or organized religion, but in whom the prophetic spirit is active. Let me cite two examples. The first occurs is an important historical study, *Religion and the Rise of Capitalism,* the work of R.H. Tawney, Reader in Economic History at the University of

London. In the concluding chapter of his book he quotes J.M. Keynes, of whom it has been said that he knew more about money and its function than any other man of our time: "Modern capitalism is absolutely irreligious, without internal union, without much public spirit, often, though not always, a mere congeries of possessors and pursuers." Then Tawney goes on with his own indictment: "It (capitalism) is that whole system of appetites and values, with its deification of the life of snatching to hoard, and hoarding to snatch, which now, in its hour of triumph, while the plaudits of the crowd still ring in the ears of the gladiators and the laurels are still unfaded on their brows, seems sometimes to leave a taste as of ashes on the lips of a civilization which has brought to the conquest of its material environment resources unknown in earlier ages, but which has not yet learned to master itself."

The other example is that provided by a local scholar, the late Elijah Jordan, professor of philosophy at Butler University for many years. Professor Jordan had more than a local reputation. Indeed one of my philosopher friends has told me that in his judgment if any American thinker is remembered 500 years from now, it will be Elijah Jordan. His last book, published in 1952, bears the title *Business be Damned*.

It is a terrific indictment of business. Professor Jordan makes it clear that he is not talking about industry, the manufacture of goods for our use; that he regards as a legitimate procedure. What he is talking about is that aspect of the process which is concerned with taking a profit as the goods pass from the manufacturer to the consumer, business as it is represented particularly in the banker and the salesman. As I read the book there were certain passages in it which reminded me forcefully of the drama, *Death of a Salesman*. The indictment is essentially the same as that set forth by the playwright, namely that the false standards, the ruthlessness of the business world bring destruction in their wake, kill what is finest in human life.

Perhaps a few sentences will show you what Elijah Jordan thought of business. "Business activity *is* essentially moral evil. There is not a single relation in business consistent with moral principles. And as business has become the dominant factor in human affairs, everybody must act by its precepts. Consequently nobody makes any pretense of guiding his actions by genuine moral principles. Morality has ceased to have anything to do with human relations. Business is destroying everything human."

Or again, from his chapter on Business and Religion: "A few years ago popular attention was given to the question what would Jesus do if he should come back to earth. Courage was lacking to give the simple answer, obvious in the life of Jesus, that he would purge the temple first, and then spend the rest of his existence working to keep the temple clean. He would deliver the church from the domination of the businessman."

Documentation has recently been given to Jordan's charge that the businessman is seeking to dominate the churches by the recent study, *Apostles of Discord*, published by our own Beacon Press. It tells, for instance, of an organization known as Spiritual Mobilization, headed by James W. Fifield, minister of the First Congregational Church of Los Angeles and financed by high officials of a number of the country's largest corporations. Reinhold Niebuhr says of its program that it is "identical with that of the National Association of Manufacturers, to which it adds merely a prayer and religious unction." And the *Christian Century*, independent religious journal, warned not long ago that the newly organized Council of Christian Churches in America is in imminent danger of being dominated by a few men of great wealth who want to use it for their own purposes.

But it is not merely religion that is endangered by business, according to Jordan. It has laid its destructive clutch on education, politics, law, and art as well. The unavoidable conclusion is that business and the good life are contradictory.

What shall we say of these charges? As I read the book, I must confess that I felt he carries his case to such an extreme that he vitiates it. There are valid criticisms of business in it, but they lose much of their force because they are constantly overstated. Perhaps this was deliberate on Jordan's part. I understand that he delighted to shock his classes, and it may be that he is resorting to the same tactics here and is trying to startle the reader out of his complacency. At least we should recognize that we cannot brush aside the criticisms of men of the stature of J.M. Keynes and Elijah Jordan as though they were of no moment.

There are, however, some brighter aspects to the picture. Jordan himself points out that man is infinitely better by nature than business will allow him to be. Certainly many of the individual businessmen I have known have been much better than the predatory creature described by these critics. Indeed, some have been highly social in their point of view, have deplored the evils of the system in which they find themselves enmeshed and have labored heroically to make of their own businesses means of serving high human ends.

In *The Saturday Review* of October 17, 1953, there was a review of the book, *America: Miracle at Work*. It told of the changes which have taken place in the American business scene since the days of Vanderbilt's famous slogan, "The public be damned!" That change is largely in the direction of a greatly increased sense of public responsibility on the part of businessmen themselves. There are, according to this review, still robber barons, large and small, in the business world, but there are also an increasing number of aggressively good citizens among the businessmen.

He cites as an example Standard Oil of New Jersey which, according to him, has evolved into a kind of model of what corporations should be like.

"Acutely aware of its obligations to its employees from top to bottom -- with full cognizance of the importance of delivering an ever increasing dollar's worth to its customers, and with a full realization of its responsibilities to stock holder (it) adds one other significant ingredient; it realizes that it is a corporation citizen of the United States and that its license to do business is issued by we, the people." You might even conclude from his description that it was ready to reverse a certain famous slogan and say: "Whatever is good for the United States is good for General Motors."

Perhaps the picture he draws is a bit too rosy, for in one of the current journals I pick up a note stating that the president of Humble Oil, a subsidiary of Standard Oil of New Jersey, has outlined a bill to be submitted to Congress, the purpose of which is to get around Supreme Court action and permit the oil industry to charge its millions of customers whatever it pleases without Federal interference. Whether or not you will regard that as good or evil will depend on your opinion as to the relation which should exist between government and industry. It happens to be my conviction that despite the improvement in the sense of responsibility on the part of business corporations we are still very much in need of the kind of controls which the oil company would abrogate.

May I share with you my own reflections on this whole problem. I am aware that my own business experience is very limited, but I have lived in this business civilization all my life, felt its impact personally, watched its effects in the lives of multitudes of others. I have no sense of infallibility in my conclusions, because I recognize that the riddle of our social-economic life is as difficult to resolve as the riddle of the universe itself.

My first criticism of the business mentality is that is fails to recognize this fact; it is sure that it has reached the true answers, it deals in finalities. In other words, it has developed an orthodoxy no whit less rigid than that of theology, and in some respects no less mistaken. It has certain dogmas that are expressed in such phrases as "free enterprise," "private initiative," competition, the "test of the market." While there is a measure of truth in these words, when they are interpreted rigidly, they cease to represent the realities of our situation.

Consider that phrase "free enterprise," which it is commonly claimed represents the very essence of our American way. When you come to examine the facts, you discover that at least in the original sense of the words, there is very little of it left. Organized labor, organized farmers, great corporations, the government -- these forces that loom so large in our economy -- are not to any large extent controlled by the simple law of supply and demand as the traditional theory insists. In practice, almost every sort of economic group gets some kind of direct or indirect subsidy or economic aid. Fortune Magazine devoted the whole issue of February, 1952, to a discussion of the government of the United States and what it called the "Service State." It gave a partial list of the services which government renders business in this country. They are so numerous and so fundamental -- all the way from protective tariffs to protecting trademarks -- that the slogan "free enterprise" seems scarcely relevant. It is only very partially a description of the actualities.

The second criticism which I have is that our business world has tragically overstressed the element of competition. There are some psychologists who insist that all competition is evil in the results it produces in personality. Rudolph Dreikurs, the psychiatrist from the University of Chicago who gave a course of lectures in this auditorium a few years ago, takes this position and says that if he could he would eliminate all competition from human life, because of the ugly results it has in human character.

This seems to me an extreme position which cannot be justified. I see no possibility of eliminating all competition and do not think it would be desirable if we could; life would be too insipid. A moderate degree of it, properly channeled, can be advantageous. But certainly it has been overstressed in our American culture to the neglect of the opposite factor of cooperation. This has been in part due to the pioneer tradition in our national history which produced the school of "rugged individualism," and in part to a false interpretation of biological theory which put an undue emphasis on competition as determining those forms of life fit to survive, and neglected the important role played by mutual assistance.

The result has been that our children have been conditioned from an early age in their homes and by the whole impact of our society to think of success in terms of winning, of being the number one man, in whatever field you are engaged. Only recently one of our top tennis players, returning from Europe, voiced the criticism of the players he had met there that they seemed to play for the pleasure of the game, rather than to win, that they were lacking in the true competitive spirit.

This has been characteristic of us, and it has been fostered by our business life with tragic results. I am thinking, for instance, of a report given by a friend of mine who made a careful study of a considerable number of inmates of one of our mental hospitals. He came across a number of instances in which he could only conclude that the patient was there because he could not adjust to the dominant competitive pattern of our business culture, but that had he found himself in a different type of civilization, he might well have enjoyed vigorous mental health and made valuable contributions to his society.

It seems to me imperative that we achieve a much larger measure of cooperation in our American society. We already have a considerable degree of it that has grown out of the necessities of our increasingly complex life. But we have accepted it only grudgingly as though it were a violation of our basic principles, our integrity. What we need to do is to exploit the possibilities of cooperation, avail ourselves far more fully than we have yet done of the advantages that accrue from doing things together for our common benefit. The degree of our interdependence has greatly increased with the progress of our technological civilization and it is going to keep on increasing as that progress continues. It is rapidly becoming a case of cooperate or perish.

The use of atomic energy is a case in point. President Eisenhower has dramatized this in his recent speech before the United Nations calling on the peoples of the world to unite in making sure that this great new power man has won, that would be so utterly destructive if used for war, shall be directed to the purposes of peace; and he has invited the cooperation of the Soviet Union to this end.

Those close to the development of atomic energy are tremendously excited about its possibilities. They see in it a source of power that lends itself as none we have ever had before to the varied uses of man. It can be made available wherever needed, in the desert, on the mountain tops, in the depths of the sea. they see in it a means whereby drudgery can literally be lifted from the life of the race. Our imagination has not yet begun to encompass the creative uses to which it can be put.

How essential it is that this great new power shall be used for the benefit of all. To ensure that this will be the case there must be a very considerable degree of social control of it. Clearly it has great possibilities of commercial exploitation and there are many who will rush in seeking to make it a means of their own financial profit. While we should avail ourselves of all the initiative and skill which such private enterprise would bring to the development of this power, we must at the same time, make very sure that the benefits are shared by all of us. The science that unlocked the secret of the atom was the product of the cooperation of men of many nations. The practical application of that knowledge was again a cooperative enterprise carried on under the auspices of the government and financed by the public funds to which all of us contributed. The results belong to all of us and we can be assured of obtaining them only by continued social control.

The situation in regard to atomic energy is but symbolic of that which exists over a much wider area. If in this society of ours, which grows progressively more complex, we are to make available to individual men and women those things which they need for the fulfillment of their lives, it must be done by the invention of social machinery adequate to the purpose. We have a good example of it in the Tennessee Valley Authority. I am aware that the TVA has been under recent attack as "creeping socialism." That seems to me but a bugaboo with which to frighten children. Actually, the TVA has commanded more admiration round the world than any other achievement of our country in recent years. Peoples in remote areas are afraid of us because of the atomic bomb; they admire us because of that democratic experiment that is TVA.

I do not mean by this praise to indicate that the single pattern presented in this one experiment is adequate to our needs. It is part of the genius of America that in practice we have not been bound by rigid theory, but have been eclectic, using those varied methods that seem best adapted to the particular need. We have intermingled government activity and private initiative, competition and cooperation, planning and improvising. That is as it should be; only the flexibility of such diverse methods is adequate to the actualities of our life. But our admixture of these diverse methods must be varied to meet the demands of changing conditions. Today that means a larger measure of togetherness.

"Society's goal is a fellowship of free men who will cooperate to use man's marvelous powers and the riches of his resources for the universal conquest of war, poverty, tyranny." And more positively for the establishment of an order that assures to every individual the opportunity to grow in fullness of human stature. This has been the goal which religious seers have envisioned across the centuries. We are as yet a very long way from achieving it. The religious task of today is to take us where we are and help us take the next difficult step toward the distant goal. Those responsible for our economic life -- industrialists, businessmen, financiers -- can contribute mightily to that advance in the degree that they see their activities as a part of our common endeavor, and use the factory, the marketplace and the exchange as instruments of the common-weal.

Just because the opportunities for fulfillment in work in the new world that is in the making are greater than ever before, it is all the more necessary that we bring to its problems flexible minds, creative imaginations, humanitarian purposes; that we correct the deficiencies and develop the possibilities. Then shall the purpose of our religion be achieved in higher degree than ever before; then shall the handiwork of our craft be indeed our prayer; then shall the workers with hand and brain and heart join to create the manifold life of the Beloved Community which is our manifest destiny.

Great Companions

The near approach of the Christmas festival invites us to consider the role Jesus will play in the religious drama as it enters the new act that is unfolding at present. It also invites inquiry into the relation of Christianity and the other great faiths of the past to the planetary religion now developing.

Certain things are obvious at once. The first is that we shall have to reject the Christ of theology. Historical studies have made it clear that this is a myth. We can trace the steps by which the man, Jesus, was transformed into a god, the Second Person of the Trinity. The whole story of the fall of man through the sin of Adam and his redemption through the sacrifice of the only begotten Son of God on the cross of Calvary is now seen to have been the invention of pious minds that were groping for a way in which to meet the spiritual needs of men.

We are not unaware that this myth embodied certain important values. It seemed true to the men who developed it, and within its framework, millions of men and women down the Christian centuries have found inspiration and incentive for lives of nobility and purity. The Christ ideal at its best has been a mighty power for good in the world. Men have poured their own aspirations, their dreams of life made perfect into this ideal as a vessel and have found them gushing forth again as a living fountain to purify and refresh them. For this we are profoundly grateful.

But there has been a debit side to this theological structure. It has been associated with an intolerant spirit which has insisted that Christ was a God and if you say he was a man we will kill you. Any deviation from the orthodox view came to be regarded as dangerous and damnable. Thousands of Jews were persecuted and put to death, not only as "Christ killers," but as heretics who believed in one God rather than three. The seeds of anti-Semitism are in the New Testament itself. It was not the Jews alone who suffered; the story of the Inquisition with all its horrors is too well known to need more than passing reference. Those suspected of unsound belief were subjected to incredible torture to give them a foretaste of what they would endure through all eternity in hell if they did not recant. Man's inhumanity to man in the name of Christianity is one of the saddest chapters in all history.

You may protest that this is ancient history; true, but much of the intolerant spirit persists today through large sections of Christendom. It is only within the past few weeks that the newspapers carried the story of a bishop of the Church of England who was bitterly denounced and repudiated by church authorities for saying that Biblical scholarship makes it clear that Jesus was a man elevated to the position of a god. You are, of course, aware that Unitarians and Universalists are denied membership in the newly organized union of the Protestant churches of this country, on the grounds that they do not believe in the deity of Jesus. The more liberal minded among the Protestants protest this exclusiveness but to no avail. It is fortunate that the orthodox mind no longer has the power to enforce its rule over the rest of us.

If we are to reject the Christ of theology, what about the man Jesus? That is a very different question! We find the story of his life and teachings an inspiration. As we read that story in the New Testament we recognize that much of it is obscure; we cannot be certain that we have a correct account of the facts at many points. We have to make allowance for the fact that it was written from a very different point of view from our own. Nonetheless, there is enough that emerges with clarity to make us sure that here was a splendid young Jew who belongs to the line of the great Hebrew Prophets who were responsible for the development of the magnificent ethical strain in their nation's religion.

Jesus was what we should call a liberal, a reformer. He sought to impress on men the fact that the important things are brotherly love and helpfulness and purity of motive rather than strict conformity to the letter of the law. His approach to whatever question he was considering was simple and human. He was close to the soil, original and direct; his sayings welled up from great depths of intuitive insight. He proclaimed the coming of the Kingdom of God which he conceived as the human family at its best writ large and made universal among men. Jesus was a Jew; he had no thought of founding a new religion, but was loyal to the end to the religion of his own people. Paul, not Jesus, was the founder of Christianity.

Fine as this man was in his ethical insights, his compassion, his readiness to lay down his life in support of his principles, we make a mistake when we picture him as a modern man, thinking in our terms. He was definitely a child of his times and his mind was shaped by the culture of which he was the product. No man, however great and original, can completely transcend his environment. Henry Cadbury, director of the Friends Service Committee, and professor in the Harvard Divinity School, has written a book on *The Peril of Modernizing Jesus.* In it he maintains that we constantly tend to read back into the words of Jesus our own thoughts and that in so doing we badly misrepresent him. Cadbury agrees with Schweitzer's statement that "the historical Jesus will be to our time a stranger and an enigma . . . He does not stay. He passes by our time and returns to his own."

Jesus, for example, was totally unacquainted with our modern scientific concepts. He knew nothing of what we call "the laws of nature"; the theory of evolution had not dawned on the mind of his time. The result is that he thought in terms of personal providence as did the other people of those days. This shows itself conspicuously in his thought of the way in which the Kingdom of God is to be established. He believed that it would come as a result of a direct intervention of God. The Fundamentalists of our day are closer to the views of Jesus in this matter than are those who try to make him out a Modernist.

"The man has never lived who can feed humanity always," said Emerson of Jesus. We can appreciate what he had in mind when we reflect not only on such differences in point of view between our time and his but also on the fact that the major problems which confront us are entirely other than those of his world. We cannot expect to find in him the answers to the questions which perplex us. To be sure, human nature remains much the same despite the changing conditions and there are certain insights, certain general principles which remain valid, and it is here that Jesus can be of assistance to us.

He was a genius of the first order and that genius expressed itself chiefly in insights into the hearts of men and a recognition of those motives, attitudes, acts which are in the best interests of men. He had a genuine feeling for the worth of human beings, "even these least," a recognition that they are to be treated as ends in themselves. He protested the propensity of men to "lord it over" others. He proclaimed that that is good that serves the wellbeing of men. "The Sabbath was made for man and not man for the Sabbath." He insisted on the supremacy of the motivation of love. Because he embodied these truths in exceptional degree in his own way of life we cherish his memory. If those who consider themselves his followers would but do his bidding instead of simply calling him "Lord! Lord!" our civilization might indeed be more worthy to bear his name.

In the light of such considerations, what is the place we are to accord Jesus in our religion today? I recognize that people differ in their requirements at this point. There are some who find it necessary to exalt a single leader to a position of supremacy, making of him a symbol to which they give their loyalty. Many who do not regard Jesus as in any way supernatural yet find it helps them to exalt him as example and commander. This meets a need in them for authority and leadership. We will not say them nay.

Yet it seems to me that such leadership is most fruitful when it is conceived in democratic terms. Democracy cannot dispense with leaders. There is a continuing need for men and women who are qualified for special services. We cannot do all things for ourselves. We delegate power to some and accept their leadership. But it is a qualified leadership, resting on the consent of those who are led. We do not abandon our own right of judgment; we retain and exercise that ourselves. The relationship within a democracy is one of companionship, co-workers, rather than ruler and ruled.

To cite a specific example, I read the essays of Judge Learned Hand, and I conclude from that reading that he is exceptionally competent in his field. He has a penetrating insight into the function of the law in our society, a genuine feeling for human rights, a sensitivity to the need of keeping our society free and flexible. Accordingly, I am glad to learn of him, to accept his guidance at certain points. This does not mean that I consider him infallible, or that I am ready to accept his leadership outside the field of his particular competence. Such leadership is necessary and widely prevalent in a democracy. It exists in many different areas and on a wide variety of levels. It is wholly consistent with a valid independence of mind and a maturity of personality.

Apply these principles to the role of Jesus and what do you get? Some years ago, George Burnham Foster startled the public with his pronouncement that "to follow Jesus is to kill the soul." What he meant, of course, was that mere conformity to a pattern established by another brings spiritual death. In order that we may have a healthy, wholesome spiritual life we must exercise our own powers, make our own decisions, be a voice and not merely an echo. Jesus serves us best, not as we blindly follow him, but as he gives us to ourselves, as he inspires us to be persons in our own right. I will avail myself of those insights in the teachings of Jesus which seem to me true. I will reject in his teachings that which seems to me false. I will derive inspiration from his courage, his loyalty to his convictions, his warm humanity, his martyr's death. At the same time, I will recognize that it is only in certain areas he can be helpful; they are important but by no means the whole of life. There is a wide range outside of it in which he is powerless to assist. I will accept him as a competent leader within the democracy of the spiritual life, and know that though this is far different from what men have expected of him in the past, it is what is required in the best interests of our spiritual development today.

Splendid as was Jesus, high as is his place in the history of religion, he by no means stands alone. We see him in better perspective when we recognize that he is one of a gallant company of such leaders. There has become popularized among us the phrase, "the greatest life ever lived," referring to Jesus. Obviously that is not an objective judgment, but represents the feelings of those who have been conditioned from early childhood to regard him not as the supreme religious leader, but also as God himself, come to earth in human form. We should not expect the adherents of non-Christian religions to concur in this judgment, as indeed they do not.

It is impossible to arrive at a valid decision as to who was the greatest man that ever lived. It is a relative matter; some are great in one direction, others in different directions. Humanity has been very rich in the great men it has produced in its many cultures. It is not necessary or desirable that we decide that one stands above all the rest. They are mutually complementary; we do well to recognize this and claim them all, for each has his particular contribution to make within the democracy of the world's spiritual life.

This I have sought to hint at in the title I have used for this sermon -- "Great Companions." In my own experience it has not been a single great leader who has companioned me and contributed to my guidance and development. There has been a varitable host of them, so many that I do not venture to name them all. Buddha and Socrates, Lao-tse and Zoroaster, Confucius and Isaiah, as well as Jesus are among those of the early centuries. They are joined by men nearer our own time: Galileo and Erasmus, Shakespeare and Tolstoi, Bach and Lincoln. And there are those who are our contemporaries, Freud and Gandhi and Schweitzer. And even some of our own acquaintance whose names may not be known to fame, but who yet have contributed more to us personally than have those of greater renown. Great companions all, eloquent of the richness and variety of our common humanity. We will claim them, every one.

In India there is a religious organization known as the Brahmo Somaj. Its relation to Hinduism is roughly the same as that of the liberal churches to Christianity. Its founders were men who had caught a vision of universal religion and they sought to convey that vision to their children by means of a song which contains the names, not only of the great spiritual leaders of their own tradition, but of all the world. Thus the children are early made familiar with the heroes and leaders of the race who represent the breadth and depth of our spiritual democracy. It is a practice we might well emulate.

All of this raises the question of the relation of Christianity to the other great religions and of all of them to that new religion which is emerging in our day. The time has gone by when we can blithely assume that our own religion is the best in the world and that it is destined to become the faith of all mankind. To be sure, there are still many who do make this assumption, but it is increasingly outmoded by the course of events today.

Something of this is reflected in the report of the Commission of the International Missionary Council published in 1952. It directs attention to the fact that not only do the non-Christian populations far outnumber Christians in the world today, but also that those populations will increase far more rapidly than do those of the Western nations. Furthermore, we are witnessing the rapid collapse of colonialism in Asia and Africa and with it a decline in the prestige of the western civilization on which the missionaries had relied heavily. There is a resurgence of nationalism among the peoples of the East and with it a renewal of traditional cultural and religious patterns. The situation is further complicated by the growth of Communism, which is itself a religion, for all its materialistic philosophy; and it has now come to dominate one third of the world's population. It is against such a background that we must review the question of the relation of the religions to one another.

Enlightened observers have long since recognized that we must abandon the mistaken notion that there is only one true religion and all others are false. William E. Hocking, in his book *Living Religions and a World Faith*, tells of the pupils in a school for the children of Japanese converts to Christianity who requested when the Christmas season came to be allowed to decorate the school room after the manner of the Japanese at their own holidays. The teacher sharply denied the request with the statement that only the Christmas tree is pleasing to God.

Hocking recognizes that that narrow, exclusive attitude must go. Indeed, he points out that in some respects other religions are superior to Christianity. Buddhists, for example, find it much easier than do Christians to believe that to search for the truth is to worship God; this is because the founder of their religion some five hundred years B.C. exemplified in his own attitudes the scientific temper of mind. A captain in the Dutch Navy who lived for fourteen years among Buddhists informed me that he found them, generally speaking, conforming their lives to the ideals of their religion more fully than is the case among Christians. Hindus are much more tolerant and inclusive than are Christians. Among them there are six distinct systems of philosophy, all of which are regarded as orthodox, a situation which would be entirely inconceivable in Christianity.

Hocking's conclusion is that Christianity will ultimately become the faith of all mankind, but that it will only be after Christianity has purged itself of some of its dross and assimilated some of the gold to be found in other faiths. I suppose it is natural for us to assume that our own religion is the one which holds in itself the promise of becoming the universal faith. Joseph Klausner, the distinguished Hebrew scholar, makes the corresponding assumption for Judaism. At the conclusion of his book, *From Jesus to Paul,* he expresses the hope that ultimately all the world will be brought to a refined and expanded Judaism.

The inevitable Christian reaction to this hope on the part of a noble Jew, the inevitable Jewish reaction to the hope on the part of a noble Christian, ought to open our eyes to the fact that both of them are in all probability mistaken. With the aspiration toward a universal faith which will unite all mankind in a single community, I find myself in hearty accord. In the close knit world in which we now live, such a unifying faith becomes highly desirable, if not imperative. Yet, I cannot believe that it is to come by the triumph of any one of the historic religions.

All of them alike have their virtues and their defects; all of them alike are strange combinations of superstitions, outmoded science, partial truths, valid ethical insights, fine ideals. All of them alike are today being subjected to forces that are bound to alter them profoundly. They are rubbing shoulders with one another in an intimacy which has never before been obtained. Such contacts have in the past been among the most potent of forces in producing modifications in religions and it would be strange if they did not do so at the present time when they exist on a vastly enlarged scale.

Even more influential is the impact of the secular world, particularly the findings of science and the development of an industrial civilization. We are aware of that impact on Christianity; we know how as a result of it there are multitudes for whom time honored doctrines have ceased to have any vitality and have been replaced by new ideas derived largely from the sciences. We know how many, particularly the best minds, have deserted the churches -- a process which has gone farther in Europe than it has in America. The same sort of process is going on among the peoples of other religious traditions. The bright young men of Asia, having appropriated the results of western science, are finding that it is compelling a modification or an abandonment of their inherited faiths. The process is to be found in many different stages of development.

We must expect that for a long time to come the various religions will persist much as they are; the momentum of a tremendous past is within them and it will not yield easily to the new forces. Catholics will continue as Catholics, Protestants as Protestants, Jews as Jews. Buddhists as Buddhists, Muslims as Muslims, and so on through the whole list. But at the same time they will undergo modification, for religions do change despite their claims to the contrary. These changes will tend to bring them closer together because they are the same forces; science is one all round the globe, and its resulting industrial civilization tends to be the same wherever it springs up. They make similar demands on the followers of all religions.

The familiar figure of people climbing the same mountain from different locations at its base is a valid one. They take different paths, they travel at varying rates, but ultimately they meet at the summit. It is even so in the religious life of mankind; we are all climbing the peak of vision. We start from very different locations, the paths we take, the trails we carve out are those determined by our respective traditions. As we approach the summit we come closer together and at along last, we arrive at the same point. We may continue to prefer the particular way by which we have come, but we have a new sense of fellowship with those who have come by other routes. The ascent has been under way for a very long time; there are those who have lagged behind, preferring to settle down at such elevation as they have achieved.

There are also those who have pushed on ahead, men and women who are particularly sensitive to the changed circumstances, ready and eager to accept the full consequences of the new conditions. They have a sense of kinship with those who have come by the other paths, acclaim their achievements and would appropriate some of the values which they bring with them. These who have climbed ahead are prone to feel that the time has come when they must cooperate in the creation of what is essentially a new religion. To be sure, it grows out of all the past history of the race, all man's universal quest for the good life in a good world. But it is a religion which is purified of all that breathes of narrowness, sectarianism, and is consciously, avowedly universal, ready to forget the names which divide and to exalt the truths, the values, the practices which unite humanity in one grand company as it pushes forward in the common quest.

We have had an instance locally of what is happening. Our good friend Rabbi Maurice Goldblatt of the Indianapolis Hebrew Temple came to the church the other day to interview Mrs. Jones, our Director of Religious Education, and to examine the curriculum material which we use in our church school. He was evidently considerably disturbed because there are some people in his own congregation who are dissatisfied with Judaism conceived in nationalistic terms; they are non-Zionists and prefer religion with a universal sweep. There is a National Council for Judaism which has this point of view, and it has recommended for use with the children of Jewish homes a considerable portion of the material used in the curriculum of our Unitarian church schools, along with other material which is more definitely oriented to the Jewish tradition.

Rabbi Goldblatt was considerably relieved when he had examined the Unitarian material, particularly because he found that where it does deal with Judaism, it does so in a manner acceptable to him. But his quandary still remained. He expressed it by saying that the question is whether one is going to be loyal to *a* religion or to religion. It is clear that his own loyalty is to *a* religion, Judaism. It would be strange were it otherwise with him, identifying himself as he does with a tradition that has commanded an exceptional degree of loyalty among its adherents, a loyalty which has been intensified in recent years by the sufferings its people have endured. Yet the tensions he is experiencing, the tensions within Judaism are signs of the time.

The same situation exists in the rest of the world. The Christian may well ask himself whether his loyalty is to be to *a* religion, Christianity, or to *religion*. I would not put the matter in quite these terms, but ask rather whether our loyalty is to be to Christianity or to the *new* religion which is developing in the world today, a religion which may well transcend Christianity and all the other religions of the past.

Our perplexity is comparable to that which exists over the relation between nationalism and internationalism. I do not want to disavow my love of my native country; despite many things which are done in the name of America of which I do not approve, she is still my country and commands my loyalty. But conditions are such in the world today that I am persuaded the highest type of patriotism requires of me that I also extend my loyalty to that new community which is struggling to be born, the community which shall comprise all the peoples of earth. In like manner I cannot disavow Christianity, though there are many things in it of which I heartily disapprove; I am a product of the culture in which it has been the most important single factor. But now we have reached that juncture at which I am persuaded we shall best fulfill the purpose at the heart of Christianity by aiding in the establishment, the growth of the greatest religion which lies beyond Christianity.

Not long ago, a man called me on the phone and inquired if this is a Christian church. He had been having an argument with one of our members who maintained that it is *not* Christian, and he was incredulous. He said that if it is not Christian he would like to join it, but he could not believe that such was the case. Would I please tell him.

It is a question for which I had no authority to give a simple "yes" or "no" in answer. All I could do was to explain to him a rather complicated situation. We are Christians in the sense that our historic roots grow back into the Christian tradition; we are sprung from the Christian church, having originated in this country in a schism within the Congregational churches of New England. We are Christian in the sense that we cherish the ethical idealism which is associated with the name of Jesus and which has always been a part of Christian teaching, though usually obscured by theological doctrine.

There are many within the Unitarian churches who insist on the Christian name even though it is denied us by the orthodox because we do not believe in the deity of Jesus. There is, indeed, among us an organized group known as the Unitarian Christians. They publish their own journal. But the very fact that they feel it necessary to organize and insist on the Christian name is indicative of the fact that there is a powerful tendency among us in the direction of the universal in religion, a growing conviction that even Christianity is but one of the sects among the religions of the world and that the time has come to transcend it in the interests of a broader, nobler, truer faith.

This strain is by no means new in the history of our church; it goes back a long way. Many of the men who sailed the famous clipper ships from New England ports in trade with the Orient were Unitarians. In their dealings with the men of those distant lands, they found them to be just as honorable, just as high minded, as any of their friends at home, despite the fact that they were not Christians. Such experiences persuaded them that it was a mistake to assume that Christianity is the one and only true religion. "By their fruits ye shall know them." They brought back with them an appreciative and sympathetic understanding of other religions. They imparted this to their home churches and it was one of the factors in the development among us of the universal point of view.

Unitarian scholars and writers early became versed in the scriptures of the Oriental religions. One thinks at once of Emerson, who saturated himself in the religious thought of India. There were two Unitarian ministers of the early 19th century who made a special study of the religions of the far east and not only published their findings but also wrote into their hymns the universal spirit which their studies induced in them. One of these was Samuel Longfellow, a younger brother of the poet; the other was Samuel Johnson. Their hymns still have an honored place among us; we joy to sing them because they have caught the accent of that grander religion toward which we are moving. Let me remind you of them by a single stanza from Samuel Johnson:

> Never was to chosen race
>   That unstinted tide confined;
> Thine is every time and place,
>   Fountain sweet of heart and mind.

This universal strain which began a century ago has developed among us under the influence of the increased contacts with the peoples of other religions, the deepened knowledge of their histories, and even more importantly because of the universalism of science which is bringing us all closer together. The result is that today a large percentage of Unitarians, ministers and laity alike, rejoice to espouse the more inclusive view. In all this we are but responding to, interpreting, giving direction to the major forces of our time. Personally I should like to have my church so conceived that the modern minded Jew, or Muslim, or Buddhist, or any other tradition, yes, and I would include those who feel compelled to disavow all the traditions, should feel as much at home in it as do those who have come by the Christian path. And all of us would be concerned not so much with the names that speak of the past as with what we are going to do together to promote the religion of the future.

Perhaps a historic parallel will help us understand what is taking place today. It was first called to my attention by a Hindu friend. Nearly 2000 years ago in the Mediterranean basin a new religion came to birth; we call it Christianity. It was not the creation of a single man but grew out of the whole life of that area of the world in that particular epoch. As a consequence of the establishment of the Roman Empire, there was taking place a great intermingling of peoples and cultures, with a resulting ferment of ideas and feelings. The peoples were distraught because of the break-up of traditional social forms; they were footloose and groping for something to which they could cling, something that would sustain them. Multitudes had lost faith in the old gods, their religions had become empty forms. There were some elements of strength in the midst of the chaotic conditions; they were to be found chiefly in the ethical idealism of the Stoic and Epicurean philosophies, but these did not reach the masses of the people.

Christianity rose in response to the needs of this situation. Paul, its real founder, synthesized in his own person the varied forces which gave the requisite answers. Christianity was an amalgam of Jewish ethical monotheism, Oriental mystery cults, and Greek speculative philosophy. It grew out of the needs and the resources of the times, and because it did feed the hungers of men it flourished and became the living heart of a culture which has endured down to our own day.

A comparable situation exists at the present hour. Only now the area involved is not the limited one of 2000 years ago, but involves the peoples of the entire earth. Again there is social confusion with the break-up of familiar forms and men are groping for security in a chaotic and revolutionary world; again the old religions are failing men, though in their desperation they seek to revive the dying faiths. Again there are elements of strength, chiefly in the ethical heritage of the race, the forward surge of democracy, and the contributions of science. The time is ripe for a new synthesis, a new amalgam, which shall do on a global scale what Christianity did in the Mediterranean.

The time is ripe for a new religion which shall grow out of the needs and resources of the present and shall flourish because it does feed the hungers of men and provide them with the inspiration for the establishment of a new and finer civilization.

Our obligation and our opportunity is to help bring this religion to birth, help it grow in stature and favor with men, making sure that it is a religion for the whole man; with an intellectual content that squares with the best thoughts of the world; with an emotional content that squares with the finest feelings of humanity and feeds the hearts of men; with a practical expression that carries the ideals formulated by love and intelligence into the everyday actions of men; and with-all, that it is clothed in garments of beauty which shall enhance its values and make it more compelling in its appeal to the loyalty of men.

At this Christmas season I would remind you that the festival belongs not to Christianity alone. Indeed Christianity appropriated it from the immemorial and universal celebrations of mankind at the return of the sun. Let us recapture this universal quality and give to the festival a meaning in harmony with the aspirations of all mankind. We are the heirs of the entire religious heritage of the race. We will refine and purify that heritage in the fires of present thought. We will pass it on enriched and fortified by the creative energies of our own souls to the end that because of it men may live and live well. This be our Christmas gift to the world.

Earlier Than You Think

Something over 40 years ago, when I was a student at the University of Jena in Germany, I made the acquaintance of Ernst Haeckel, the distinguished scientist widely known in this country through his book *The Riddle of the Universe*. At the time I knew him he was living in retirement in his home on Ernst Haeckel Strasse. He had been the leading German interpreter of Darwin's theory of evolution, and had established in Jena a museum which contained the most complete display of the evidence for that theory then in existence.

One day when I was visiting Professor Haeckel he received two visitors from England. They were none other than a granddaughter and grandson of Charles Darwin, the young man bearing the same name of his world-renowned grandfather. The two young people were of about my own age and Professor Haeckel took the three of us on a personally conducted tour of his museum.

Having had this personal contact with Charles Galton Darwin, I was naturally much intrigued a few months ago to see the announcement of the publication of a new book by him bearing the title *The Next Million Years*. Of course, I at once secured a copy. The present Charles Darwin has followed the family tradition and become a scientist. His special field is physics and he has been one of the pioneers in nuclear studies.

The book is interesting but not on the whole very reassuring to those of us who would like to think that better things are in store for man in his long future. His major thesis, briefly stated, is that we cannot expect much change in human nature in the next million years, with the consequence that the life of mankind will go on essentially the same as in the past. In fact, he is inclined to think that the present will prove to have been one of the golden ages of humanity; that we are building up a great technological civilization at the cost of depleting our resources to the point of exhaustion, and those who come after us a few generations hence will have to accept a much reduced standard of living.

The reason he alleges for this pessimistic outlook is that man is essentially a "wild" animal and will not submit to being tamed to the point where his major problems can be resolved. If he were a domestic animal, that is, if he would submit to a master, it might be possible to breed him and tame him to the point where a rational order could be imposed on him. But he isn't, the wild strain is ineradicable. It is at once his glory and his despair.

As a consequence he will go on reproducing his kind in greater numbers than his resources can support and that will result in holding the individual life cheap. Man's inhumanity to man will continue to make countless thousands mourn. Civilization will continue to be spotty, flowering in one place, withering away in another, but never entirely lost. There will be times when an uneasy world government will be established but it will not last for long.

There are some brighter aspects to the picture he paints. Man's knowledge will accumulate vastly beyond anything we know, the level of his intellectual achievement may at times exceed our present attainment and periodically there may come fresh golden ages. But on the whole, he concludes that the pattern of the future will correspond more or less closely to that of China in the thousands of years of her history. Not a very alluring prospect.

Here is a direct challenge to the validity of the religion of human fulfillment which I have insisted throughout this series is destined to be the faith of man as he moves forward into the next stage of his development. It comes not from any reactionary source, but from a man who is himself versed in science and is forward looking in his views. Is there any adequate answer to him? I think there is. It seems to me that I detect certain fallacies in his reasoning, notably at the point where he insists that it is because man is a "wild" animal rather than a domesticated one that he will be unable to resolve his major problems and avail himself to the full of his opportunities for development. I agree that man does not want to submit to a master, but it does not seem to me that Professor Darwin takes into adequate consideration the fact that man is capable of self-discipline and hungers to achieve an inner mastery however much he may revolt against a will imposed on him from without. Perhaps if man cannot tame himself, woman will do it for him!

Be that as it may, I am aware that there is much in the condition of the world today to breed pessimism, despair in the minds and hearts of men. The rapid advance of Communism is a case in point. With some of the social aspirations of Communism, persons of discrimination and sensitivity may well have a profound sympathy. However mistaken its methods may be, it does represent on the part of multitudes who respond to it a genuine and sincere effort to achieve a better, more equitable, more secure way of life. But when those aspirations become linked with totalitarian methods, a rigid dogmatism that will brook no heresy, a ruthless application of the philosophy that the ends justify the means, when it becomes the incentive for aggression on the part of vast nations with tremendous populations and resources, then it constitutes a more colossal menace to the values we hold most precious than were the Nazis under Hitler's leadership.

Having said that, honesty compels me to state that I am almost equally disturbed by the reaction of our own people to the forward surge of Communism as a world power. It is a sorry spectacle to see our great nation with its tremendous power, its boundless resources, so largely dominated by a fear psychology. It is a time for us to heed the admonition of the late President Roosevelt that the only thing we need to fear is fear itself. It is a tragic spectacle to watch our elected officials elevate to a national policy, in the name of safeguarding our liberties, methods which are the very antithesis of these freedoms, methods which fail to discriminate between those sensitive persons who are idealists and humanitarians genuinely devoted to the values of democracy and those who are actually subversives. It is inevitable that some who have been the victims of these methods should feel utterly disillusioned and prostrated, feel that the light has gone out of their world. My heart goes out to them; my heart responds to the invitation on a New Year's card from Rabbi Louis Greenberg. He writes: "I invite you to join me in valiantly insisting that *all* totalitarians (the *extreme* Rightists and the *extreme* Leftists) begin ceasing and desisting." Fortunately there are still those among us who dare raise their voices in such protests -- witness the editorial on spies in the current *New Yorker*!

Yes, ours is a world bristling with formidable problems. In addition to the conflict between Communism and the West there are other large areas of strife. Think of Africa with its 200 million still living in primitive conditions; the whole continent is now seething with revolt as its people begin to enter the modern world and claim their share of its good things. What a long, hard struggle that portends, complicated as it is by racial antagonisms. Think of the terrific population pressures that are resulting as fecund peoples respond to the stimulus that attends industrial development. Think of the religious antagonisms and hatreds which still divide the peoples of earth. No easy optimism is possible in the face of all this.

It is not strange, indeed, that many are much more pessimistic than is Professor Charles Darwin. There are multitudes who are overwhelmed by a situation they do not understand; they make no effort to relate it to any comprehensive explanation, they make no plans, no efforts to correct it, but simply live from day to day as best they can. There are others who are caught up by a futilitarian philosophy; they maintain that civilizations, like individuals, are born, mature, and die, and ours is now in the process of decay; they anticipate that we will hasten the end by an atomic war. There are those who turn to traditional religion in their despair and announce that man of himself is hopeless, that it is only as God intervenes in history as he did when he gave a revelation of his truth in the Bible, as he did when he sent his son into the world, that there is any redemption for the race.

None of these attitudes satisfy the requirements of my mind. Often I wonder why it is that despite the evils I can see so clearly, the violence I deplore, the gigantic proportions of the obstacles in our way, I still continue to hope and expect great things of mankind in the future. Is it that I refuse to admit the significance of the facts, deluding myself? I cannot believe that such is the case. Is it sheer animal faith, an emotional necessity to "cleave ever to the sunny side of doubt?" Perhaps, in part. But, of course, I am convinced that there is a rational basis for my optimism. Let me share with you some of the factors which contribute to its establishment.

The first is the historical perspective. I agree with historian Charles Beard, who said that the study of history made on him the ineradicable impression that something creative is going on in mankind's trek across the ages. The story is by no means a clear one of continuous advance. It is very mixed; there have been losses as well as gains; we will not deny the evils, the cruelty, the degradation that has been part and parcel of the process. There has seldom been any clear cut conception of where we are going, little planning as to the means that are to bring us forward. Such direction as we have achieved has been largely unconscious, groping, growing out of the necessities of immediate needs. But for all that humanity has been on the march; there is a direction in history, a direction which stems from what man is and what he desires to become. And he has made progress, difficult as it sometimes is to observe and measure it.

On the material side that progress is obvious. Through the agency of the sciences, man has won an incomparably greater degree of control over the forces of nature than he has ever enjoyed before. He has made more strides in agriculture in the past century than in all the previous millenniums during which he has been cultivating the soil. And that is but one example out of many which could be cited. As far as we can now determine, there is no limit to the extent of his further conquests in this direction.

There is, of course, the danger that he may use the very power he has won to destroy himself. With atomic and hydrogen bombs an actuality, that is a possibility that cannot lightly be dismissed. The consideration of this point brings to mind an incident that warns how far wrong attempts at prophecy may be. In 1928 English biochemist J.B.S. Haldane published a book called *Possible Worlds*. In it he addresses the question as to whether man is likely to develop his weapons to the point where he will destroy himself. Let me give you his answer: "Unless atomic energy can be tapped, which is wildly unlikely, we know that it will never be possible to box up very much more rapidly available energy in a given place, than we can already box up in a high explosive shell . . . I think therefore that the odds are slightly against such a catastrophic end of civilization." How mistaken can we be! Professor Haldane would have done well to heed his own words earlier in the book where he wrote: "In forecasting scientific research, there is always one general law to be noted. The unexpected always happens." Less than 20 years after he had proclaimed the atomic bomb "wildly unlikely" it wiped out Hiroshima.

Material progress, while it has such dangers, is not to be belittled or written off as meaningless. It is a product of the spirit of man, of man the master of things, and therefore has its spiritual as well as its material significance.

How is it, however, when we turn to those values which are more specifically of the inner life, through which and in which we chiefly live? Have men become more intelligent, more just, kindlier, more imbued with good will toward their neighbors, with the passing of the centuries? Have societies become better organized, more effective in providing the conditions favorable to the development of all their members?

These are highly debatable questions and I am by no means unaware of what can be said in support of a negative answer. But again I am convinced that on the whole there has been decided progress in these areas. This becomes more apparent when we contrast what we know of primitive man with the conditions that exist in our better communities today. Read an account by an anthropologist of life among some of the primitive peoples extant today and compare it with your own experiences. I am confident you would not want to exchange your lot for that of these people who are representative of a stage in which all men existed at one time. The race has come a long way since man first emerged as man a half million years ago.

Even within the historic period, only about 6000 years, I should say that there has been a definite improvement. To be sure there arose in those earlier centuries individuals of as great stature morally and intellectually as any we are producing today. We are not transcending such men as Ikhnaton, Zoroaster,

Euripides, Jesus, Marcus Aurelius. And there have been certain periods when local cultures have attained a brilliance we can scarcely match. One thinks of the Athens of Pericles. Yet even when we have made due allowance for such facts as these, it remains true that there has been advance.

In a measure the poet's prayer, "Make no more giants, God, but elevate the race at once," has been answered. A larger percentage of the world's population is educated today than ever before and has access to the accumulated knowledge of the past. The conscience of the world does not accept as readily as it once did the atrocities of war, the ruthlessness of economic competition and exploitation. The position of woman has greatly improved over the time when she was regarded as a piece of property owned by man. There is a greater recognition of the rights of children than the past has known. Read some of the Old Testament passages on the relations between parents and children and you will be shocked. Democracy -- certainly in its ideals and to some extent in its practice -- is a great improvement over the authoritarian regimes of the past. Poverty has been greatly reduced for considerable sections of mankind; labor shares in the increased wealth and measurably in the direction of the economic life. Much of the drudgery is being transferred to the backs of machines; our leisure is increased. We live longer, have conquered much pain and disease. It is perhaps impossible to draw up a balance sheet, but for all its difficulties, I would not trade our own era for any of which I have read in the pages of history.

Another factor of great significance has entered the human situation: We have become conscious of the possibility of progress. We no longer accept resignedly things as they are, but conceive of ways in which they can be bettered and deliberately set ourselves to achieve that improvement. There is not just a single destiny ahead of men, but a choice of destinies depending on our own actions. The degree of our freedom in this respect may not be very great, for there is undeniably a large measure of determinism in human affairs. Yet that element of choice is real and can become increasingly important as we recognize it, plan our own destiny and work to bring our plans to fruition.

This thought brings to mind some lines from Browning in "Bishop Blaughram's Apology":

> The common problem, yours, mine, everyone's
> Is -- not to fancy what were fair in life,
> Provided it could be -- but finding first
> What may be, then how to make it fair
> Up to our means.

The same idea is expressed in Walter Lippmann's fine definition of the ideal as "that which is at once possible and desirable in the real." In our plans for the future of humanity we must avoid at once the Scylla of the Utopian, the visionary, and the Charybdis of the unimaginative, the pedestrian. In the spirit of Browning's lines, let us look at the possibilities that lie ahead, taking courage from the progress already achieved as a portent of what may yet come to pass.

Our first resource is time. It is this which led me to adopt as the title of this sermon the phrase "Earlier than you think!" A contemporary scientist has said that 600 million years ago our ancestors were worms; 10,000 years ago they were savages; in a few million years our descendants may excel us as much as we do the jellyfish. I cite this statement not because I wish to speculate on what our successors may be like in that remote time, but rather to remind us of the scale of time with which we have to deal.

Astronomers tell us that if the sun will but be careful in his journey among the stars, and they anticipated no calamity in this respect, the conditions on this earth home of ours will be such as to maintain life for about a million million years. It is hard for us to think in such terms. But at least we can recognize that it means man is only at a very early stage of his pilgrimage. He has been man only about half a million years and he has 10 million times that long before him We are still writing the first letter in the first word of the saga of his long journey. Do we have enough imagination to be concerned about the kind of a world our descendants beyond our great-grandchildren will inherit? It is the kind of imagination we need to cultivate to the point where it makes a difference in our actions.

Within this immeasurable future that stretches ahead of us we have certain materials with which to work. Part of them are external to ourselves; the resources of our earth home. It is conceivable, some are saying today that it is probable, that man shall yet lay his scepter on the stars and command the resources of other portions of the universe, but let us be conservative and stay earth-bound in our speculations. We know that we have scarce begun to exploit its possibilities and that even now we are entering an exciting new era.

But I am more interested in what man is going to do with the resources in himself because the possibilities there are even more alluring than those of space travel. Can man bring about an improvement in his own biological nature? Your biologist will tell you that is the crucial question because it is only as we anchor the gains we make in our biological heredity that we can be confident they will endure. Can we develop a science of eugenics to the point where it will enable us to produce a race of men who average as high in their endowment as the most superior among us do today?

Clearly we are not going to resort to the method of the stud farm and secure our superior race by selective breeding. That is repugnant to our feelings on a variety of grounds. Yet we cannot dismiss lightly the possibility of improving our racial quality on a voluntary basis. We know that a selective process of mating has been going on always on the basis of individual and social preferences. Men and women have married those who possessed what they regarded as desirable qualities, health, beauty, intelligence, stable character, etc. It is entirely conceivable that as our knowledge of heredity grows, as we are able to foretell with some degree of accuracy what the probable results of a given marriage will be in terms of the quality of the children, we shall develop a eugenic conscience and people will insist on adding to the list of qualities which constitute the basis of their selection of mates, thus effecting the desired racial improvement. Charles Darwin (the grandson) tells us that it takes about a million years to produce a new species. That is why he limits his discussion to "The Next Million Years" in which he is confident man will remain man. It may be that by then we shall have produced a race of supermen to whom the strictures of the present are no longer applicable.

But our more immediate concern is with what can be made of man as he now is, for I am sure that none of us will concede that he is doing the best of which he is capable. I am speaking here in general, rather than individual terms, though I think that the generalization is applicable to each one of us.

This is largely a social problem. There are some social conditions favorable to the fullest development of the capacities of men, others that are repressive. It was no accident that Athens flowered in a remarkable civilization in the fifth century B.C. and that Greece in a period of two centuries of that era gave to the world perhaps the most remarkable galaxy of genius ever produced. There were definite conditions known to historians which contributed largely to this result; most conspicuous was the fact that the mind of man enjoyed an exceptional degree of freedom.

How can we make sure of establishing the social conditions that are most favorable to the development of a high civilization, productive of the finest type of humanity? In the past this has come about largely as a matter of happenstance, not by deliberate intent. But now we are beginning to develop a tool which may enable us to plan for it and bring it about our own creative effort. This is to be accomplished by bringing the scientific method to bear on the problems involved.

There is now developing a whole group of sciences which concerns itself with man himself, man as an individual and man in society. Many are skeptical of the value of these sciences. This is apt to be the case with scientists in the older fields of physics and chemistry, and to some extent of biology. They are inclined to deny that psychology, sociology, economics, anthropology and so forth are true sciences at all. It must be acknowledged that they are as yet in their infancy, that they are dealing with an immensely complicated and difficult area and in the very nature of the case cannot meet many of the requirements of the older sciences. Nonetheless, they are attempting to bring the scientific method to bear on this most important of all fields. Already they have some notable achievements to their credit; already they are being given practical application in a wide variety of ways. It is not too much to anticipate that as they mature they will contribute importantly to the establishment of those conditions under which the potentials of human life have the maximum opportunity of fulfillment. How far we shall be able to carry this process only the future can disclose, but it is perhaps the most promising of all the lines of endeavor man is now pursuing.

A highly imaginative prophecy of what the end result might be is provided by J.B.S. Haldane in his *Possible Worlds*. Perhaps when you remember his words about the release of atomic energy being "wildly unlikely," his prophecy in this other respect will be discredited for you in advance. Nonetheless, I give it for its suggestiveness.

> In the rather improbable event of man taking his own evolution in hand -- in other words, of improving human nature, as opposed to environment -- I can see no bound at all to his progress. Less than a million years hence the average man or woman will realize all the possibilities that human life has so far shown. He or she will never know a minute's illness. He will be able to think like Newton, to write like Racine, to paint like Fra Angelico, to compose like Bach. He will be as incapable of hatred as St. Francis, and when death comes at the end of a life probably measured in thousands of years he will meet it with as little fear as Captain Oates or Arnold Von Winkelried. And every minute of his life will be lived with all the passion of a lover or a discoverer. We can form no idea whatever of the exceptional men of such a future.

The passage has a Utopian flavor beyond anything I would venture, yet who shall dare to pronounce it "wildly unlikely?"

I have come to think that while it is stimulating now and again to lift our eyes to such distant and alluring horizons, we are better advised for the most part to concentrate on the immediate task of taking the next step ahead. Grandiose dreams have their role to play, but humanity comes forward by solving the pressing problems of the present. My feeling about our situation today is that we are like a man floundering in a bog when solid ground is only a short distance away. If only he could extricate himself he could move rapidly forward.

The potentialities of the present are vast beyond all computing, but we are prevented from availing ourselves of them by certain conditions that are for the most part hangovers from the world we are trying to leave behind us. The most obvious of these is the threat of war made inconceivably destructive with the weapons of the atomic age. But closely associated with this is the upsurge of new nationalism in various parts of the world, and the increasing pressure of expanding population. We have at our disposal the means of resolving these difficulties in our own generation. If we do so, Tagore's figure of the eaglet that has broken his shell and is preparing to soar in a grand new world may well prove prophetic. If not, the upward sweep of humanity will be indefinitely delayed.

This confronts us with the practical problem of what it is that we can do to assure the outcome our hearts desire. The answer is manifold, but there is one aspect of it that is particularly pertinent to our purpose in this church, and supremely important. It is that we shall help to create and establish in the minds and hearts of men that religion which shall be to them their marching song, their victory morale as they strive to reach that better world which we see as at once desirable and possible to us. That has always been the function of religion -- to give soul to the culture out of which it developed and within which it was a creative and directive force. To do this effectively today, our religion must grow out of our own ground, have the force of our own generation within it. No hereditary faith can serve us.

Let me here dispose of the notion that to make a religion out of man's purpose and effort to build for himself a good life in a good world is to blaspheme, is to set man up in the place which belongs to God alone. This is the charge constantly preferred against it by the priests of things as they are. Actually such a religion is not at all incompatible with a due humility and reverence on the part of man. We know full well that we did not create this incredibly marvelous universe; we know full well that all the resources with which we have to work are ours only by virtue of our membership in the vast cosmic order that brought us here and sustains us, providing us with such opportunity as is ours; we know that this is true of our own endowment of intelligence, ingenuity, devotion as well as of the forces external to ourselves which we seek to master. We are at once humble and proud. Actually, were I God I think I should deem it not blasphemy but the fullest worship that my human children undertook to make the most out of the heritage I had given them; I should feel that they were growing into maturity and ready for partnership with me in the unending task of creation.

But it will not suffice simply to proclaim this religion of the human enterprise in intellectual terms. We must give it body, organs through which it may work. It has been characteristic of all religions that they have developed their rites and ceremonies, their festivals and holy days, their theologies and priesthoods, their churches and temples. All these have appeared in a wide variety of forms depending on the particular circumstances out of which they have grown.

The new religion will be no exception to this; it too must develop its forms to meet the varying needs of man. This is hard for many men of the modern mind to appreciate. Because they see clearly how hollow and meaningless so many of the forms of the traditional religion have become they are impatient and ready to throw them all out as sheer superstition. This is a mistake; these forms have met genuine psychological needs on the part of men; they have performed indispensable functions without which the religions would have been futile, impotent.

Some students of the history of religions are convinced that "cult," that is the forms and ceremonies, has been the most important part of the religions. The function which it has performed has been that of conveying the essentials of the religions to men in such wise that they would penetrate deeper than the conscious intellectual level and reach the depths of the emotional, the unconscious life where they are most effective. Symbols, dramatic acts to be performed, creeds to be learned, institutions to command loyalty, these and much besides have given the religions a universal appeal they could not otherwise have secured. It is unrealistic to think that a modern religion can flourish and exercise the influence it should in the absence of such forms.

The proponents of that modern secular religion known as Communism have been astute enough to recognize this. Hence they have provided their movement, which they intend shall conquer the world, with its arsenal of forms and ceremonies, its pictures of Lenin and Stalin, and now presumably of Malenkov, its scriptures in the writings of Marx and his later interpreters, its symbol of the hammer and sickle, its red flag, its public ceremonies and festivals, its priesthood in the membership of the Communist Party, its object of supreme worship -- the State. Communism has all the marks of the historic religions and much of its strength lies in this fact.

There are dangers to this aspect of religion; the danger that the forms shall become ends in themselves, meaningless repetitions which have had the life squeezed out of them, a substitute for and a hindrance to a vital faith; they are often perverted to unworthy ends. They need constantly to be subjected to critical examination, revitalized, fresh forms created out of growing experience. But there is no substitute for them; we cannot dispense with them. Just what forms the new religion will take we cannot predict with any certainty; they may be radically different from anything the past has produced. they will have to grow out of the intellectual, the aesthetic, the moral, the practical impulses that constitute the living heart of the religion. And we may be well assured that they will come if only our religion is vital.

We need not be discouraged because as yet this religion has not taken on the forms, attained the body, that enable it to command the imagination of men. It exists for the most part latently in the gropings of men's minds, their hopes, their purposes. It will fast enough become manifest and articulate. It is earlier than you think. All the great religions of the past had their days of small things when they existed only in the minds and hearts of a few men and women. Christianity did not spring full blown into being and power, but was centuries in the process of development. It must be even so with the faith that is growing out of the present and will command the future.

But come it will, and I covet for us, for the little bands of liberals, the insight and the dedication that shall make of us pioneers of this religion. It is an incomparably great service we are in a position to render at the point where man's need is greatest -- the need for the vision to discern the path humanity must take in order to fulfill its high destiny, the need for the inspiration, the courage, the skill to travel that road. Let us make our contribution, humble though it be, to that mighty end, a song in our hearts, the song of the Open Road:

> They go! they go! I know that they go, but I
>   know not where they go;
> But I know that they go toward the best --
>   toward something great. (Whitman)

Books from Humanist Press
P.O. Box 1188, Amherst, NY 14226-7188
Tel. (800) 743-6646

The Philosophy of Humanism
(2nd edition, revised)
Corliss Lamont
$16.95 paper

Freethought Across the Centuries:
Toward a New Age of Enlightenment
Gerald A. LaRue
$27.95 cloth, $19.95 paper

The Genesis of a Humanist Manifesto
Edwin H. Wilson
$12.95 paper

Humanism as the Next Step
(2nd edition, revised)
Lloyd Morain and Mary Morain
$10.00 paper

Confronting Church and State:
Memoirs of an Activist
John M. Swomley
$12.95 paper

The Humanist of the Year Book
Mildred McCallister and Lloyd Kumley
$9.95 paper